Political fictions

Political fictions

Michael Wilding

Department of English
University of Sydney

Routledge & Kegan Paul

London, Boston and Henley

First published in 1980
by Routledge & Kegan Paul Ltd
39 Store Street, London WC1E 7DD
9 Park Street, Boston, Mass. 02108, USA and
Broadway House, Newtown Road,
Henley-on-Thames, Oxon RG9 1EN
Set in Journal 10pt by Columns
and printed in Great Britain by
Unwin Brothers Limited
The Gresham Press, Old Woking, Surrey

British Library Cataloguing in Publication Data

Wilding, Michael

Political fictions.
1. English fiction — 19th century — History and
criticism 2. English fiction — 20th century —
History and criticism
I. Title
823'.8'09   PR871

ISBN 0 7100 0457 5

to Jack Lindsay

Contents

	Note on references	ix
	Acknowledgments	xi
	Introduction	1
1	The false freedoms of *Huckleberry Finn*	21
2	*News from Nowhere*	48
3	*The Iron Heel*	91
4	*The Rainbow*: 'smashing the great machine'	127
5	*Kangaroo*: 'a new show'	150
6	*Darkness at Noon*	192
7	*Nineteen Eighty-four*: rewriting the future	216
	Bibliography	247
	Index	255

Note on references

Page references following quotations are to editions specified in the bibliography. For the convenience of readers using different editions of the novels discussed, chapter references and where applicable part or volume references are also given. Hence (I:2:34) means Part or Volume I, chapter 2, page 34 of the edition specified; (5: 67-8) means chapter 5, pages 67-8 of the edition specified. The abbreviation CE refers to George Orwell's *The Collected Essays, Journalism and Letters*, and PW refers to William Morris's *Political Writings*.

Acknowledgments

The author and publishers would like to thank Jonathan Cape and Harold Matson Inc. for their kind permission to quote from *Darkness at Noon* by Arthur Koestler, and Mrs Sonia Brownell Orwell and Martin Secker & Warburg for their kind permission to quote from *Nineteen Eighty-four* and *The Collected Essays, Journalism and Letters* by George Orwell.

Introduction

Political fictions can take many forms. What we can call a political novel might also be called a novel of society or a novel of colonialism, an historical romance, a utopian fantasy or a fable. Political fiction is not something to be narrowly defined. Categories overlap.

When Morris Edmund Speare wrote his study *The Political Novel* (1924), it was on the parliamentary political novel that he particularly focused.

> What is a Political Novel? It is a work of prose fiction which leans rather to 'ideas' than to 'emotions'; which deals rather with the machinery of law-making or with a theory about public conduct than with the merits of any given piece of legislation; and where the main purpose of the writer is party propaganda, public reform, or exposition of the lives of the personages who maintain government, or of the forces which constitute government. In this exposition the drawing-room is frequently used as a medium for presenting the inside life of politics. (ix)

For Speare the political novel was 'an important offshoot' from the tree trunk of the historical novel (17) and drew on the ' "novel with a purpose" ... a form already well launched in the history of English letters' (29). But while recognizing these connections and extensions, Speare was none the less concerned to establish a narrow definition. It was a narrowness that corresponded with the narrow social elite that peopled the drawing-rooms of those novels. 'The writer in the world of politics is not dealing with a common human-ity', Speare declared:

> Dickens and Thackeray, and Henry James, as social writers, deal with men and women as men and women: the variety of common

1

> human emotions they may report is endless, and the more usual
> and familiar they are to us the better is it for those writers. But
> the political novelist, if he is to be true to his craft, must be
> dominated, more often than not, by *ideas* rather than by
> *emotions*. The people who play his leading parts are above the
> common average of intelligence. They are endowed not with
> common joys and common sorrows, but are men and women
> sophisticated in their tastes, highly trained in the complex world
> of affairs and of diplomacy, dealing at first hand with problems
> of theology, of education, of economic barter and exchange,
> of philosophy. (23)

The elitist social assumptions at the base of Speare's narrow attempt
to define a genre are unconcealed. He attempts the literary equivalent
of those scholars who saw history as being concerned only with
kings and statesmen.

But there are novels that deal with politics that do not exclude
'common humanity'. Lawrence's *Kangaroo* deals with party-political
leaders, with self-proclaimed elites — but his protagonist, Somers,
never forgets that he is the son of a working man; political issues are
discussed and worked out with representatives of 'common humanity'
like Jack and Jaz as well as with the politicians; and the novel moves
beyond the drawing-room restraints to speculate on the forces of
telepathic communication, vertebral consciousness and the unintel-
lectualized currents of feeling that mobilize mass action. Emotions
are kept in balance with ideas, not dominated by them. William
Morris's *News from Nowhere* totally rejects the 'take me to your
leader' orientation of elitist political thought. It presents a world
free from leaders, politicians, and political institutions — but it is a
freedom achieved by the implementation of a conscious political
programme. And Mark Twain, by focusing on a runaway slave and
the runaway son of the town drunkard, is able to give us a fuller
picture of the political forces of the American South in *Huckleberry
Finn* than if he had confined his novel to the drawing-rooms of the
Shepherdsons and the Grangerfords. Would we want to exclude
these works from a discussion of political fictions?

Irving Howe's *Politics and the Novel* (1957) offers a wider range
of approach than Speare. No longer are we confined in the narrow
world of constitutional history.

> By a political novel I mean a novel in which political ideas play a
> dominant role or in which the political milieu is the dominant
> setting — though again a qualification is necessary, since the word

2

'dominant' is more than a little questionable. Perhaps it would
be better to say: a novel in which *we take to be dominant*
political ideas or the political milieu, a novel which permits this
assumption without thereby suffering any radical distortion and,
it follows, with the possibility of some analytical profit. (17)

None the less Howe, like Speare, works within tight restrictions. He
may say 'that I meant by a political novel any novel I wished to
treat as if it were a political novel' (17), but when he writes 'novel'
there is a narrow assumption that a 'novel' is always the bourgeois
realist novel. It is a significant limitation. 'From the picaresque to
the social novel of the nineteenth century there is a major shift in
emphasis', Howe writes, and he marks a further shift in emphasis
between the 'social' and the 'political' novel:

> The ideal social novel had been written by Jane Austen, a great
> artist who enjoyed the luxury of being able to take society for
> granted; it was *there*, and it seemed steady beneath her glass,
> Napoleon or no Napoleon. But soon it would not be steady
> beneath anyone's glass, and the novelist's attention had
> necessarily to shift from the gradations within society to the
> fate of society itself. It is at this point, roughly speaking, that
> the kind of book I have called the political novel comes to be
> written — the kind in which the *idea* of society as distinct from
> the mere unquestioned workings of society, has penetrated the
> consciousness of the characters in all of its profoundly
> problematic aspects, so that there is to be observed in their
> behavior, and they are themselves often aware of, some coherent
> political loyalty or ideological identification. (19)

And in arguing against 'the notion that abstract ideas invariably
contaminate a work of art and should be kept at a safe distance from
it', Howe writes:

> ideas, be they in free isolation or hooped into formal systems,
> are indispensable to the serious novel. For in modern society
> ideas raise enormous charges of emotion, they involve us in our
> most feverish commitments and lead us to our most fearful
> betrayals. The political novelist may therefore have to take
> greater risks than most others, as must any artist who uses large
> quantities of 'impure' matter. (20-1)

But none of this is the exclusive preserve of the realistic novel. The ideas and phrases which Howe uses in defining the political novel apply as readily to Swift's *Gulliver's Travels* (1726) as to any of the nineteenth- or twentieth-century works of realism with which he deals. The 'feverish commitments' and the 'most fearful betrayals' resulting from political ideas are there in Gulliver's commitment to the ideology of the houyhnhnms and his rejection, his betrayal, of humanity. While the 'coherent political loyalty or ideological identification', which Howe argues that the characters of a political novel possess, is evidenced in Gulliver's conversations with the King of Brobdingnag. Gulliver's commitment to the political system of England and his eulogies of its procedures provoke first mirth, when the King having heard Gulliver's account 'could not forbear taking me up in his right Hand, and stroaking me gently with the other; after an hearty Fit of laughing, asked me whether I were a *Whig* or a *Tory*' (II:3:91); and later they produce contempt in the King's famous denunciation — 'I cannot but conclude the Bulk of your Natives, to be the most pernicious Race of little odious Vermin that Nature ever suffered to crawl upon the Surface of the Earth' (II:6:116).

Seeing the political novel as a development of the social novel, Howe is inclined to emphasize the social, the naturalistic connections of political fiction. The assumption is that the political novel is a variety of nineteenth-century bourgeois realism. But an equally important non-naturalistic tradition of the fable, the imaginary voyage and the utopian narrative leads through Swift to William Morris, Jack London, H.G. Wells, Eugene Zamyatin, Aldous Huxley and George Orwell. Here the tradition of the transferable political fable persists — a fable drawing on observations of a specific reality, projected into a geographically or temporally distant context, and designed to be readily applicable to a range of different social situations. Discussing the origins of the historical novel, Georg Lukács wrote in 1962:

> even the great realistic novel of the eighteenth century, which in its portrayal of contemporary morals and psychology, accomplished a revolutionary breakthrough to reality for world literature is not concerned to show its characters as belonging to any concrete time. The contemporary world is portrayed with unusual plasticity and truth-to-life, but is accepted naïvely as something given: whence and how it has developed have not yet become problems for the writer. This abstractness in the portrayal of historical time also affects the portrayal of historical

place. Thus Lesage is able to transfer his highly truthful pictures of the France of his day to Spain and still feel quite at ease. Similarly, Swift, Voltaire and even Diderot set their satirical novels in a 'never and nowhere' which nevertheless faithfully reflects the essential characteristics of contemporary England and France. These writers, then, grasp the salient features of their world with a bold and penetrating realism. But they do not see the specific qualities of their own age historically. (19-20)

And the fable tradition continued. George Eliot and Disraeli, Stendhal and Dostoevsky developed political fictions from the major realistic strand of the nineteenth century. But as traditional realistic modes came to be less appropriate for political perceptions, novelists concerned with the political turned back to the fable and the utopian fantasy. But they were able to turn back to them with a developed awareness of the social and historical specificities developed by the great realists. So that though *Gulliver's Travels* might well seem unrelated to *Felix Holt* or *Beauchamp's Career*, it is importantly part of the context and tradition of *News from Nowhere*, *The Iron Heel* or *Nineteen Eighty-four*.

If by political fictions we mean imaginative prose works that say something useful or interesting about politics, then we need to move beyond the narrow confines of realism. Yet the realistic mode has been dominant in critical surveys of the novel, both in English bourgeois culture, with Leavis's *The Great Tradition*, and in European marxist culture, with Lukács's studies. It has been a conservative stress. And the force of the Leavis-Lukács emphasis demonstrates the challenge that realism was under from other forms representing and expressing the vision of other class or sub-class groups. There would be no need to assert the centrality of realism so strongly and so dogmatically unless it were already under attack. These challenges to the dominance of realism are reflected above all in political fictions. Fiction dealing with politics successfully is responsive to the forces of society; these forces manifest themselves in the cultural area, have their aesthetic expression. In political fictions we would expect to find not only the political conflicts of social choices, but also the aesthetic conflicts of fictional choices.

Speare and Howe restrict their concerns to realism. Yet a dissatisfaction with realism can be seen throughout the fictional productions of this century. *News from Nowhere*, *The Iron Heel*, *We*, *Brave New World*, *Animal Farm*, *Nineteen Eighty-four* constitute far more than a peripheral departure from a central 'realism'. The search in political fiction, as in all fiction, is for the appropriate,

Introduction

expressive form. From Morris's analysis of realism in *News from Nowhere* to Brecht's running argument with Lukács, the limited nature of realism has been demonstrated. 'Realism' is a particular formalism — partial, historically based, class-determined. Its name claims a totality and finality that as a form it does not possess. It is but one mode among many, and no longer the mode which those progressive writers concerned with political and social issues would choose. Its continued dominance way after it has ceased to be a vital mode of literary production is preserved by the schools and universities, the party apparatchiks and bureaucrats in order to resist and exclude other, newer modes that by the very fact of their being other and newer are feared to be disruptive: modes that would challenge the established literary order.

The fable and the utopian fantasy were reactivated as alternative modes to inflexible realism. But there was another early mode, romance, that was brought back into a relationship with realism to evolve a new mixed mode. The dialectical tension of romance and realism created new formal possibilities at the same time as expressing perceived polarities in the political life. The pattern that recurs constantly through English language political fiction is a vision of two polar opposites of political engagement: on the one hand the romance of individualistic activity, gestures at the hero as politico, on the other hand the documentary realism of detail, researched statistics, intellectual theory and exposition. In George Meredith's *Beauchamp's Career* (1875) and D.H. Lawrence's *Kangaroo* (1923) they are represented as the Scylla and Charybdis of political alternatives — between which the new problematic novel steers its tentative passage. Both Meredith and Lawrence self-consciously exploit the appropriate fictional modes to capture these alternative positions: they produce fictions that are an amalgam of romance and documentary realism, two modes that create some powerful tensions between them. They are formal tensions enacting the tensions within the consciousnesses of the novels' protagonists.

Meredith presents a protagonist, Nevil Beauchamp, who 'with every inducement to offer himself for a romantic figure . . . despises the pomades and curling-irons of modern romance' (4:34). An aristocrat by birth, conducting his early military career with an appropriate romantic individualistic impetuosity, he destroys that image by setting out on a career as a Radical parliamentary candidate. Nevil's problem of the effective conversion of quasi-feudal romantic enthusiasm into radical political action becomes the problem of making an effective political novel. The novel begins as a romance, but the romantic is constantly frustrated:

I am reminded by Mr Romfrey's profound disappointment in the
youth, that it will be repeatedly shared by many others: and I
am bound to forewarn readers of this history that there is no
plot in it. The hero is chargeable with the official disqualification
of constantly-offending prejudices, never seeking to please; and
all the while it is upon him the narrative hangs. (4:33)

Meredith identifies the problems of his protagonist in the fictional
world with the writer's own problems in presenting politics in
fiction. Romance is unrealistic; realism is unromantic. The romantic
action constantly collapses into bathos; realistic recording of society
becomes boring. But out of the tension something else emerges: the
drama of consciousness. A new mode is born.

Those happy tales of mystery are as much my envy as the popular
narratives of the deeds of bread and cheese people, for they both
create a tide-way in the attentive mind; the mysterious pricking
our credulous flesh to creep, the familiar urging our obese
imagination to constitutional exercise. And oh, the refreshment
there is in dealing with characters either contemptibly beneath
us or supernaturally above! My way is like a Rhone island in the
summer drought, stony, unattractive and difficult between the
two forceful streams of the unreal and the over-real, which
delight mankind — honour to the conjurors! My people conquer
nothing, win none; they are actual, yet uncommon. It is the
clockwork of the brain that they are directed to set in motion,
and — poor troop of actors to vacant benches! — the conscience
residing in thoughtfulness which they would appeal to; and if
you are there impervious to them, we are lost . . . (47:479-80)

Lawrence comes out with something very similar in *Kangaroo* where
his protagonist Somers likewise has romantic dreams of political
activity, fantasies of leadership — and where the novel's action is
indecisive, bathetic:

Chapter follows chapter, and nothing doing. But man is a
thought-adventurer, and his falls into the Charybdis of ointment,
and his shipwrecks on the rock of ages, and his kisses across
chasms, and his silhouette on a minaret: surely these are as
thrilling as most things. (15:312)

Both writers are trying to steer a course between the adventure of
plot and mystery and romance, and the novel of bourgeois realism

7

with its itemization of and concentration on the mundane — property, objects, fishing catches. For both of them it is the inner, the mental drama, the drama of consciousness that is important — Lawrence's 'thought-adventure', Meredith's 'clockwork of the brain'.

'Politics in a work of literature is like a pistol-shot in the middle of a concert, something loud and vulgar, and yet a thing to which it is not possible to refuse one's attention', Stendhal wrote. Certainly both Meredith and Lawrence found their political material disruptive of the comfortable aesthetic that novel-reading concert-goers or concert-going novel-readers liked. Both were concerned to alter the formal possibilities of fiction so that it could represent an experience of politics without distortion of the experience. If it was going to be a pistol shot then it was to be a pistol shot — not a cap-gun or a pistol in a sound-proof chamber. In dealing with political materials they made necessary innovations in the current conventions of the novel, they opened up the form. The changes they made were not in the direction of Joycean avant-gardeism but in the proportional allocation of space and energy to 'story', 'plot', 'documentation', 'romance' and 'ideas'. For both of them the emphasis was to be placed not on the reader's conventional expectation of plot or narrative, but on the 'clockwork of the brain', on the 'thought-adventure', the inner drama, the modification of consciousness.

The confrontation of the hopes of romance with the mundane actualities of realism runs throughout political fiction. It is a pattern that arises from the nature of political engagement. The formal polarities arise from the situation, the politics, the character choices. This is not an abstract formalism. An examination of the formal characteristics of these novels leads directly to the political situations. The individual protagonist is offered the choices — indeed is sometimes oppressed and overwhelmed by one or the other of the possibilities. Huckleberry Finn is dominated by Tom Sawyer's romantic vision of 'adventure' and his experience on the river journey is in large part a process of demystification. And the exposure of romanticism moves beyond the exposure of Tom's contained, make-believe 'rebellion' to an exposure of the ideology of the American South. That two of the main instruments of this demystification are those rogues called the King and the Duke stresses the political meanings of the romantic masquerades. In *Huckleberry Finn* romanticism is exposed by realism. In *News from Nowhere*, conversely, the 'realism' of the way we live now is exposed by the romance of the Guest's vision of the communist future. In *The Iron Heel* Avis's romantic narrative of her socialist-leader husband is qualified by the objective annotation of the future editor: romantic aspiration and documentary realism are held in balance.

Romance and realism are not the only components of the mixed mode in political fiction. In *Darkness at Noon* the aristocratic interrogator, Ivanov, trails with him the romance of revolution, heady theoretical discussions in late-night café society; he is replaced by the realistic bureaucrat, Gletkin. And then both romance and realism are distanced by Koestler, who resurrects the note of classical tragedy for his material. This is not a choice that emerges dialectically from the opposition of romance and realism, but something superimposed. Just as Fielding felt he had to give credibility to his realistic narrative of bourgeois social values, *Tom Jones*, by dressing it in the trappings of classical epic, so Koestler feels the need to elevate his theme by giving it the aura of classical tragedy; as if the political were not valid on its own, as if the novel had insufficient credibility for the serious reader. It is the attitude of an intellectual who distrusts both politics and fiction, uneasy in both areas yet feeling the need to express himself in those modes. It is an aesthetic choice that reveals the conservative, non-dynamic world-view that Koestler presents, for all his understanding the detail of the dialectical debate between Rubashov and his interrogators. In effect Koestler is saying, the forms of art were determined in the world of classical Greece, they are absolutes, no new forms to challenge them can evolve. Similar strategies haunt Conrad's political fictions. *Nostromo* has a recurrent epic note that establishes its backward-looking anti-progressive mood. Both Conrad and Koestler use classicism to break the romantic lure of revolutionary politics. Orwell, similarly concerned to discredit revolutionary commitment in *Nineteen Eighty-four*, uses 'realism' in its extended popular sense of 'kitchen-sink' squalor to destroy those fragile glimmerings of romance that briefly rise in Winston Smith's life — the possibility of romantic love, the possibility of romantic conspiracy.

But realism has an ambiguous role in this novel of the world of doublethink and newspeak. *Nineteen Eighty-four* is about politics so its form is not hermetic and autonomous, but pegged down to, reaching into and supplemented by the documentary. Lawrence quoted actual documents in *Kangaroo* and incorporated them in a collage process — clippings from the Australian press. Orwell, writing about a 'future', has to invent his documents (though commentators have remarked how Goldstein's imaginary book *The Theory and Practice of Oligarchical Collectivism* is closely indebted to Trotsky's *The Revolution Betrayed*). And with his 'documents' Orwell extends the scope of his novel. He has to invent the details of his future society to establish the world of his novel, but he does not restrict his invention to materials to be dramatically realized. He draws on the tradition of the imaginary book, the book as object, to employ resources beyond the range of the 'realistic' novel. He moves beyond the 'realism' of character or setting, to the different order of realism of the incorporated excerpts from Goldstein's book, and the appendix of newspeak. He draws on the tradition of *Gulliver's Travels*, with its proliferation of dedications and prefaces, and *The Iron Heel* with its footnotes, using the full resources of the book as an object to simulate realism.

But it is a playing with 'realism' that takes Orwell to the edges of modernism. And commentators, of course, have complained, as if the simple narrative of *Nineteen Eighty-four* was its whole point. Alex Zwerdling complains that the excerpts from Goldstein's book are 'like so many lumps in the porridge, and though they are brilliantly written, they can hardly help distracting the reader's attention from the narrative and diluting its force' (206), and he objects similarly to the appendix on newspeak. Richard Gerber complains of 'the impression that there is still a good deal of undigested material, that there is too much political and social theory' (129).

But to reject the Goldstein excerpts and the newspeak appendix as undigested, excessive political material is to refuse to read the novel Orwell wrote. The careful, conscious and literary calculation that went into the novel can easily be neglected. The often-remarked simplicity of Orwell's style masks a conscious programme of critically reinterpreting earlier political fictions. The disruptions of the narrative strengthen rather than weaken the novel, they draw attention to the critical nature of the narrative. It is not simply carrying us along, it needs to be checked against the documentation which Orwell incorporates, against our memory of other political fictions. We are referred to the newspeak appendix by an asterisk early in the first chapter: straightaway the fictional 'realism' is disrupted by reference to appended documentary material — introducing a different language, a different verbal texture. The potential of romantic narrative (Winston alienated from all-powerful state, what will he do?) is cut across by the intrusion of documentary realism.

The incorporation of documentary materials into the political novel is important to establish the texture of the created society, to provide the data for the sociology. Winston Smith, working on *The Times* newspaper, would seem the ideal protagonist; he readily has access to social information, he has an overview of society that transcends the limitations of his own personal experience: he is in a much better position to mediate information for the novel than an alienated visiting foreigner like Somers in *Kangaroo*.

But in the society of 1984 things are different. Winston's occupa-
tion is rewriting news items so that history reads consistently in the
light of various political changes. The documents that Winston has
access to are useless. 'As soon as all the corrections which happened
to be necessary in any particular number of *The Times* had been
assembled and collated, that number would be reprinted, the original
copy destroyed, and the corrected copy placed on the files in its
stead' (I:4:35). Periodically the novel is studded with statistics that
Winston has to shape for *The Times* — the basis of documentary
information. But 'statistics were just as much a fantasy in their
original version as in their rectified version. A great deal of the time
you were expected to make them up out of your head' (I:4:36). The
documentary impulse of political fiction is constantly frustrated in
Nineteen Eighty-four. The documents are all suspect. Goldstein's
book turns out to have been written not by the mythical opponent
of the regime, but by O'Brien and other inner party members.

The formal choices and confrontations of political fictions
represent life choices, political confrontations. The mixed mode is
not unique to political fiction. But with political fiction it is easier
to see the political choices behind the opposing modes. These are
not decorative, aesthetic, abstract conflicts: the aesthetic clash
carries the force of ideological clash, class struggle. Huck Finn's
own vernacular idiom offers the verbalization of a very different
social base from the authorial, traditional prose of the earlier
Adventures of Tom Sawyer (1876). *The Rainbow* demonstrates a
shift from the almost pastiche George Eliot—Thomas Hardy opening chapters to the more schematic, argumentative, less 'realized'
open form in the latter part, looking forward to *Women in Love* and
Kangaroo — marking a major shift in life values, life possibilities.
And to examine the political fictions of Twain or Lawrence is to
understand better their 'non-political' writing — is to be forced to
ask, indeed, if any of their writing is 'non-political'. This study is
concerned to help resituate the political interests of such writers
as central to their vision. *Huckleberry Finn* and *The Rainbow* are
basic texts in educational syllabuses. Yet their radicalism has been
consistently denied and suppressed. It is a radicalism that needs to
be restored to centrality in reply not only to conservative suppression but also to distortions by the 'left'.

Huckleberry Finn is consistently presented as a child's book or as
a religious book or as anything else but a radical exploration of the
social forces of the American South during and after slavery. T.S.
Eliot's introduction to the novel ignores the social analysis and

stresses the mythical quality of the river, presenting it as a sort of god. He associates the novel with Conrad's *Heart of Darkness*, an indictment of imperialism that literary critics have preferred to treat in a depoliticized way.

> Thus the River makes the book a great book. As with Conrad, we are continually reminded of the power and terror of Nature, and the isolation and feebleness of Man. Conrad remains always the European observer of the tropics, the white man's eye contemplating the Congo and its black gods. But Mark Twain is a native, and the River God is his God. It is as a native that he accepts the River God, and it is the subjection of Man that gives to Man his dignity. For without some kind of God, Man is not even very interesting. (xv)

Eliot's conservative, religious mystification has had its influence. Edwin Bowden even maintains 'that religious principles themselves are never mocked' in *Huckleberry Finn* (40) — yet surely the way Huck talks about God and Heaven and Hell shows the incongruity, unbelievability and unnecessity of them? In so far as Twain deals with God, it is to show the extent to which religious belief maintains the structure of Southern society; God is a manifestation of social oppression. As the seventeenth-century radical Laurence Clarkson put it, sin was invented by the ruling class to keep the poor in order. Bowden extends the conservative 'religious' reading into a desocializing of the novel: he sees isolation as its central concern. But though Huck himself may be seeking freedom from certain persecuting forces, freedom is not the same as isolation. It is important that Huck never achieves isolation, that all the way down the river he encounters the brutal, slave-owning society of the South. Certainly Huck himself passes few explicit criticisms of the society, but this should not divert us from seeing society as a major concern of the novel and from recognizing the social comment made by the novel. For what Twain magnificently does is analyse the components of the ideology of the South: the combination of a Christian piety that yet never extends its charity towards blacks, of silent brutality elevated to feuds of honour, and of a romantic rebelliousness that always directs rebellion away from the realities of the society. Yet even those critics who have recognized the force of Twain's analysis of the slave-owning South, have still tried to depoliticize the novel. James M. Cox argues in his *Mark Twain: The Fate of Humor*:

Huck's revolt seems on the face of things a genuinely tame
performance. He is involved in a subversive project which has the
reader's complete approval — the freeing of a slave in the Old
South, a world which, by virtue of the Civil War, has been
declared morally reprehensible because of the slavery it
condoned. Huck's rebellion is therefore being negotiated in a
society which the reader's conscience indicts as morally wrong
and which history has declared legally wrong. (169)

But it is clear enough that slavery is not Twain's immediate or only
theme in *Huckleberry Finn*. Huck's escape is paralleled with Jim's,
but Huck is the centre of the book, the narrating consciousness.
Jim's escape from literal slavery serves to underline and define the
nature of Huck's escape from the same society. When Twain wrote
slavery had been abolished, but the South was still determined by
those same economic, social and ideological factors. Slavery was an
ultimate, dramatic expression of that society, but it was the society,
not the specific issue of slavery, that Twain presented. He offered a
radical account of the social and ideological forces of the South,
and this needs to be stressed against the continual attempts to
depoliticize the book. Cox, for instance, goes on to argue:

Comfort and satisfaction are the value terms in *Huckleberry Finn*.
Freedom for Huck is not realized in terms of political liberty but
in terms of pleasure. Thus his famous pronouncement about life
on the raft: 'Other places do seem so cramped and smothery, but
a raft don't. You feel mighty free and easy and comfortable on a
raft.' (178)

But Twain does not separate political freedom from 'pleasure'. They
are parts of the same total well-being. Huck's positives of 'free and
easy and comfortable' are undoubted political positives; their negation, 'cramped and smothery', are the expression of imprisonment.
The images of imprisonment run throughout the book, defining the
achieved freedoms. The cells of *Darkness at Noon* and *Nineteen
Eighty-four* are there to receive Huck and Jim at every stage — Huck in
Pap's hut, Jim tied up on the raft or locked up in Aunt Sally's shed.
    The attempts at depoliticization do not only come from conserva-
tive critics. Orwell, who for years was seen as a radical commentator
on literature and society, is particularly responsible for the way in
which radical writers like Twain, Lawrence and Jack London have
been discredited, their politics distorted, their literary achievement
undermined. He argues that:

Introduction

Mark Twain had some pretensions to being a social critic, even a species of philosopher. He had in him an iconoclastic, even a revolutionary vein which he obviously wanted to follow up and yet somehow never did follow up. He might have been a destroyer of humbugs and a prophet of democracy more valuable than Whitman, because healthier and more humorous. Instead he became that dubious thing a 'public figure,' flattered by passport officials and entertained by royalty, and his career reflects the deterioration in American life that set in after the Civil War. (CE, II:55:371)

But it is a dangerous sort of criticism: conceding that there was a radical aspect gives the hint to exploratory readers to look for evidence of expressed radicalism. Orwell claims that 'Twain, except perhaps in one short essay "What is Man?", never attacks established beliefs in a way that is likely to get him into trouble' (CE, II:55:372). It is an extreme and serious charge, and one that is utterly false. The banning of *Huckleberry Finn* by the Concord library was trouble enough for a writer, even if the grounds now seem absurd. And Twain deliberately courted trouble in denouncing King Leopold's policies, and US complicity, in the Congo. As soon as E.D. Morel asked him in 1904, Twain committed himself to the Congo Reform Association, writing the immensely powerful *King Leopold's Soliloquy*. Conrad dealt with the Congo atrocities in *Heart of Darkness*, but in a letter to his publisher Blackwood (31 December 1898), assured him that though 'the subject is of our time distinctly' it was 'not topically treated' (*Letters to William Blackwood and David S. Meldrum*, 33); he refused Roger Casement's request to commit himself to the public campaign against Leopold's imperialist horrors. The Congo is never named in Conrad's novel. Orwell's attempt to discredit Twain collapses not only in the face of a crea- tive polemic like *King Leopold's Soliloquy*, but also before any adequate reading of *Huckleberry Finn*, where the 'iconoclastic' and the 'revolutionary vein' stand revealed.
    Orwell likewise offers a misreading of Lawrence. He claims that:

What he is saying is simply that modern men aren't fully alive, whether they fail through having too narrow standards or through not having any. Granted that they can be fully alive, he doesn't much care what social or political or economic system they live under. He takes the structure of existing society, with its class distinctions and so on, almost for granted in his stories, and doesn't show any very urgent wish to change it. All he asks is

14

that men shall live more simply, nearer to the earth, with more
sense of the magic of things like vegetation, fire, water, sex,
blood than they can in a world of celluloid and concrete where
the gramophones never stop playing. He imagines — quite likely he
is wrong — that savages or primitive peoples live more intensely
than civilized men, and he builds up a mythical figure who is not
far from being the Noble Savage over again. (CE, II:31:235)

But Lawrence is very concerned about social, political and economic
systems. The whole import of his continuing argument is that industrial capitalism is totally destructive of mankind, not only in its
economic exploitations, but destructive of the totality of human
experience. His subject is the alienation that industrial capitalism
produces. And his interest, as this Etonian ex-colonial policeman
and broadcaster of wartime imperialist propaganda to India puts it,
in 'savages or primitive peoples', is to search for alternative possibilities, new directions, in cultures other than his own. Celluloid and
concrete and gramophones are not his preoccupation, they are the
notation which Huxley uses in *Brave New World* for *frissons* of
bourgeois taste-horror. Lawrence sees well beyond the superficial
manifestations of the system; he has no Edwardian nostalgia for
fine bindings or brick walls or string quartets: he knew the price of
such 'superior' taste, he came from the exploited proletariat that had
financed it. It is not mere materials he rejects; he rejects the mental
and social structures that have generated and confirmed the alienations of contemporary industrial capitalist existence. Born into the
English industrial working class, Lawrence experienced the ultimate
alienations of British society. Indeed, his alienation expresses itself
succinctly in his denial of his class in his first novel, *The White
Peacock* (1911), where he draws on autobiographical materials but
transfers them into a bourgeois context. Even Ursula, whose experiences in school-teaching and at university draw on Lawrence's own,
is given a determinedly non-proletarian background in *The Rainbow*.
    But what possibility was there for writing about the proletariat
in non-revolutionary England? All that could be expressed would be
alienation. He does use the material in *Sons and Lovers* and the
experience of social alienation there is transformed into a dynamic
to escape the limiting conditions of English working-class existence.
But having escaped from the destructive environment of the industrial proletariat, Lawrence does not abandon his class ties. In *The
Rainbow* he turns to examine the forces that oppress the proletariat.
He formally continues the English novel tradition of bourgeois
realism and writes about the comfortable bourgeoisie: gentlemen

farmers, managers, intellectuals, officers. But his mode is one of critical realism; he is analysing, not commemorating, let alone endorsing, this world. He proceeds to demystify and reject it. In the end he cannot bear to write about it — he sets his fiction in Italy, Australia, South America. Since most English literary criticism is the product of the bourgeoisie, however, the terms of Lawrence's rejection have not been fully understood. The Brangwens are regularly interpreted as a family in ideal, pastoral, unalienated, direct contact with working the land — when in fact Lawrence establishes them in the specific social context as prosperous farmers, very soon 'gentlemen farmers', the employers of the rural proletariat we never see.

Of course the attempts to depoliticize, deradicalize, Lawrence and to absorb him into a reactionary, elitist, high bourgeois, lifestyle cult had inevitably to occur. Dr Leavis writes in *D.H. Lawrence: Novelist*:

> The colliery, of course, is not merely the colliery; it is 'the great machine that has taken us all captives.' We have, in this later part of *The Rainbow*, the very world of *Women in Love*; the distinctive themes and tones of the later book, and the same sense of the plight of human life in an industrial civilization. (148)

Leavis sees 'industrialism' as the theme, as the evil; but he refuses to see the economic and political context of industrialism. Lawrence is made to look like a bourgeois environmentalist and his political direction is obscured. Leavis continues on *The Rainbow*, 'a more serious criticism, perhaps, bears on the signs of too great a tentativeness in the development and organization of the later part; signs of a growing sense in the writer of an absence of any conclusion in view' (150). But the apocalyptic note of a proletarian uprising is the necessary and inevitable conclusion of the movement of the novel, a vision planned and fulfilled.

Lawrence is so present as a force in twentieth-century writing that it is easy to forget how early some of his works were written. *The Rainbow* was published in 1915; there had never been a successful proletarian revolution by 1915; Lawrence offers an apocalyptic vision as his faith in the inevitable necessity of such an uprising — two years before 1917. He was not writing a futuristic work like *News from Nowhere*, but a novel set in contemporary society. His hostile critics of the left tend to write as if he turned his back on a revolution which, when he wrote *The Rainbow*, had still not occurred.

The apocalyptic note places Lawrence in the line of the radical thinkers of the English Revolution — the tradition of Winstanley and the Diggers and of the various radical religious groups of the mid-seventeenth century. The positive, radical aspects of Lawrence's social thinking continually need to be reaffirmed. The more narrowly materialist of his leftist critics seize on Ursula's conviction that life has a soul as evidence of Lawrence's mystifying idealist habits of thought. But Lawrence's stress on the non-logical, non-conventionally intellectualizable aspects of existence was not a mystifying emphasis. 'He is one of a great crowd of thinkers who have held to the notion that there is a consciousness other than the mental, and that modern civilization has repressed it', Frank Kermode reminds us (87). In *Kangaroo* he goes on to develop his case that there are many other forms of communication, of perception, of feeling than our conventional science and psychology can at the present quantify and isolate. To deny these qualities simply because our logic or our science cannot analyse or comprehend them is illogical and unscientific. The impetus of his writing is to reach out and understand and experience more; not to reduce the world into those small fragments that our limited intellectual procedures have so far been able to understand or preserve. This is a progressive, not a regressive impetus.

The radical component of Lawrence's thought has been obscured not only by the attentions of conservative critics, but also by the widespread rejection of his work by the left. Discussing 'Healthy or Sick Art?' in *Writer and Critic*, Lukács declares 'the ultimate in modern decadence we owe to D.H. Lawrence' (106). 'The parallel between Lawrence's terminology and that of the Nazis has often been pointed out', John Strachey wrote in *Literature and Dialectical Materialism*. 'Lawrence was a typical — indeed, the archtypal — member of the school of "the fascist unconscious"' (18). Terry Eagleton perpetuates this view in *Criticism and Ideology*:

> Lawrence was a major precursor of fascism, which is not to say that he himself unqualifiedly accepted fascist ideology. He unequivocally condemned Mussolini, and correctly identified fascism as a spuriously 'radical' response to the crisis of capitalism. Lawrence was unable to embrace fascism because, while it signified a form of Romantic organistic reaction to bourgeois liberalism, it also negated the individualism which was for him a crucial part of the same Romantic heritage. This is the contradiction from which he was unable to escape, in his perpetual osciallation between a proud celebration of individual autonomy and a hunger for social integration. (158-9)

17

Introduction

At least Eagleton makes it clear that Lawrence 'was unable to embrace fascism', though he still stresses fascism before he stresses individualism. It is the wrong emphasis. The individual is more important than any system of authority throughout Lawrence's writings. And it is the radical aspect of that individualism, its rejection of repressive systems whether bourgeois democracy, or fascist totalitarianism, that needs to be emphasized.

Twain and Lawrence are writers whose work is preserved on educational syllabuses throughout the English-speaking world; they are transmitters of our consciousness; but the radical component of that consciousness has been obscured. William Morris and Jack London were marxist writers whose work is rarely found on educational syllabuses. Occasionally they surface as Morris the pre-Raphaelite decorative artist, or Jack London the adventure and animal story writer; their works that deal explicitly with marxist revolution, *News from Nowhere* and *The Iron Heel*, have effectively been suppressed. Neither Morris nor London is discussed by Speare or Howe in their studies of the political novel. Morris's biographer, J.W. Mackail, wrote in 1899 of *News from Nowhere*:

It is a curious fact that this slightly constructed and essentially insular romance has, as a Socialist pamphlet, been translated into French, German, and Italian, and has probably been more read in foreign countries than any of his more important works in prose or verse. (II: 256)

Philip Henderson is even more dismissive:

It would be an insult to Morris's intelligence to suppose that he really believed in the possibility of such a society, where the only work that appears to be going on is a little haymaking at Kelmscott. And yet one frequently finds *News from Nowhere* seriously discussed as though it were a blue-print for a communist future. (386)

Jack London receives a different sort of critical dismissal — the variety reserved for the self-taught, working-class writer. His writing is dismissed as vulgar, crude, clumsy. His experimentalism is ignored because the forms in which he experimented were appropriately popular forms, not conservative literary ones.

A radical literary criticism has a number of immediate tasks. It needs to re-establish the radical vision of such writers as Twain and Lawrence. It needs to restore works like *News from Nowhere* and

18

The Iron Heel to a central position in any thinking about political fictions. And it needs to look at some of those works that have a perpetuated role in educational syllabuses and literary discourse as the considered view of ex-leftists, now basking in the seen light. The fact of once having been left and being so no longer is presented as the mark of the objective credibility of Koestler or Orwell. It is important to expose the literary strategies by which they present their message, to reveal the politics of these works, and to explore how they attempt to exercise their palpable design on us. Koestler works within a surface context of European alienation: Kafka and Beckett represent one set of relevant connections, Conrad stands as an earlier figure in the tradition. Leavis, rarely endorsive of any post-Lawrentian fiction, comments enthusiastically on Koestler in *The Great Tradition*, associating him with this reactionary mode.

> It is relevant to note here that in the early hey-day of Wells and
> Shaw, Conrad wrote *Nostromo* — a great creative masterpiece
> which, among other things, is essentially an implicit comment
> on their preoccupations, made from a very much profounder
> level of preoccupation than theirs. And it is also relevant to
> venture that in Mr Arthur Koestler's very distinguished novel,
> *Darkness at Noon*, we have the work of a writer — also, we note,
> not born to the language — who knows and admires Conrad,
> especially the Conrad of *Nostromo* and *Under Western Eyes*. (32)

It is one of Leavis's few comments about a living fiction writer, and it indicates the ready acceptance that the conservative modernism of Koestler's work achieved; the drama of the individual conscience in the minimal setting leads back to the world of Conrad and behind that, George Eliot and Dostoevsky. This study concludes with Orwell not because he is in the forefront of any fictional experiment, but because his work serves as an anthology of devices from earlier political fictions; he has a few trappings of modernism, but generally comparison with the earlier works to which he alludes indicates their radicalism and his conservatism.

A radical criticism needs to be responsive to a radicalism of form as well as content. Marxist criticism has not traditionally been happy in this area. Marx, Engels, Lenin, Plekhanov, Trotsky, Lukács, all preferred the products of nineteenth-century realism to any other available fictional modes. As a result, works of radical content and radical form have tended to be neglected by both conservative and radical critics. The fictions dealt with here demonstrate a search for alternatives to realism — through vernacular picaresque, dream

vision, imaginary book, found manuscript, collage, utopian projection, dystopian fable, neo-neoclassicism, and through various mixed
modes. This is not an attempt to offer an alternative 'great tradition'
or indeed any tradition at all. The varieties of experiment are all
different in nature. But what they predominantly share is a constant
search for the appropriate mode, radical both formally and politically, revolutionary as fiction as well as in the transmitted consciousness, the better to transmit that consciousness.

1

The false freedoms of *Huckleberry Finn*

When Huck refers to 'sivilization' in *Huckleberry Finn* (1885) the spelling cannot be explained as an attempt by Mark Twain to render phonetically one of the different dialects he tells us in his 'Explanatory' he was 'painstakingly' representing. No variant pronunciation is indicated but a number of ironic points are made. What is first testified to is Huck's ignorance; but it is more than a merely book-learning, correct-spelling ignorance, it is an ignorance that shows his separation from the correctness of the widow's world. He doesn't even know how to spell civilization. But the spelling indicates the ironical judgment that the sivilization Huck observes isn't really civilization. We are offered not just a mis-spelling but a homophonic pun, and a pun making an evaluation. The two words may sound alike but are, the spellings suggest, distinct. The ideal values of civilization are not present in this specific sivilization, which embodies a debasement of those values. Maybe there never can be an ideal civilization in practice, maybe they are always going to be sivilizations. The specific society Huck denotes as sivilization may well feel his uncivilized ignorance is testified to by his mis-spelling; but by denoting it as sivilization, Huck has already passed a contemptuous dismissal of it. Huck's spelling has exposed an ambiguity in human values, and the spelling insists on this ambiguity — in the same way that we can talk of humane behaviour and how it is not always found in human behaviour. The spelling of sivilization, then, and more explicitly the phrase in chapter 6, 'sivilized, as they called it' (76), establishes firmly Huck's alienation from the society which he finds so cramping, and implies an evaluation that his observations of the society certainly support.

Huck's alienation is sufficient to make him not only uncomfortable in sivilization, but to try and escape it. He can only cope with living with his father by escaping to the woods, and he makes similar

21

brief escapes when he is in the widow's household — 'before the cold weather I used to slide out and sleep in the woods, sometimes, and so that was a rest to me' (4:65). *Huckleberry Finn* opens with Huck's account of how he has tried to run away from the widow. The necessity for escape is a theme present in the novel from the very beginning. And it is not only individuals Huck is fleeing from: they are fully realized individuals, but they represent certain basic aspects of Southern society — the sivilization from which Huck feels alienated, is alienated. Huck must escape all his persecutors fully to escape sivilization. But because the aspects his persecutors embody are basic ones, he encounters these same characteristics throughout his journey down the river.

These basic characteristics of the Southerners naturally relate to the basic social and economic feature of Southern society — slavery. It is significant that when Huck flees, it is in company with the slave, Jim. He is not attempting in the early stages of the book to set Jim free; rather they are both seeking their freedom at the same time. The contemporaneity of their escapes emphasizes the identity of their escapes. Huck is fleeing from certain individuals whose attitudes cramp him; these attitudes, the book shows us, provide the ideological bases for the slavery that Jim is fleeing. Jim's literal escape from literal slavery serves to illustrate, to provide an emphatic metaphor for, and to some degree to define, Huck's own search for freedom.

Huck and Jim are running away, but Huck wants more than a merely negative escape from things. He continually expresses his alienation by the word 'lonesome' which suggests not only that he feels cut off from society, but that ideally he would like to belong somewhere. He wants not a recluse's isolation but the companionship of civilization. Running to the woods provides only a temporary respite. It is because Tom Sawyer can offer Huck the lure of *belonging* to a group (the robber band) and a group, moreover, that seems to be an alternative to the widow's sivilization, that Huck returns from hiding.

What we find though, is that Huck never does find a civilization to which he wants to belong. He is always ready to believe in one. And in *Huckleberry Finn* we see society constructed on a series of seeming alternatives. Huck, a perpetual optimist, is always ready to believe that whenever one way of life is cramping, the alternative will offer freedom. The brilliance of Twain's social analysis in *Huckleberry Finn* lies in this indication of the essential alliance of seemingly dissimilar attitudes. The widow and Miss Watson provide the first example.

Sometimes the widow would take me one side and talk about Providence in a way to make a body's mouth water; but maybe the next day Miss Watson would take hold and knock it all down again I judged I could see that there was two Providences, and a poor chap would stand considerable show with the widow's Providence, but if Miss Watson's got him there warn't no help for him any more. (3:60-1)

Their attitudes to selling Jim are similarly different, as Jim tells Huck:

I hear ole missus tell de widder she gwyne to sell me down to Orleans, but she didn' want to, but she could git eight hund'd dollars for me, en it 'uz sich a big stack o' money she couldn' resis'. De widder she try to git her to say she wouldn' do it . . . (8:96)

Yet even though the widow seems more humanitarian here, on the basic issue of the institution of slavery they are in inhumane agreement. They never question that issue. Their Providences represent the same values and present not different attitudes, but alternative methods of securing the same attitudes; on the one hand bribery, on the other coercion, with the same end in view. Huck is to be sivilized either by the lure of a Providence that will 'make a body's mouth water' or by threats of 'the bad place'. The widow and Miss Watson are the originals of that soft policeman-hard policeman duo; they are a basic feature of authority systems, they fulfil an archetypal structural role in the maintenance of any system of social order.

Within the total context of sivilization, the joint, shared aim of the widow and Miss Watson is to sivilize Huck, to train him in the ways of society.

Miss Watson would say, 'Don't put your feet up there, Huckleberry' and, 'don't scrunch up like that, Huckleberry — set up straight' and pretty soon she would say, 'Don't gap and stretch like that, Huckleberry — why don't you try to behave?' Then she told me all about the bad place, and I said I wished I was there. (1:50)

Having begun by trying to teach Huck to spell, Miss Watson has gone on to reprimand him for bad manners; and that leads so naturally and easily to moral instruction and threats of hellfire. The associations are not accidental. Similarly on Huck's return from hiding, the widow's laments had been religious and her positive attempts at reformation had been those of fitting Huck to polite society.

> The widow she cried over me, and called me a poor lost lamb, and she called me a lot of other names, too, but she never meant no harm by it. She put me in them new clothes again, and I couldn't do nothing but sweat and sweat, and feel all cramped up. Well, then, the old thing commenced again. The widow rung a bell for supper, and you had to come to time. When you got to the table you couldn't go right to eating, but you had to wait for the widow to tuck down her head and grumble a little over the victuals, though there warn't really anything the matter with them. (1:49-50)

The 'poor lost lamb' is in keeping with her piety, and the tucking down her head to grumble is fittingly ambiguous. She may be saying grace, or she may be looking at and complaining about the food; the action of tucking down the head and the 'grumble' would apply to either, inextricably involving the religious and the social. The combination produces sivilization.

Good manners at table is more here than just an indication of a child's disliking the restraints of the adult world. That aspect is present — the child's vision questioning the absurdities of adult behaviour. But the adult behaviour being questioned is a specific sort of behaviour — Christian slave-owning society in the American South. Twain is concerned to capture the *signs* of this society, to record the denotations of manners, and relate the style of this society to its social and economic base. The association of good manners with Christian piety indicates the nature of Christianity in this society. That it is associated with 'correct' table manners indicates the shallow comprehension of Christianity — that is the immediate satirical evaluative point. But the further point is the important one — that Christianity as it is understood here provides the ideology for the social world. It provides a set of images and a set of social controls in the form of threats of hellfire for people who break its code. It is here as the ethical support for the economic system of slavery — the slavery that allows the social niceties and indeed necessitates them — necessitates the existence of the 'style' of the South so that time will be filled up while the slaves do the work.

We see the effects of Christianity as used in the South in microcosm on Huck; it makes him feel 'all cramped up'. The image is one of physical constraint, forcible loss of liberty. It directs us outward to the larger losses of liberty in the institution of slavery.

The widow and Miss Watson have no doubts about slavery at all — nor do they switch off their Christian beliefs when considering slavery. Rather, Miss Watson insists on bringing Christianity *to* the slaves. 'Miss Watson she kept pecking at me, and it got tiresome and lonesome. By-and-by they fetched the niggers in and had prayers . . .' (1:51). The attempts to make Huck well-mannered, the Christianity, and the slavery are all collocated in these two sentences. Sivilization is, in one range of its attitudes, epitomized here; and Huck feels his alienation from it, feels, in his recurrent term, 'lonesome'.

The most dramatic indication of the conscription of Christianity as an ideological component in the perpetuation of slavery is given in the episode at the end of the raft's voyage, when the King and Duke have sold Jim back into slavery to Silas Phelps. In Huck's struggle with his conscience about what to do, we see in action those values that are analysed in the opening chapters, see how the social mores of the opening section apply all the way down the river. If Huck were to help Jim to get free, he would break the social code. 'It would get all around, that Huck Finn helped a nigger to get his freedom; and if I was ever to see anybody from that town again, I'd be ready to get down and lick his boots for shame' (31:281). But breaking the social code is breaking the moral, Christian code. To help 'a nigger get his freedom' is to sin and to deserve hellfire:

> it hit me all of a sudden that here was the plain hand of
> Providence slapping me in the face and letting me know my
> wickedness was being watched all the time from up there in
> heaven, whilst I was stealing a poor old woman's nigger that
> hadn't ever done me no harm, and now was showing me there's
> One that's always on the lookout, and ain't agoing to allow no
> such miserable doings to go only just so fur and no further . . . .
> (31:281-2)

Huck's use of the pious phrases of his moral teachers has often been remarked on. It shows his indoctrination. But at the same time the vernacular context in which Huck puts the Christian concepts makes the concepts look ridiculous. Twain has captured a fine ambiguity here. And this becomes active in the way Huck's own untaught syntax leads him into an amazing ambiguity that sums up his moral dilemma, just as his untaught spelling of sivilization implied a moral judgment. He is expressing his sense of guilt at stealing the slave from the 'poor old woman' who has never hurt Huck, whom Huck has no cause to hurt. Huck, of course, is being hypocritically pious;

he has several reasons for disliking the poor old woman, and she has certainly done him a lot of harm in her cramping him, pecking at him — harm that is emblematic of and of course a basic component of the larger harm of which he may not be conscious — the moral indoctrination to which she has subjected him; the forcible conditioning, which goes under the name of a good, Christian education. Huck is in a mood of confessional wallowing rare for him though typical of the South we are shown. He has even been conditioned into that now.

What Huck's sentence syntactically expresses, though, is that the 'nigger' has never done Huck any harm — not that the widow hasn't done him any harm. And of course Jim hasn't done Huck any harm; so how can Huck return him to slavery? Further, Jim has positively cared for Huck — has done more than the negative 'hadn't ever done me no harm', so that that phrase works as a powerful litotes. Huck's emotions are working in the direction of this meaning and this sympathy towards Jim, while his indoctrinated social and moral Christian 'conscience' is expressing a false devotion to Miss Watson. Because his 'conscience' isn't his innate, intuitive and experiential conscience. And so, just as Huck's uncertainty about his sivilized conscience allows his heart and emotions to direct his actions so that he'll '*go* to hell', his uncertainty about his sivilization-taught syntax allows his heart and emotions to express themselves. Unable to pray he reflects 'It was because my heart warn't right; it was because I warn't square; it was because I was playing double' (31:282). The 'double' directs us to the verbal ambiguities expressive of this dilemma between his personal and his social-Christian value systems.

The final decision is a difficult one for Huck. He consciously choses 'wrong'. 'All right, then, I'll *go* to hell' (31:283). This is very different from most nineteenth-century fiction. The opposition between individual and society recurs continually; and the individual is often enough presented as making a decision to go against society. But the individual is generally convinced of the essential rightness of his or her decision, and knows that society is wrong.

The implication is that society is wrong here too. But Huck himself doesn't know that. For him the problem is nightmarish. Everything tells him that he is wrong. It is only his sound heart, his good feelings, and his developed relationship with Jim on the raft that make him decide to help free Jim. He is sure it will mean his own damnation — his own exclusion from society and everlasting torment in hell. But he makes his choice.

Not only, then, do the widow and aunt not offer alternative ways of life, but together they embody certain aspects of the society of the South. They feel themselves, however, in opposition to Pap Finn. At first Huck accepts this distinction. After his father has kidnapped him, he comes to enjoy Pap's way of life; he feels a freedom from sivilization, the freedom he had sought when he first escaped from the widow, now embodied in a positive way of life, not consisting of a negative running away.

> It was kind of lazy and jolly, laying off comfortable all day, smoking and fishing, and no books nor study. Two months or more run along, and my clothes got to be all rags and dirt, and I didn't see how I'd ever got to like it so well at the widow's, where you had to wash, and eat on a plate, and comb up, and go to bed and get up regular, and be for ever bothering over a book and have old Miss Watson pecking at you all the time. (6:75)

Huck, though, isn't free. At the widow's he had 'felt so lonesome I most wished I was dead' because he was locked in, punished, solitary. And with Pap too he is soon locked in, punished and solitary. 'But by-and-by pap got too handy with his hick'ry, and I couldn't stand it. I was all over welts. He got to going away so much, too, and locking me in. Once he locked me in and was gone three days. It was dreadful lonesome' (6:75).

These literal imprisonments occur throughout the novel. Huck is locked up by the widow and by his father. Jim is tied up on the raft and locked up in the novel's final episode. They provide the images of what the book is about — they establish a recurrent metaphor of imprisonment, of denial of freedom — contrasting with the ideal of the raft with its openness, its lack of confinement, with no one pushing it but time and the river.

What at first seemed to be alternative ways of life for Huck are shown to be very similar in their restrictions on freedom. Their similarities are emphasized even more by the fact that each imprisonment is so vulnerable to assault from the other. Huck was for a while happy enough with the widow because he was away from Pap 'and that was comfortable for me; I didn't want to see him no more'. When he suspects that Pap may turn up, he gets very worried; and indeed Pap does turn up and carry Huck off. But Huck gets equally worried after he has settled in with his father when he hears that

> people allowed there'd be another trial to get me away from him and give me to the widow for my guardian, and they guessed it would win, this time. This shook me up considerable, because I didn't want to go back to the widow's any more

and be so cramped up, and sivilized, as they called it.
(6:76)

Both states of imprisonment can be seen by Huck to represent a
freedom — in comparison to the one he has left; but as soon as one
is accepted, the other is seen as a threatening force that will imprison
him again. With both so easily and equally seen as threatening, it is
on the parallel restrictions of freedom of the two states that emphasis
finally rests for the reader, not on the false freedoms that mislead
Huck.

The way of life of the brutal Pap Finn is parallel to rather than in
opposition to the polite Christianity of the widow and Miss Watson.
Certainly he is pretty rough; certainly he does not possess many of
the trappings of social living (unlike the widow's, 'there warn't no
knives and forks on the place'); and he dresses in a fashion unacceptable to the widow and Miss Watson:

> As for his clothes — just rags, that was all. He had one ankle
> resting on t'other knee; the boot on that foot was busted, and
> two of his toes stuck through, and he worked them now and
> then. His hat was laying on the floor; an old black slouch
> with the top caved in, like a lid. (5:69)

Yet these cast-offs have at least once belonged to society. They are
worn-out rags — like those Huck wears when he is with Pap. They
show Pap Finn is at the very bottom of the society that supports
the widow and Miss Watson quite comfortably. But being at the
bottom is a place — society needs someone on the bottom.

Freedom from sivilization is shown not in worn-out clothes but
in the nakedness of Huck and Jim on the raft. There in discarding
clothing they discard society and all its values: 'we was always naked,
day and night, whenever the mosquitoes would let us' (19:179).
It is not an idyll; there are mosquitoes. But it is a genuine freedom.
If you're going to get rid of the mosquitoes then you are going to
have to make certain compromises with sivilization — put on clothes,
use mosquito repellent, clear the breeding grounds. Either that or
put up with the mosquitoes.

Freedom from sivilization brings its own hazards. But it is a
genuine freedom. Whenever society impinges on Jim and Huck's
vulnerable freedom, they are clothed again. Huck is given a set of
clothing by the Grangerfords; when he returns to the raft he throws
it away. The two con-men the King and Duke intrude on the raft
and the Duke suggests that Jim in order to remain free should be

dressed up 'in King Lear's outfit'. Society has intruded and Jim has to dress to its requirements, dress here in the dissimulative way appropriate to the crooked plans and behaviour of the King and Duke.

Pap Finn still wears clothes, for all their roughness; he is still part of Southern society. His membership is indicated most strikingly and importantly by his fury at the existence of the free negro. The episode has no importance in the 'plot' — no importance that is to Huck's escape, which is often seen as the interest of the book, the *narrative*. And it has no importance to any description of what Huck suffers at the hands of Pap. We see Pap's brutality to his son often enough — there is no necessity to expand on this. The point of this episode is to show that it is the same brutality that is the basis of his attitude towards blacks, that supports slavery. The violence of this episode is one of the forces that maintains slavery, the violence that claims for itself some moral superiority. 'And to see the cool way of that nigger — why, he wouldn't a give me the road if I hadn't shoved him out o' the way' (6:78). The same evening Pap gets drunk and delirious and attacks Huck with a knife. Huck leaves the next day.

The Christian support of slavery we have seen demonstrated in the widow and Miss Watson. But belief in Christianity alone could not maintain slavery. It can provide an ideology of the chosen of God, or of God's natural order; but more than an ideology is needed. The requisite acting out of the belief, the necessary brutality and human contempt towards blacks (as towards his own son) is shown in Pap. His behaviour is a necessary complement to the widow's and Miss Watson's, not despite but because of his brutality. All down the river we will see the piety of sivilization allied with violence. It is there in the sermon to the Shepherdsons and Grangerfords, the men all with their guns 'between their knees' or 'handy against the wall', while the sermon is 'all about brotherly love, and such like tiresome-ness' (18:169); it is there in the moral righteousness that prompts the townspeople to try and lynch Sherburn for shooting Boggs, and the King and Duke for duping the Wilkes family, and in the towns-people who tar and feather the King and Duke for their misde-meanours. So quite naturally Pap's qualities are in fact shared by the widow and Miss Watson. When Huck returns from his first escape, 'the widow she cried over me, and called me a poor lost lamb, and she called me a lot of other names, too, but she never meant no harm by it' (1:49). It is not clear whether the other names are of the same order as the pietistic 'poor lost lamb'. Huck's dry comment 'she never meant no harm by it' might indicate they were, or might equally indicate they were abusive names such as his father might use. Both interpretations are possible; and because both are equally valid interpretations, the verbal ambiguity becomes a moral ambiguity basic to Twain's picture of the South. Pap and the widow speak the same language (even if the widow might seem not to, she can swear as well as Pap). Similarly Miss Watson and Pap are both motivated by the same money ethos of this society; they are both ever-eager to make a buck — despite their seeming outsider status from the bourgeois commercial norm. Miss Watson might seem too ethereal and ladylike to let money considerations be her primary concern but when an opportunity turns up that she can take, she takes it; she plans to sell Jim down the river for $800. That is why Jim runs away. And Huck runs away from his father who has imprisoned him to get hold of his money. The two seeming alternatives of Pap and the widow and Miss Watson are in accord.

Consequently, to gain his freedom, Huck has to escape the widow and Miss Watson, and his father. Whichever one he tries to find 'freedom' with, he is sure to be discovered and abducted by the other. He meditates on this when he has finally escaped to Jackson's Island. 'I got to thinking that if I could fix up some way to keep pap and the widow from trying to follow me, it would be a certainer thing than trusting to luck ...' (7:83). It is this paralleling of the persecutions of the widow and Pap that is suggested in Twain's phrasing in *Life on the Mississippi* (1883), when he refers to

> Huck Finn, son of the town drunkard of my time out west, there. He has run away from his persecuting father, and from a persecuting good widow who wishes to make a nice, truth-telling, respectable boy of him; and with him a slave of the widow's has also escaped. (25)

The passage suggests, too, the way in which Pap is not an outsider but a figure in the social setting — 'the town drunkard'. James M. Cox (1954) has claimed that 'Huck is, in the deepest sense, an outcast. Although Tom is an orphan, he at least has relatives who recognize his credentials and have adopted him. Huck has only Pap, the drunkard, the outcast himself ...' (236). Cox is correct in stressing the way in which Huck has a self-image of being an outcast; hence his 'lonesomeness' that impels his search for belongingness with Tom's robber band. But to see Huck's father as an outcast is to misunderstand the social vision Twain presents; Huck's father very much has a role in the society — he is not just the drunkard, as Cox describes him, but the town drunkard. That is how Twain sees him.

The false freedoms of *Huckleberry Finn*

As Richard P. Adams stresses, Huck's 'background is about as purely poor-white as it could be' (296), and he quotes an important passage from *A Connecticut Yankee*, looking forward to nineteenth-century America:

> when the 'poor whites' of our South who were always despised and frequently insulted by the slave-lords around them and who owed their base condition simply to the presence of slavery in their midst, were yet pusillanimously ready to side with the slave-lords in all political moves for the upholding and perpetuating of slavery, and did also finally shoulder their muskets and pour out their lives in an effort to prevent the destruction of that very institution which degraded them.

Poor whites like Pap Finn are pauperized, degraded, exploited — and bamboozled into supporting the system that causes that very pauperization, degradation and exploitation.

The other important feature of Twain's account of *Huckleberry Finn* in *Life on the Mississippi* is the way that slavery is put firmly in the forefront of the social picture. Twain stresses that the widow from whom Huck flees is the widow from whom the slave flees. Jim and Huck are put on a par in their search for freedom, just as Pap and the widow are put on a par in their hostility to it. In his notebook Twain described the book in a way that stressed the distance between the morality of sivilization and the goodness of the alienated, outsider Huck. It was 'a book of mine where a sound heart and a deformed conscience come into collision and conscience suffers a defeat.' But this moral schema is firmly situated in a social context, the conscience has been 'deformed' by the values of 'sivilization'.

The sense of freedom that the raft seems to offer is one shared by both Jim and Huck. After the experience of the Shepherdson-Grangerford feud, Huck says:

> I was powerful glad to get away from the feuds, and so was Jim to get away from the swamp. We said there warn't no home like a raft, after all. Other places do seem so cramped up and smothery, but a raft don't. You feel mighty free and easy and comfortable on a raft. (18:176)

But it is as false and vulnerable a freedom as any other Huck has tried. Already the raft had been run down by a steamboat. In the chapter following Huck's reflections on feeling 'mighty free and

31

easy' the King and Duke arrive. Society and the things of society cannot be avoided.

The raft offers very much a negative freedom, too. It is like Huck's running off to the woods from the widow's. It provides no positive, free way of life. It offers us a negation of the society of the South, but the negation of the negation is needed for us to find freedom positively presented. Certainly Jim does have an objective in being on the raft — to reach Cairo; but the raft drifts past it. With the arrival of the King and Duke, even their negative freedom is circumscribed. The Duke soon suggests: 'Whenever we see anybody coming, we can tie Jim hand and foot with a rope, and lay him in the wigwam and show this handbill and say we captured him up the river . . .' (20:195). Certainly Jim is tied up in order to be kept free. But his captivity is as real a captivity as ever. In simulating captivity he is experiencing it even more directly; it is one of the recurrent images of the book, being locked up or tied up; and here the imprisonment occurs on the wide, open 'freedom' of the raft and river. And the acted captivity becomes actual when Jim is sold on the strength of the handbill printed to assure his freedom.

Not only is the raft vulnerable to the forces hostile to freedom (it is the King and the Duke who sell Jim), it also becomes an implement in the power of such forces. Since the freedom of the raft is undirected, it is susceptible to being directed in ways hostile to freedom if strong enough anti-freedom forces appear. It is not a state of positive freedom that can repel intrusion; with no dynamic of its own, simply drifting with the current, it cannot resist anti-freedom forces. It is used as readily by the King and Duke to exploit the towns down the river, as it is by Huck and Jim to flee. The raft is committed neither to freedom nor to captivity. Its most important feature here is that it can only drift on the back of some stronger force — time, the current.

Through the raft's drifting, Huck and Jim come into contact with the society of the South, a society no different from the one that they are fleeing. The Grangerford episode is representative of events down the river, and illustrates those aspects of sivilization already indicated. The emphasis on polite behaviour, especially on a Sunday, after the manner of the widow and Miss Watson is made clear by young Buck Grangerford's asking Huck, 'Do you like to comb up, Sundays, and all that kind of foolishness? You bet I don't, but ma she makes me' (17:157). The piety of the widow and aunt is paralleled by the late Emmeline Grangerford's religiosity, and by the books in the Grangerford household; conspicuous are the Bible, *Pilgrim's*

Progress, and a hymnal. This element is brought out more significantly in the sermon on brotherly love.

> Next Sunday we all went to church, about three mile, everybody
> a-horseback. The men took their guns along, so did Buck, and
> kept them between their knees or stood them handy against the
> wall. The Shepherdsons done the same. It was pretty ornery
> preaching — all about brotherly love, and such-like tiresomeness;
> but everybody said it was a good sermon, and they all talked it
> over going home, and had such a powerful lot to say about faith,
> and good works, and free grace, and prefore-ordestination, and
> I don't know what all, that it did seem to me to be one of the
> roughest Sundays I had run across yet. (18:169)

In the shoot-out that follows the next day the same adjective is used: 'I reck'n dey's gwyne to be mighty rough times' (18:173), the Negro Jack predicts. It is an adjective Huck had earlier applied to the widow Douglas's attempts at sivilizing at the very beginning of the book; 'it was rough living in the house all the time, considering how dismal regular and decent the widow was in all her ways' (1:49). It is one of Huck's significant terms, one of the ways he characterizes aspects of sivilization. And on all occasions it is an outsider who makes the comment — not a WASP member of this society. The association of the theology and the violence by this same adjective that has already been applied to the widow's sivilizing, is a sardonic meaningful ambiguity. Brutality and piety are once again firmly identified. And the rougher the preaching, the rougher the violence of the shooting. There is more than the obvious irony of the held guns contrasting with the topic of the sermon. The verbal associations in 'roughest Sundays' and 'rough times' suggests that piety and brutality are naturally characterizable by the same adjective; the guns are *naturally* taken into church — it is no longer an irony.

But the shooting has its basis in more than just brutality. Its ideological validation is found in another basic characteristic of the society, one hinted at in the description of the Grangerfords' parlour curtains 'with pictures painted on them, of castles with vines all down the walls, and cattle coming down to drink' (17:163). What is suggested here is a certain mode of chivalrous, Scottish baronial, highland cattle, idealized romanticism. The vines might suggest some Mediterranean fortress castle, a perpetual prisoner immured within; the drinking cattle evoke Scottish baronialism. Both suggestions from the curtains find their parallels in the behaviour of the

Southerners; the delight in legends of the suffering prisoner, the romantic trappings, that we find in Tom Sawyer, and in the King and the Duke; the delight in revenge, in robber barons' chivalry, in family honour, that we find in the feud. The two aspects are closely linked, indeed merged. This conception of honour, courage, chivalry is inextricably involved with striking a pose, romantic rhetoric, tear-jerking sentimentalism. It provides an ideological focus for the tearful piety and for the brutality of the South — so that the Shepherdson-Grangerford feud is waged with the mindless violence that we can see in Pap Finn, though 'ennobled' by a conception of honour and chivalry associable with the pious nonsense of Emmeline Grangerford on the one hand, and, tellingly, on the other hand with the histrionics of the King and the Duke. Just as Pap Finn and the widow and Miss Watson seem to be abysses of respectability apart, yet united in their basic attitudes, so too do Emmeline Grangerford and the King and the Duke seem separated by an unbridgeable chasm; but her attitudes and their attitudes are aspects of a certain Southern aesthetic, part of the overall ideology of the South.

In *Life on the Mississippi* Twain makes some explicit comments about these various components of Southern ideology. After discussing the advances brought about by the French revolution, he writes:

> Then comes Sir Walter Scott with his enchantments, and by his single might checks this wave of progress, and even turns it back; sets the world in love with dreams and phantoms; with decayed and swinish forms of religion; with decayed and degraded systems of government; with the sillinesses and emptinesses, sham grandeurs, sham gauds, and sham chivalries of a brainless and worthless long-vanished society. He did measureless harm; more real and lasting harm, perhaps, than any other individual that ever wrote. Most of the world has now outlived good part of these harms, though by no means all of them; but in our South they flourish pretty forcefully still. Not so forcefully as half a generation ago, perhaps, but still forcefully. There, the genuine and wholesome civilization of the nineteenth century is curiously confused and commingled with the Walter Scott Middle Age sham civilization and so you have practical, common-sense, progressive ideas, and progressive works, mixed up with the duel, the inflated speech, and the jejeune romanticism of an absurd past that is dead . . .

> If one take up a Northern or Southern literary periodical of forty, or fifty years ago, he will find it filled with wordy, windy,

flowery 'eloquence', romanticism, sentimentality — all imitated
from Sir Walter, and sufficiently badly done, too — innocent
travesties of his style and methods, in fact. (265-7)

The attitudes that Twain indicates are all embodied in the Grangerford
household, with the 'sham gauds' of the decorations, the 'wordy,
windy, flowery "eloquence", romanticism, sentimentality' of
Emmeline, the 'sham chivalries' of the feud that shows on a large
scale the idiot brutality of the duel. The last shootings that Huck
sees are provoked by the 'jejeune romanticism' of the elopement.
What the episode does is dramatically isolate and emphasize this
third facet of the ideology of the South, and place it alongside the
religiosity and the brutality as a major theme in Twain's analysis.
Romantic chivalry provides the sanctification of violence; it is the
ideological resolution of the alliance of the Christian pious and the
brutal; and like the other two forces, it is something typical of the
entire South. Twain refers to *Don Quixote* and the way in which the
good work it did has been nullified in *Life on the Mississippi*.

> A curious exemplification of the power of a single book for good
> or harm is shown in the effects wrought by *Don Quixote* and
> those wrought by *Ivanhoe*. The first swept the world's
> admiration for the medieval chivalry-silliness out of existence;
> and the other restored it. As far as our South is concerned, the
> good work done by Cervantes is pretty nearly a dead letter, so
> effectually has Scott's pernicious work undermined it. (267)

In *Huckleberry Finn* Tom cites *Don Quixote* to show Huck how
the Sunday school party they ambush is in fact Spaniards and Arabs.
'He said if I warn't so ignorant, but had read a book called *Don
Quixote*, I would know without asking. He said it was all done by
enchantment' (3:62). Tom's models for the conduct of his gang are
to be the correctly chivalrous and romantic — and such is the need
for a code of the romantic that he takes it from *Don Quixote*,
finding the images of action he wants, blissfully unaware of the
satire he is missing, arrogantly superior to the 'ignorant' Huck. The
values Tom finds in Cervantes are the values associated with him
elsewhere. When Jim and Huck find the wrecked steamboat, Huck
says 'Do you reckon Tom Sawyer would ever go by this thing?
Not for pie, he wouldn't. He'd call it an adventure' (12:122). We
find out in the next chapter that the steamboat is called the *Walter
Scott*. And the language Huck uses to describe the boarding Tom
would have made is significant: 'he'd land on that wreck if it was his

35

last act. And wouldn't he throw style from it?' (12:122). 'Act' carries the histrionic connotations here — playing at chivalry, bravery, honour — and associates Tom with the two professional actors, the King and Duke and their 'style'. But the consequences of this sort of 'style' reach way beyond Tom's childish games. As Twain put it in *Life on the Mississippi*, 'Sir Walter has so large a hand in making Southern character, as it existed before the war, that he is in a great measure responsible for the war' (266). Foner argues that 'Twain even charged that Scott had caused the Civil War' (1972, p.262). But that it is not quite what Twain claims; had he claimed that, then Foner's comment that 'this personal devil interpretation of American history was superficial' (262) would indeed be correct. But Twain distinguishes between cause and ideological rationalization. As Foner observes, 'An analysis of Twain's post-Civil War writings reveals that he understood clearly that the foundation of slavery had been the profit motive' (258), and Foner demonstrates the continuity of analysis underlying Twain's hostility to slavery and to imperialism. The profit motive underlying slavery caused the war. But the writings of Sir Walter Scott, as Twain saw so clearly, provided the ideology, the ready-made, romantic model for the life-style based on that barbarous system of economically motivated exploitation. And in its validation of that life-style, the Scott ideology gave it a strength — like the ethical idealism of London's Iron Heel plutocracy — that led it into the war.

Tom, of course, has never represented true freedom. He is not a persecutor like Pap and the widow, yet he is equally inhibiting of Huck's freedom, and for a long time Huck is not able to realize this. Indeed, Huck never does formally conceptualize this in his narration. Twain leaves it an ambiguity of the book as to whether Huck finally realizes Tom's true nature; or prefers not to think about it, and directs his attention to very different values — implicitly evaluating Tom negatively, but without having to say so and reject a once good friend.

Tom's romanticism is not, as it first seemed to Huck, an escape from the persecutions of society, but a product of the seemingly contradictory forces that create the society's ideology. Tom is a safety-valve ensuring the perpetuation of the society, by seeming to offer an alternative, a rebellion. But it is a rebellion firmly placed within its useful social role by sivilization, it is one of the components of that very sivilization. The night Huck had been told of Moses and the Bulrushers, been pecked at, told of the good and bad place, and finally sat 'lonesome' at his window, Tom had come offering a sort of escape to the robber band. But to participate in this seeming alternative to sivilization, Huck had first to belong to sivilization. He had already followed Tom's demands to 'go back to the widow and be respectable' (1:49). Even after that he was nearly disallowed membership of the band as he had no parents he could promise to kill. It is an effective irony that Huck's lack of social appendages should be used to prevent him from joining an anti-social force. But of course it isn't an anti social force. 'Ben Rogers said he couldn't get out much, only Sundays, and so he wanted to begin next Sunday; but all the boys said it would be wicked to do it on Sunday, and that settled the thing' (2:59). Not only is one potential robber locked up all the week except Sundays, but the other potential robbers refuse to rob on days unacceptable to this Christian society. The organization of the gang is equally lacking in freedom. Everything has to be done according to the rules. They must ransom even if they don't understand the word because, as Tom says, 'Do you want to go to doing different from what's in the books, and get things all muddled up?' (2:57).

Tom's inadequacies as a source of freedom for Huck are obvious to the reader. Tom shares the attributes of the society against which he 'rebels', and his is only a childhood disobedience, unopposed to the bases of sivilization. Huck and Tom may seem to form an alliance of youth against age — but there is room within sivilization for youthful games and adventures and Scottian romanticism. It is the alliance that ignores age differentials — that between Huck and Jim — that is in opposition to the basic codes of society.

Tom's inadequacies are not obvious to Huck, though. Certainly he is not impressed by the Sunday School attack and the theory of the genie of the lamp. 'So then I judge that all that stuff was only just one of Tom Sawyer's lies. I reckoned he believed in the A-rabs and the elephants, but as for me I think different. It had all the marks of a Sunday school' (3:64). Leo Marx has argued that with this statement 'Huck parts company with Tom. The fact is that Huck has rejected Tom's romanticizing of experience; moreover he has rejected it as part of the larger pattern of society's make-believe, typified by Sunday school' (222).

But Huck, though he certainly disbelieves Tom's account, does not reject Tom. Huck himself uses lies all down the river, and he passes no disapproval of Tom's lying here, nor does he express any sense of being cheated. The emphasis before the last section of the book is always on admiration for Tom. Though Huck occasionally refers to Pap and the widow and Miss Watson when he's on the raft, it is never to regret their absence. But when he escapes from his father's hut, he comments: 'I did wish Tom Sawyer was there, I knowed he would take an interest in this kind of business and throw in the fancy touches' (7:85). The 'fancy touches' may arouse our doubts about Tom, but the 'did' in 'I did wish' emphasizes Huck's tone of regret that Tom isn't with him. Huck kills a pig to use its blood to make it seem as if he has been murdered when he escapes from his father's cabin, when Huck tells him 'the whole thing', Jim 'said Tom Sawyer couldn't get up no better plan than what I had' (8:95). Both Huck and Jim naturally value Tom's abilities, and so for all their doubtful comments on Tom's schemes in the final chapters, they are nevertheless deceived enough by his image to go along with him in them.

Yet Tom's conforming characteristics have been present from the beginning of the book, and our last sight of him before Huck's journey placed him firmly within the total society of the village in one perfectly expressive symbolic picture. Huck is hiding on the island watching the ferry-boat that is carrying the searchers for the body. 'Most everybody was on the boat. Pap, and Judge Thatcher, and Bessie Thatcher, and Jo Harper, and Tom Sawyer, and his old Aunt Polly, and Sid and Mary, and plenty more' (8:90). Though Miss Watson and the widow are absent, the judge who was to act for them in regaining Huck from his father is there as their representative. Tom here is put in alliance with, not in opposition to, the other members of his society. And the implications of this image are demonstrated on the river voyage. Huck begins to notice how Tom's characteristics turn up elsewhere in sivilization. He had not been upset by Tom's 'lies' about the 'A-rabs', but when the King and Duke arrive he says: 'It didn't take me long to make up my mind that these liars warn't no kings nor dukes, at all, but just low-down humbugs and frauds' (19:185-6). Lying is now seen to be associated with roguery, and Huck passes an explicit moral judgment, unlike anything he has said before. But these lies are, of course, a way of seeing the realities of sivilization – these palpable liars give a lead on the less obvious 'low-down humbugs and frauds'. 'What was the use to tell Jim these warn't real kings and dukes? It wouldn't a done no good; and besides, it was just as I said; you couldn't tell them from the real kind' (23:218). Lying, romantic rituals, performances are associated with roguery now. Huck has already identified the King and the Duke as being like his father, 'his kind of people' (19:186) – allying them with the forces of brutality, as well as with their proclaimed romantic rituals. Romanticizing and posing are, by the end of the raft voyage, no longer able to be seen as charmingly childish, as originally they had seemed in Tom. Now they are in a new, far more serious context.

The concluding chapters of the book identify Tom finally and inescapably with the world and values of the King and Duke, and the Shepherdsons and Grangerfords — and through them with Pap and (via Emmeline) the widow and Miss Watson. Though the manner of the last section suggests again that Tom is merely childish, this is a suggestion that is qualified by the full experience of the river. The things Tom represents are childish, are 'romantic juvenilities', but the return to the boys' adventure story manner does not involve any lessening in seriousness for the novel's concerns. The adventure story manner is Tom's consciousness — but that is placed in the wider awareness, the developed consciousness of Huck, that the book has cumulatively created. We now see the materials of the book's opening in a context widened and deepened by the experiences of the river voyage, and we see how Tom, and the romanticism he represents, reduce the serious issue of freedom to a childish game, to play — in the word's full ambiguity associating it with both childishness and with the 'acting' of the King and Duke. Leo Marx objects that 'the most serious motive in the novel, Jim's yearning for freedom, is made the object of nonsense' (217). But the *motive* is not made the object of nonsense. Tom's behaviour and the methods he uses to 'free' Jim are shown to be nonsensical; but the motive of the escape for freedom remains as vitally important as ever. Its importance underlines how the romantic rebellion which Tom plays at will never produce freedom, how, indeed, it is not rebellion. Romanticism is here put in direct contact with the issue of slavery — just as Christian piety had been in Huck's struggle with his conscience, and racist brutality had been in Pap's rage at the free Negro. All three forces combine to inhibit genuine freedom. Out of Tom's romantic game, serious meanings emerge.

The raft voyage showed in action the basic forces of the society that were analysed and isolated in the opening chapters. And it is these forces that we naturally find again in the last section of the book. Whatever Huck may have learned about respect for human individuality on the raft, he is able to fall back easily and perhaps even unconsciously into the thought patterns of society. When asked if anyone was killed in his invented steamboat explosion, he says: 'No'm. Killed a nigger,' and Aunt Sally replies 'Well, it's lucky; because sometimes people do get hurt' (32:291). There are no worries about slavery or about the sanctity of Negro life at the Phelpses. Uncle Silas, too, brings Christianity to the slaves — he 'come in every day or two to pray with' Jim (36:321). The piety is the same as ever. Aunt Sally tells how someone injured on a steamboat 'turned blue all over, and died in the hope of a glorious resurrection' (32:291). It is part of the Southern language. Huck's reaction to this world is, in the midst of Tom's plots, to get away as before. 'I begun to lay for a chance; I reckoned I would sneak out and go for the woods till the weather moderated' (37:326). The raft in its drifting has brought Huck and Jim inevitably no nearer to any positive freedom than when they began. Tom's conforming characteristics are brought out, as James M. Cox has pointed out, even more emphatically by his adopting the name of Sid Sawyer, 'the Good Boy of *Tom Sawyer*; he was the eternal prude, the darling of a puritan Sunday School' (237). Tom as ever insists on following the books, going by the rules, and on not offending society. Just as the robbers had said it was wrong to steal on Sundays, so Tom prohibits certain sorts of theft. A water melon is not to be stolen, but

> as long as we was representing a prisoner, we had a perfect right to steal anything on this place we had the least use for, to get ourselves out of prison with. He said if we warn't prisoners it would be a very different thing, and nobody but a mean ornery person would steal when he warn't a prisoner. (35:314)

Huck is amazed, of course, that Tom should want to help Jim escape since he 'was a boy that was respectable, and well brung up; and had a character to lose; and folks at home that had characters' (34:304). He realizes how closely Tom is integrated with society on the issue of slavery. But when Tom offers to help, he nevertheless believes in Tom's sincerity. He does not imagine that Tom's rebelliousness is *only* a game.

Tom's games in the opening chapters were harmless enough. What Huck hasn't done is relate them to the games that might have had serious consequences on the river. For Huck himself has learnt not to play any more Tom-like tricks after the incident of Jim's being bitten by a rattlesnake. That showed the physical dangers of Tom's style of behaviour. There are also moral, spiritual dangers. When Huck gets separated from Jim in the fog, he regains the raft and tricks Jim into believing it was all a dream — a dream whose meanings Jim begins to interpret. Huck points to some leaves and branches showing that the raft's collision with one of the islands in the fog was not a dream at all — and Jim brilliantly continues his interpretation of dreams to present a moving assessment of Huck's behaviour.

> 'What do dey stan' for? I's gwyne to tell you. When I got all wore out wid work, en wid de callin' for you, en went to sleep, my heart wuz mos' broke bekase you wuz los', en I didn' k'yer

no mo' what become er me en de raf'. En when I wake up en
fine you back again', all safe en soun', de tears come en I could
a got down on my knees en kiss' yo' foot I's so thankful. En all
you wuz thinkin' 'bout wuz how you could make a fool uv ole
Jim wid a lie. Dat truck dah is *trash*; en trash is what people is
dat puts dirt on de head er dey fren's en makes 'em ashamed.'
(15:142-3)

Another in the developing sequence of incidents that shows the
nastier side of lies, once simple, Tom Sawyerish games, it is crucial in
changing Huck's attitudes to game-playing at other people's expense.
Game-playing of the Tom Sawyer variety always is at someone
else's expense, it begins to emerge. When Huck had wanted to
board the wrecked *Walter Scott* it was because Tom would have
done it. 'He'd call it an adventure' (12:122). But it turns out dan-
gerously. 'I told Jim all about what happened inside the wreck, and
at the ferry-boat; and I said these kinds of things was adventures;
but he said he didn't want no more adventures' (14:132). The word
now carries serious overtones. For Tom, though, an adventure
remains just something exciting; he demands to know all about
Huck's trip 'because it was a grand adventure, and mysterious, and
so it hit him where he lived' (33:295). And when Tom is asked why
he had wanted to set Jim free when he was already free he replies,
'Why, I wanted the *adventure* of it; and I'd a waded neck deep in
blood . . .' (42:365).

But there are two sorts of adventure. Tom's irresponsible ones —
freeing a free slave, playing games with people; and there are those
with a purpose, like the raft voyage down-river. Tom cannot see the
difference; all that matters is the excitement, not the result — as the
'A-rab' ambush showed. And there is likely to be more excitement
the less the result matters. The last chapters show the dangers of
playing the game of adventure in a serious context, playing the game
— and Henry Nash Smith has remarked on the 'devastating pun'
(133) — of Evasion (*Mark Twain: the Development of a Writer*).

As Tom is playing the game of Evasion, it is natural that none of
his plans work. The attempt to dig out Jim with case knives is too
arduous so Tom decides 'we got to dig him out with the picks, and
let on it's case-knives' (36:319). The final escape is disastrously
bungled and the game results in the shooting that isn't only a game,
and Tom is wounded. 'Tom was the gladdest of all, because he had a
bullet in the calf of his leg' (40:348). The gun-law of the Grangerfords
intrudes naturally, and it is only luck that prevents an equivalent to
the death of Buck in that earlier game.

The genuine seeker after freedom doesn't have time for the romantic posturings and ineffectualities of Tom. Nor can he afford to trust the literary rebels, the romantic poseurs; like Scott, they turn back progress, they are in effect (and often in intention) reactionary. The genuine escaper must insist on escaping. A series of important echoes point to Tom's preoccupation with the *act* of escaping. There are the inscriptions Tom orders Jim to carve on the wall:

> 3. *Here a lonely heart broke, and a worn spirit went to its rest, after thirty-seven years of solitary captivity.* 4. *Here, homeless and friendless, after thirty-seven years of bitter captivity, perished a noble stranger, natural son of Louis XIV.*
> Tom's voice trembled, whilst he was reading them, and he most broke down. (38:332)

The phrases and the emotion we have seen too clearly before. The innocent quality of Tom's early posing is now seen for what it is — reactionary, monarchically-oriented gesturing, identified with the phoneyness of the King and Duke — the pair who sold Jim back into slavery. The Duke's early lament was: ' "Some day I'll lie down in it and forget it all, and my poor broken heart will be at rest." He went on a-wiping' (19:182). And the King, also sobbing, claims: 'your eyes is lookin' at this very moment on the pore disappeared Dauphin, Looy the Seventeen, son of Looy the Sixteen and Marry Antonette' (19:184). But it is not just that Tom's behaviour and attitudes conform to sivilization's. His schemes parody the ways in which Huck had grown aware of Jim as an individual and come to understand the nature of the society; and they parody, too, stages in his struggle towards freedom. For his adventure Tom wants rattlesnakes in Jim's hut — and this is more than just part of his ridiculousness. It recalls Jim's being bitten by rattlesnakes in Huck's Tom-like trick. Tom has another scheme: 'when Louis XIV was going to light out of the Toolerie a servant girl done it' (39:340) — delivered an anonymous letter, that is. Tom wants to disguise Huck as just such a servant girl. Apart from the association with the King's proclaimed father somewhat tarnishing the associations of the episode, the scheme recalls the occasion when Huck did indeed have to disguise himself as a girl to find out about the dangers of being followed before he and Jim left Jackson's Island. Frank Baldanza has argued that without advanced planning, and spurred by momentary impulses, Mark Twain — in all probability unconsciously — constructed whole passages of *Huckleberry Finn* on an aesthetic principle of repetition and variation. Because the process was unconscious, it does not attain the regularity of Proust's employment of the Vinteuil theme . . . . (277-8)

But the correspondences are too meaningful to be seen as merely unconscious; and the role is not merely one of aesthetic patterning. The aesthetic is integrated with the social meaning of the materials. Baldanza remarks:

One could nearly make a parlor game of searching out minor correspondences like Huck's dressing as a girl when he visits Mrs Loftus, and Tom's later insistence on Huck's assumption of the 'yaller wench's frock' when he delivers the note to the Phelpses. The very proliferation of such repetitions, in fact, proves that Twain had no control over them and that they simply flowed from his pen as exuberant impulse. (281)

But the very proliferation proves no such thing. Twain was not interested in empty aesthetic surfaces; that is the province of the King and the Duke and other such fraudulent old world, theatrical, cultural artists. Twain's use of repetition and variation is directed to the revelation of the development of Huck's consciousness, to indicating the progressive stages of Huck's attainment of freedom. The variations are not merely random, they are dynamic and progressive. The change shows us things; it is not cyclic and conservative, like Conrad's vision of revolution succeeded by revolution in *Nostromo*. Each variation takes us to or indicates the existence of the next stage in a development; Tom is fixed in cyclic repetitions that trivialize and etiolate crucial stages in Huck's escape; but Tom's static repetitions are to be seen in the context of the urgent and progressive dynamic of the movement towards growth and freedom (the two things are paralleled and identified) in Huck and Jim. Baldanza recalls

how Huck early in the book saws his way out of his father's cabin undetected because he works behind a blanket that is stretched over the wall; toward the end of the book, Jim's escape is managed through a hole dug beneath the cabin, again disguised by a hanging blanket. (278)

This is not mere empty aesthetic patterning; it is a patterning that underlines the parallels and the discrepancies between the real search for freedom and the unreal game that Tom plays. Huck describes the crucial incident of his escape:

> I reckon I had hunted the place over as much as a hundred times; well, I was 'most of all the time at it, because it was about the only way to put in the time. But this time I found something at last; I found an old rusty wood-saw without any handle; it was laid in between a rafter and the clapboards of the roof. I greased it up and went to work. (6:75)

For Huck the escape is a matter of urgency. For Tom, freeing Jim is a game and his treatment of the situation is very different. Huck goes to get a couple of case knives with which to dig Jim out. Tom asks for another.

> 'Smouch three,' he says; 'we want one to make a saw out of.'
> 'Tom, if it ain't unregular and irreligious to sejest it,' I says, 'there's an old rusty saw-blade around yonder sticking under the weatherboarding behind the smoke-house.'
> He looked kind of weary and discouraged-like, and says:
> 'It ain't no use to try to learn you nothing, Huck. Run along and smouch the knives — three of them.' So I done it. (35:317)

Huck's suggestion certainly is 'unregular and irreligious'. Tom insists on regularity, following the rules of escaping; and the romantic rules are those of a society that is supported by religion, whose religion is a mixture of Christianity and Scott romanticism. Tom isn't serious in his 'freeing' of Jim; Jim could never be freed this way, so the religious code of society that sees freeing a slave as a sin (remember Huck's struggle with his conscience on this issue) will not be broken.

False freedom must be sought for in a 'regular' way and the regular way is the romantic one of making a knife into a saw, rather than of using a convenient saw-blade. Our memories of that first escape, and the use Huck made of the saw-blade so fortunately found, emphasize the unseriousness of Tom's attitudes here, his lack of concern for freedom, his lack of freedom in being so rule-bound himself. Someone who really wants to get free does not worry about the rules, forgets — or has no time to remember — that in correct romance saws are made from knives. Huck takes whatever is on hand and gets right into it. 'I greased it up and went to work.' But Tom, who has no intention of getting free or freeing anyone else, who has no intention of leaving his society, concentrates on the adventure of it, the game, the hocus-pocus romanticism. What he does has to look good, has to be regular. Because for Tom there will never be any need to use the knife made from a saw, after all.

The ending of *Huckleberry Finn*, then, is structured in such a way with these echoes and correspondences that the seeming freedom which Tom offers is firmly discredited and finally repudiated. From the beginning Huck was confronted by a sustained pattern of a choice of two false freedoms. Tom's role as an alternative to his father or to the widow or to Miss Watson is at last discredited. He isn't an alternative to any of them any more than any of them is in any sense an alternative to any other of them. Piety and politeness, brutality, romanticism are not different ways of life but are all aspects of this one world of the slave-owning South.

Tom's rebellion is a convenient one for sivilization; it serves as a safety-valve — it gives the illusion of freedom without in any way disturbing society's basis or fabric: 'and I couldn't ever understand, before, until that minute and that talk, how he *could* help a body set a nigger free, with his bringing-up' (42:366). At last Huck is in a position to understand — to understand that Tom never would help anyone escape. At the end of the book he is in a position to try again for his own freedom — his father and Miss Watson are dead; the specific restraints are going — gone if Tom is seen as consciously discredited in Huck's eyes. Perhaps he can now gain his freedom as Jim has finally gained his freedom. Certainly at the end of the book Huck hasn't got what he expected in his escape from the restrictions of the adult world. The specific restrictions put on him by Pap, the widow and Miss Watson, and Tom are simply things that exist throughout this society; so even if he is free of the restraints of those specific people, society still lives by the same values; his childhood escape is into an adult world of identical restrictions, identical social forces. We thought we were drilling into the bank but it turned out to be the prison. The only way to get true freedom is to grow aware of the false freedoms, and reject them.

The pointlessness, the ineffectualness, the playing of games that Tom demonstrates in this last section show us that someone like Tom will never be free — he is so bound to the trappings and rules of pseudo-rebellion. He is an important type for the political novel, and for political literature in general. The radical whose radicalism is only that of surface, magazine subscriptions, signing petitions, while living the comfortable bourgeois intellectual life, accumulating a library of marxist literature (don't we all). As Ed Sanders puts it in

The false freedoms of *Huckleberry Finn*

Investigative Poetry: 'if I go to prison, what will happen to my 15,000 books?' (13). The only way Jim and Huck will get freedom is by themselves — either individually or with each other. You don't get freedom by enlisting the help of the Toms. Tom has no interest in freeing Jim, it's only a game, the pretence of romantic escape. Jim is free already in fact — and Tom's attitude is shown in his not disclosing this: Tom in effect *prolongs the slavery* which Jim experiences, by keeping him locked up when he could announce the fact that Jim has been freed. He wants his game, he doesn't care about the people he involves in it, and the point of the game is to prolong Jim's slavery.

Huck and Jim seemed free on the river; why does Twain refuse to liberate them, why plunge them back into sivilization at the book's end? Because drifting on a raft achieves nothing. Jim is freed not by running away but by good luck, a change of heart; Huck is freed by lucky deaths. They would have been freed if they had stayed at home. They are in effect no more free than if they had stayed at home — because society is just like things were at home. The freedom they had on the raft was a passive freedom, the raft drifted downstream, they hardly directed anything themselves.

So in one sense to confirm the meaning of the book the ending is deliberately unsatisfactory; the endings are 'happy' by the totally transparent conventions of the Victorian plot — not by anything that was worked out in the narrative, not by anything organic and dynamic. Miss Watson's change of heart and freeing of Jim is totally unconvincing, an absurd fictional cliché.

The point Twain is making is that escape to the raft, undirected negative escape *from* things, isn't an escape after all. The freeing of Huck and Jim is the result of quite separate circumstances. Jim is no longer a slave, but the society remains unchanged; slavery persists; people remain brutal. Jim got his personal freedom, but this is no solution to the problems raised by the novel — the picture of Southern society that Twain has presented to us. As long as you have that sort of society, you will get this sort of clichéd-ending novel.

But there is another ending. Here the focus is on the circumstances that allow Huck now to see through society totally. He has freed himself from the mystifications; now he can go off and seek for a positive freedom; just as Jim, released from the shackles of slavery, now is in a position to seek for a positive freedom as an individual. And that freedom cannot be gained by drifting. It must be worked for actively. As the raft escape was the negation of Southern society, so the projected future of Huck is the negation of that negation — a reassertion of his freedom on a higher level, a positive search, not a drift.

Instead of just temporarily escaping sivilization by disappearing to the woods for peace, Huck's final decision is a positive one, one that repudiates his world, and turns his negative alienation from it into a positive move towards a new world; the possibility of creating a new society in the uncivilized frontier. This time he will not drift but make an active move. The analysis of society which the novel has given is a despairing one; even the freeing of Jim and Huck is a freeing we can only despair at — such arbitrary, lucky acts are all that can be hoped for in this sivilization. And lucky things don't happen for most people. But Huck has learned a lot; his consciousness has changed; he is in a better position now than at the book's beginning. The ending is a positive note, drawing on and given hope from Huck's perpetual optimism. 'But I reckon I got to light out for the Territory ahead of the rest, because Aunt Sally she's going to adopt me and sivilize me and I can't stand it. I been there before' (43:369).

2

News from Nowhere

At the core of William Morris's *News from Nowhere* (1890), the nineteenth-century narrator — the Guest as he is called — talks about the future society he has awoken into. He talks to Old Hammond who as a one-time 'custodian of the books' at the 'Museum' (8:232) is interested in the past and the evolution of the new society — unlike most of those who live happily in the new society, freed from the burden of history. In chapter 11, 'Concerning Government', Hammond and the Guest have a crucial discussion.

> 'Do you want further explanation?'
> 'Well, yes, I do,' quoth I.
> Old Hammond settled himself in his chair with a look of enjoyment which rather alarmed me, and made me dread a scientific disquisition: so I sighed and abided. He said:
> 'I suppose you know pretty well what the process of government was in the bad old times?'
> 'I am supposed to know,' said I. (11:258)

News from Nowhere is a political fiction, it is a projection of a future society. Its full title makes this clear: *News from Nowhere or an epoch of rest being some chapters from a utopian romance*. The Guest may prefer 'rest', but 'utopian romance' indicates the unavoidable political. The opening words of the first chapter tell us that the Guest is a member of 'the League' — the Socialist League which Morris helped to found in 1884 after leaving the Social Democratic Foundation. *News from Nowhere* was originally published as a serial in the League's weekly journal, *The Commonweal*. The political context — moreover, a committed political context — is total. And yet the narrator 'dreads' a scientific disquisition on political structures, 'sighs' at the prospect of it — even though he asked for it;

and asked for it, indeed, with a hesitant 'well, yes . . .', and replied equally hesitantly to questioning about his knowledge of the politics of his own time, 'I am supposed to know'.

Oh, the groans at having to deal with politics. The passage is crucial in revealing the split in the consciousness of people like Morris. They are involved in political activity, they are working towards a just society — but what a wretchedness it all is, what a time-waste it all is, taking time from living and creating, if only we could get directly into the utopian situation. Yet the only way to get there is through the dreariness of political organization and activity, unless you dream it. But even when Morris writes his beautiful dream vision of a utopian future, he drags his narrator out of the sunny experience of it, and for the central part of the book the narrator is forced to confront the dreariness and the misery of the stages by which it was reached, and the underlying structures of it. Morris deals with all that as quickly and briefly as he is able — but he still feels the obligation to deal with it. *News from Nowhere* is presented to us as a dream, but it is not an indulgent day-dream, however much the dreamer would in one part of his consciousness like it to be. After tasting the society experientially, he has to face up to theory, strategy, analysis — all those things he had been arguing about 'up at the League' on the evening of his dream, all those things that the nineteenth-century intellectual shrank from in dread even though in theory he believed in them.

> When the hope of realising a communal condition of life for all men arose, quite late in the nineteenth century, the power of the middle classes, the then tyrants of society, was so enormous and crushing, that to almost all men, even those who had, you may say despite themselves, their reason and judgment, conceived such hopes, it seemed a dream. So much was this the case that some of those more enlightened men who were then called Socialists, although they well knew, and even stated in public, that the only reasonable condition of Society was that of pure Communism (such as you now see around you), yet shrunk from what seemed to them the barren task of preaching the realisation of a happy dream. (17:288)

Even though humanely, emotionally committed to a socialist solution, the narrator is one of those who shrinks, dreads, sighs at the idea of political analysis; the likelihood that any of this theory will issue in action and achieve the desired change in society, seems as remote as a dream.

The dread and the sigh are in part a response to the prospect of a scientific disquisition — to theory, to analysis. Morris had written his fair share of lectures and essays on socialism. But who wouldn't prefer to read romance to essay, fiction to lecture?

Apparently some wouldn't. In *Culture and Society* Raymond Williams comes out with a strange — though not unique — assessment of Morris:

> I would willingly lose *The Dream of John Ball* and the romantic socialist songs and even *News from Nowhere* — in all of which the weaknesses of Morris's general poetry are active and disabling, if to do so were the price of retaining and getting people to read such smaller things as *How we Live, and How we might Live*, *The Aims of Art, Useful Work versus Useless Toil*, and *A Factory as it might be*. The change of emphasis would involve a change in Morris's status as a writer, but such a change is critically inevitable. There is more life in the lectures, where one feels that the whole man is engaged in the writing, than in any of the prose and verse romances. These seem so clearly the product of a fragmentary consciousness — of that very state of mind which Morris was always trying to analyse. Morris is a fine political writer, in the broadest sense, and it is on that, finally, that his reputation will rest. The other and larger part of his literary work bears witness only to the disorder which he felt so acutely. (159)

This depreciation of Morris's 'literary work' leaves him as a strangely and disablingly flawed writer. He aimed for a wholeness, an integration in his work — and if the corpus of his work is to be seen as fragmented how can the wholeness which he reached towards and advocated be communicated in a convincing way? If his work does not demonstrate the wholeness in which he believed, how can that wholeness be believed in as an attainable end? To reject the 'literary' work' in favour of a few of the essays and lectures, is in effect to reject the message of those essays and lectures. E.P. Thompson's *William Morris: Romantic to Revolutionary* works from similar assumptions to Williams.

News from Nowhere is the creative summation of Morris's thinking on society, art, life: the expression of the inseparability of society, art, life. Morris was a creative artist, not only an 'intellectual'. And yet his initial responses to and thoughts about socialism had been couched in theoretical, 'intellectual', non-poetic non-fictional modes. He could not but have been aware of the paradox — or, to put it more negatively, of the split in his consciousness: his literary creativity and his political beliefs separated. With *News from Nowhere* he attempts to unify the materials of his lectures with the creative mode in which he was happiest, the romance. He attempts to integrate the separated aspects of his consciousness; his vision of a communist utopia is of a time and place in which man's different aspects and capabilities would be integrated — not separated and specialized and fragmented as in nineteenth-century capitalist society. Projecting, then, this future integration he projects a different sort of art — one in which theory and feeling, dream and reality, would not be separated, one in which theory would not be boring, one in which the dream would not be defined as unattainable: an art counter to nineteenth-century art, the negation of that negation of human possibilities.

Edward Bellamy's *Looking Backward 2000-1887* (1887) provided the stimulus. Reviewing the 1889 English edition, Morris expressed his revulsion with the machine civilization values he found in Bellamy's socialism.

His scheme may be described as State Communism, worked by the vast extreme of national centralisation. (200)

A machine life is the best which Bellamy can imagine for us on all sides; it is not to be wondered at then that his only idea of making labour tolerable is to decrease the amount of it by means of fresh and ever fresh developments of machinery.

I believe that the ideal of the future does not point to the lessening of man's energy by the reduction of *labour* to a minimum, but rather to a reduction of *pain in labour* to a minimum, so small that it will cease to be pain. (201)

Morris drew on the ideas he had been formulating in his lectures — ideas about the relationship of art to society, and of the relationship of art to labour without pain — creative labour; and he embodied them in a fictional form to counter Bellamy's future projection.

It is necessary to point out that there are some Socialists who do not think that the problem of the organisation of life and necessary labour can be dealt with by a huge centralisation, worked by a kind of magic for which no one feels himself responsible; that on the contrary it will be necessary for the unit of administration to be small enough for every citizen to feel himself responsible for its details, and be interested in them . . . That variety of life is as much an aim of true Communism as

51

equality of condition, and that nothing but an union of these two will bring about real freedom. (200-2)

Bellamy's novel provided one stimulus for Morris to react against. But his fight was not only with fellow socialists. His vision was in opposition to the main currents of establishment art and thought of his day. The form of the great nineteenth-century English bourgeois novels of George Eliot, Dickens, Thackeray, Trollope reflect the nature and requirements of that society. The readers required to see in fiction the confirmations of their own value systems — the detailed presentation of individuated characters; the complexities of multiple social interactions; the meaningfulness of one event leading to another, plots in which things tied up. This way was confirmed the necessary belief in bourgeois individualism, in a free society in which people mixed and socially moved in a social Darwinism, and in a sense of purpose, that it was all worth doing, that bourgeois life was meaningful — either to God or to the artist. The artist stands in for God for those whose faith has evaporated, to assure them that there are aesthetic absolutes, and that the design of bourgeois life is innately aesthetically pleasing.

By rejecting that whole nineteenth-century fictional mode for *News from Nowhere* Morris indicates how he has rejected the society that generated and required that mode. Patrick Brantlinger has pointed out how '*News from Nowhere* is a conscious anti-novel hostile to virtually every aspect of "the great tradition" of Victorian fiction' (34). But Brantlinger is unable to detach himself from that 'great tradition' to see the achieved strengths of *News from Nowhere*. He goes on to say it

is not 'a great work of fiction' judged by ordinary standards. The only 'great tradition' of which it is a part is exemplified by *Utopia* and *Arcadia*. Because it appeared first in *Commonweal*, the journal of the Socialist League, and because it is not much more than a fictional elaboration of ideas which Morris set forth in his lectures and essays, perhaps we should describe it as a piece of socialist propaganda, and let it go at that. (39)

Why be trapped by 'ordinary standards', why does *Commonweal* serialization invite a reductive judgment, why postulate some narrow 'great tradition'? That 'fictional elaboration of ideas' was a huge achievement, not something to be so easily dismissed. Brantlinger finally plays with the idea that the romance

was written in an age which Morris himself believed all genuine
art impossible. So, far from being an example of or even a
foreshadowing of the art of utopia, perhaps *News from Nowhere*,
in Morris's own terms can only be described as a work of
non-art. (48)

But such academic concept games cannot obscure the fact that *News
from Nowhere* has survived as an immensely popular, immensely
moving art work for the best part of a century. The anti-novel
aspects are certainly present and provide a telling critique of bourgeois critical realism. But it is as a positive, an inspirational, romance
that *News from Nowhere* has attracted the majority of its readers.
As Northrop Frye has stressed:

> William Morris should not be left on the side lines of prose
> fiction merely because the critic has not learned to take the
> romance form seriously. Nor, in view of what has been said about
> the revolutionary nature of the romance, should his choice of
> that form be regarded as an 'escape' from his social attitude.
> (305)

Rejecting nineteenth-century industrial capitalism and the bourgeois art forms it produced, Morris turned to the dream for his prose
fiction. It is as if by entering into a dream a new fictional form can
be found. His fiction arises not from the dominant social values of
nineteenth-century England and their endorsive requirements, but
from the dreamed utopia. By choosing the dream mode he immediately rejects bourgeois realism; he borrows the medieval vision
form for a future insight — by-passing the present.

So most of the expected features of nineteenth-century prose
fiction are missing from *News from Nowhere*. Plot — what plot? The
narrator goes home from a League meeting, wakes the next morning
into some other era, talks to a few people, is taken to meet an old
man who tells him how society got to this point, then the narrator
goes up the river Thames to the hay-making, meets a few people on
the way, seems to be falling in love with a young woman called
Ellen; and when the destination is reached, he goes along to the
hay-making dinner, finds no one can see him any more, the future
vision fades away, and he is back in the nineteenth century.

Nothing is rounded off — the materials of the future vanish and
nothing is resolved. Because the future will be open, unresolved,
open for continual movement and change; not closed off like the
nineteenth-century bourgeoisie would have had it with life

possibilities rounded off neatly like the marital pairings at the end of the representative novel; and not like Bellamy's solution in *Looking Backward* where the future is organized, fixed, rigidly determined by the inadequacies of a late nineteenth-century vision. These aesthetic choices, as Raymond Williams reminds us in *Marxism and Literature*, are social choices:

> Certain stories require, conventionally, a pre-History and a projected ('after' or 'ever after') history, if their reading of cause, motive, and consequence is to be understood. The exclusion of such elements, like their inclusion, is not an 'aesthetic' choice — the 'way to tell a story' — but a variable convention involving radical social assumptions of causation and consequence. (Compare the final 'settlement' chapter in early Victorian English novels — e.g. Gaskell's *Mary Barton* — and the final 'breakaway' chapter in English novels between 1910 and 1940 — e.g. Lawrence's *Sons and Lovers*.) (176)

And so events are inconsequential in *News from Nowhere* because the tone of this future society is inconsequential. There are no imperial ambitions, no capitalist aims of generating greater surplusses, no drive towards continual consumer commodity production, no myths of technological progress, no religious crusades. At last there is time for people to walk and talk, to meet and wander off, to live; there is no social treadmill of compulsion forcing people along — providing the narrative impetus for the novel.

There is, however, movement in *News from Nowhere*: the boat journey up the Thames to the hay-making. Importantly this is a deliberate, conscious, chosen movement up-river — not a downstream drifting like *Huckleberry Finn*. It is a movement of engagement, not escape. It puts a dynamic into the world — the future society is not static like the world of a Jane Austen novel. It is a journey to a new society, to a new life, to a new art — though this is only present as a haunting suggestion; the romance is not heavily symbolic or allegoric. After all, the new society is already in existence when the narrator awakes in the Hammersmith house downriver.

It is also a personal work of art here. The river journey was one which Morris had made himself more than once. It starts from the site of his own London house at Hammersmith, transmuted as Henderson points out to 'the Gothic house he would doubtless have much preferred' (225), and ends up at his other house, Kelmscott Manor in Oxfordshire. The personal note is present because Morris's personal feelings and his communist aims were united. In the same way Jack London was to put his rebel socialists in hiding on the site of his own Californian ranch in *The Iron Heel*. The ideal of the impersonal, objective artist of nineteenth-century fiction, not personally involved but controlling a cast of a thousand puppets, etc., is rejected by London and Morris in their socialist romances. They reintegrate their own private dreams with their socialist visions; they break down the taboos on personal feelings, they refuse to respect the distancing frame that the novel had been given. It is part of the de-alienating, re-personalizing process to which Morris is committed.

News from Nowhere has no wills, inheritances, illegitimacies, lawsuits, rising in the world, falling in the world, bankruptcy, success, property, religion, stigma, exile, outcasts, shame, railway trains, stage coaches, huntsmen, cathedral intrigues, wars, universities, etc. — none of the staple materials of nineteenth-century fiction.

Rejecting bourgeois society, Morris rejects its obsessions and materials as material for art; and in the rejection he rejects bourgeois realism. He has to create a new art to express his vision of a new society. Of course, Morris is still firmly rooted in the nineteenth century so the aesthetic of *News from Nowhere* cannot be a pure utopian aesthetic. It is an approximation to what might be a future art in a future society, a projection from the consciousness of someone who rejects the society and art of the nineteenth century and who has a theoretical base from which to predicate a future. It is the product of an aspect of nineteenth-century bourgeois society — it expresses the aspirations of a sub-section within that class; its aims are determined by nineteenth-century society since it is to be the negation of that very nineteenth-century industrial capitalist society.

So some nineteenth-century bourgeois values still emerge. There is a recurrent emphasis on acquisition objects, artefacts. John Berger in *Ways of Seeing* has indicated how

> many oil paintings were themselves simple demonstrations of what gold or money could buy. Merchandise became the actual subject-matter of works of art . . . a demonstration of more than the virtuosity of the artist. It confirms the owner's wealth and habitual style of living. (99)

In the Nowhere utopia, Morris stresses, there is no merchandise, no money or exchange symbol; things are not sold; the Guest is constantly having to suppress his automatic response to reach into his pocket to pay for something. But at the same time as satirizing the Guest's conditioning by commercial society, these recurrent incidents are there to emphasize the value of the objects that don't need to be paid for — and it is bourgeois value. Simply wanting tobacco, the Guest ends up with 'a red morocco bag, gaily embroidered' to keep it in and 'a big bowled pipe . . . carved out of some hard wood very elaborately, and mounted in gold sprinkled with little gems . . . like the best kind of Japanese work, but better' to smoke it in (6:217).

In Morris's utopia there are no more tawdry cotton prints but elegant red morocco tobacco pouches, gaily embroidered. People dress strikingly, colourfully. Their pipes are beautiful, carved and decorated. Morris's intention is to make a critique of nineteenth-century shoddy commercialism, of ill-made, ill-designed, ugly products, products made without love or good feeling. It was a critique he made throughout his life, both by attack on what was badly designed and made, and by the positive example of the design work of Morris & Co. The problem with Morris & Co., however, was that their products were available only to the wealthy bourgeois. Good taste had its economic base; the work was expensive — and its purchasers bought it to demonstrate what things of good taste their gold or money could buy: how solid they were economically and artistically. And so though Morris tries to create a utopia in which good design and good workmanship produce these beautiful arte-facts which are available for everyone with no commercial trans-action, none the less the stress on the artefacts themselves reminds us that Morris's socialism was built on to a bourgeois consciousness. From the beginning there is a continual awareness of objects and artefacts — the boatman's 'little silver bugle horn' and his belt 'of filigree silver-work' (2:191); the 'delicately made glass' of the guest-house table (3:194). At Bloomsbury 'the glass, crockery, and plate were very beautiful to my eyes, used to a study of medieval art; but a nineteenth-century club-haunter would, I daresay, have found them rough and lacking in finish' (16:284): here is beauty for the true connoisseur, the bourgeois as art-critic rather than the bourgeois as club-haunter.

Contrast Morris with Jack London. *The Iron Heel* is concerned with the ideas of socialism, with confrontations, drama, action — there is almost nothing about objects and artefacts in this socialist vision. London's consciousness was quite differently formed — proletarian childhood, supporting himself and his mother from the age of thirteen; he achieved considerable wealth as a successful author, but his writings show none of that *object* stress. With Morris, however, we are constantly reminded of the bourgeois artefact collector, art as the ideology for property acquisition — attitudes of mind and behaviour that would have appalled him and that he would have rejected.

And so the beautiful breakfast on the morning of the Guest's awakening into the utopia has this disturbing, dual quality. It is both the idealized light summer meal of ideal country fruits and home-made bread — the simple life, away from adulterated, processed and unfresh foods of the big city, stuffy Victorian breakfasts; it is a rural idyll, the pastoral of garden nature. 'The bread was particularly good, and was of several different kinds, from the big, rather close, dark-coloured, sweet-tasting farmhouse loaf, which was most to my liking, to the thin pipe-stems of wheaten crust, such as I have eaten in Turin' (3:194). But it is also the aesthetic of the still life, the heaped foods commemorated in oils. Morris has excluded game — pheasants and hares — the whole death note of meat-eating. But there is still the suggestion of the consumer's feast — as Berger puts it 'the edible is made visible . . . . It confirms the owner's wealth and habitual style of living' (99). One of the three graceful young women comes in

> with a great bunch of roses, very different in size and quality to what Hammersmith had been wont to grow, but very like the produce of an old country garden. She hurried back thence into the buttery, and came back once more with a delicately made glass, into which she put the flowers and set them down in the midst of our table. (3:194)

An aesthetic combination of glassware, flowers, and food — the food and style taste ritual elevated to art ritual; the ritualized art commemorates a bourgeois style of living, with attendant young women ministering to the consumer. It is a ritual not a self-service. His is a vision determined by having had servants. And it is a sexist vision consistently — women are in service, housework and such-like ministering roles throughout the novel. The personal nature of Morris's vision of a socialist future is continually stressed by commentators. The class basis of that personal vision is rarely remarked. But it would be wrong to stress the bourgeois components of the stress on beautiful objects, at the expense of Morris's socialist vision of those objects. Beautiful artefacts can be made only as a result of the workman's pleasure in his labour; labour without creative pleasure is slavery; industrial capitalism has developed a system by which each labourer works on only repetitive fragments of a whole object, and the object's design was determined by the basic consideration of realizing the maximum profit by the cheapest means. Old Hammond explains:

the ceaseless endeavour to expend the least possible amount of
labour on any article made, and yet at the same time to make as
many articles as possible. To this 'cheapening of production,' as
it was called, everything was sacrificed: the happiness of the
workman at his work, nay, his most elementary comfort and bare
health, his food, his clothes, his dwelling, his leisure, his
amusement, his education — his life, in short — did not weigh
a grain of sand in the balance against this dire necessity of 'cheap
production' of things, a great part of which were not worth
producing at all. (15:276)

What results from this capitalist mode of production is a disregard
for the product — the emphasis is on cheap production and on
marketing.

How could they possibly attend to such trifles as the quality of
the wares they sold? The best of them were of a lowish average,
the worst were transparent make-shifts for the things asked for,
which nobody would have put up with if they could have got
anything else. It was a current jest of the time that the wares
were made to sell and not to use. (15:279)

Morris comes to socialism from this horror at the shoddy product.
Building the Red House, back in 1860, he finds that the available
materials for furnishing and design are tawdry or inadequate — so
has to design and manufacture his own. He has to become acquainted
with the production processes. His socialism begins to develop
when he realizes the intimate connection between the shoddy
products which he abhors, and the appalling conditions in which
the products are made. In his lecture 'Art Under Plutocracy' which
he delivered, to controversy, at University College, Oxford, in 1883,
he wrote:

Now the chief accusation I have to bring against the modern state
of society is that it is found on the art-lacking or unhappy labour
of the greater part of men; and all that external degradation of
the face of the country of which I have spoken is hateful to me
not only because it is a cause of unhappiness to some few of us
who still love art, but also and chiefly because it is a token of
the unhappy life forced on the great mass of the population by
the system of competitive commerce.
  The pleasure which ought to go with the making of every
piece of handicraft has for its basis the keen interest which every

healthy man takes in a healthy life, and is compounded, it seems
to me, chiefly of three elements: variety, hope of creation, and
the self-respect which comes of a sense of usefulness; to which
must be added that mysterious bodily pleasure which goes with
the deft exercise of the bodily powers. (PW, 68)

Now this compound pleasure in handiwork I claim as the
birthright of all workmen. I say that if they lack any part of it
they will be so far degraded, but that if they lack it altogether
they are, so far as their work goes, I will not say slaves, the word
would not be strong enough, but machines more or less conscious
of their own unhappiness. (PW, 68)

At the basis of Morris's socialism is the assumption that creativity
is a quality of all men, and that the pleasure of creative work produces art; the denial of creative joy in work produces ugliness and
tawdriness. We can see this clearly enough when the work he is
talking of is the production of artefacts — the silver filigree buckle,
the delicate glass vase, the morocco tobacco pouch. But Morris not
only extends the nineteenth-century concept of 'art' out of mere
'high seriousness' and the elite arts into artefacts and crafts — he
extends it further still to include all labour. In 'Art Under Plutocracy'
he asks his audience

to extend the word art beyond those matters which are
consciously works of art, to take in not only painting and
sculpture, and architecture, but the shapes and colours of all
household goods, nay, even the arrangement of the fields for
tillage and pasture, the management of towns and of our
highways of all kinds; in a word, to extend it to the aspect of
all the externals of our life. (PW, 58)

And so in *News from Nowhere* we are shown this Ruskinian extension of 'art' to 'man's expression of his joy in labour' (PW, 67). This
concept is the book, it permeates every aspect of the future society.
Rowing up the Thames, the Guest observes Clara watching Dick:
'She looked at him fondly, and I could tell that she was seeing him
in her mind's eye showing his splendid form at its best amidst the
rhymed strokes of the scythes' (22:331). Here is the socialist union
of art and labour, creative unalienated labour; the romantic union
of the separated arts. The visual impression, painting and sculpture
yet alive, of the 'splendid form'; the poetry of motion in 'the rhymed
strokes'; and the productive labour of the hay-making. It is a

synthesis of all those disunified fragments, united at last, free from
the enforced separations of capitalist society.

What then of traditional 'high art' in the communist future?
Morris allows a role for the traditional artist, but it is a very small, a
lessened role. What need is there for art when life itself is suffused
with art, is art? What need for the solace of art when life has few
ills that need solace? Ellen, whom the Guest meets on his up river
journey, says to her grandfather:

> 'Books, books! always books, grandfather! When will you
> understand that after all it is the world we live in which interests
> us; the world of which we are a part, and which we can never love
> too much? Look!' she said, throwing open the casement wider
> and showing us the white light sparkling between the black
> shadows of the moonlit garden, through which ran a little shiver
> of the summer night-wind, 'look! these are our books in these
> days — and these,' she said, stepping lightly up to the two lovers
> and laying a hand on each of their shoulders; 'and the guest
> there, with his oversea knowledge and experience — yes, and even
> you, grandfather . . . .' (22:336-7)

That evening, after this denunciation of books, 'Ellen showed us to
our beds in small cottage chambers, fragrant and clean as the ideal
of the old pastoral poets' (22:340). Poetic ideals are lived experience here, there is no need of a separated art, the creative force has
now gone into life itself. Why paint landscapes of hay-making when
you can be in the landscape at choice, when hay-making isn't a
mystery denied the factory-bound or desk-bound urban dweller, but
an activity in which the entire population can take part if they wish?
Why turn to poems as opiates when life has the richness that poets
imagined:

> the sky, in short, looked really like a vault, as poets have
> sometimes called it, and not like mere limitless air, but a vault so
> vast and full of light that it did not in any way oppress the spirits.
> It was the sort of afternoon that Tennyson must have been
> thinking about, when he said of the Lotos-Eaters' land that it was
> a land where it was always afternoon. (27:371)

Morris revealingly misquotes. Tennyson wrote

> In the afternoon they came unto a land
> In which it seemed always afternoon.

Tennyson's Lotos-Eaters live a life of illusion; but for Morris there is no indeterminate 'seemed afternoon' (maybe it was, maybe it just looked that way, maybe it's the drugs, maybe drugs are reality); Morris remembers his poetic touchstone as declaring that it *was* always afternoon; that is how he remembers this poetic utopia, a definite escape world, drained of any disturbing doubts or ambiguities.

Morris offers us a minor *Golden Treasury*; we have Keats's casement open wide, we have Shelley's vault of the sky, we have the ideal cottage of the 'old pastoral poets', we have Tennyson's eternal afternoon, all resplendently actualized for us. Poetry has become life, there is no need for the separated art of writing poetry. What once could be grasped only by the visionary few, insights, touchstones of peace and harmony, and had to be experienced at second hand as 'art' by the rest of the world, is now available to be experienced by everyone. Art is no longer elitist and inaccessible and providing joy just for a moneyed, literate few. There are now no mediations between the values carried by art and the experiencing of them. Whatever art embodies is now available for everyone, and the concept of 'art' is unnecessary, art is life now.

In the final chapter of *News from Nowhere* Morris indicates the ultimate bond of art and life, the drama of the seasons. It is something the Guest initially finds it hard to understand: ' "How strangely you talk," said I, "of such a constantly recurring and consequently commonplace matter as the sequence of the seasons" ' (32:396). And even when he interprets what is enjoyed 'as a beautiful and interesting drama', he is still viewing it as an alienated, conventional observer of high art. For, as Dick stresses, the experience of the seasons is far more than simply 'interesting' of 'beautiful', an alienated artefact for assessment; it is something experienced, something participated in, not something watched as through a proscenium arch and described as merely 'beautiful and interesting'. 'I can't look upon it as if I were sitting in a theatre seeing the play going on before me, myself taking no part of it,' Dick explains, 'but I mean that I am part of it all, and feel the pain as well as the pleasure in my own person. It is not done for me by somebody else, merely that I may eat and drink and sleep; but I myself do my share of it' (32:396-7). And the Guest contrasts this with:

the days I knew: in which the prevailing feeling amongst intellectual persons was a kind of sour distaste for the changing drama of the year, for the life of earth and its dealings with men. Indeed, in those days it was thought poetic and imaginative

to look upon life as a thing to be borne, rather than enjoyed.
(32:397)

There is no need for alienated spectator-art in Morris's utopia; no
need for art as consolation for a life to be endured rather than
enjoyed. Here man is not alienated from nature, from other men,
from his labour, from his creativity. Man is able to experience
nature again, to enjoy his labour creatively, to experience that integration that before could only be gestured at by art — by art that
itself was a specialized and alienated product of the fragmentation of
unhappy life. Conflicts and contradictions, the destructive separations of 'work' and 'leisure' have been removed.

In *News from Nowhere* work is creative, work is pleasurable, and
there is a prevailing holiday note; but the holiday is the Guest's
escape from nineteenth-century alienated industry — the inhabitants
of Morris's future combine the holiday mood with the productive
hay-making. And though the mood is gentle, free from conflict, the
result is not stasis. The stress on the drama of the seasons is a stress
on dynamic — the constant mutation of the seasons, flux, transition.
The pleasures of work, of art, of nature are unified, are simultaneous,
are inseparable here.

There are some 'artists' in the traditional nineteenth-century
conception of the word in Morris's utopia. At Bisham the Guest and
Dick and Clara go ashore from the river:

> The folk of the place, however, were mostly in the fields that
> day, both men and women; so we met only two old men there,
> and a younger one who had stayed at home to get on with some
> literary work, which I imagine we considerably interrupted. Yet I
> also think that the hard-working man who received us was not
> very sorry for the interruption. Anyhow, he kept on pressing us
> to stay . . . . (24:350)

Even though the social norm is to participate in the communal hay-
making, the individualist artist is free to pursue his individualism.
And in this idyllic world he is hard working, and yet at the same
time not annoyed at the interruptions. But such individualism is
rare; it is allowed, tolerated, acceptable — but the majority of people
clearly participate in shared activities. Indeed, the implication is
that the young man is feeling lonely because of his alienated craft of
literary composition; he is glad to be interrupted — he needs to
communicate with people. Like Morris himself, he does not mind
persons from Porlock visiting: he does not barricade himself against

the world.

Certainly when we go further up river, the artists we encounter next are communal artists — not the traditional nineteenth-century high art practitioners. The Obstinate Refusers, as they are called, a group who refuse to participate in the communal hay-making, because they wish communally to finish building a house. Morris is again stressing that there is no coercion in this society — those who do not want to make hay are free to pursue other activities. And amongst the Obstinate Refusers we encounter the obsessive artist, Philippa, who insists on going on with her work while the visitors talk because she lost the opportunity to work earlier through being ill — 'I am sure you won't think me unkind if I go on with my work' (26:362).

In 'Art Under Plutocracy' Morris postulates two types of art, the Intellectual and the Decorative. He argued

that in all times when the arts were in a healthy condition there was an intimate connexion between the two kinds of art; a connexion so close, that in the times when art flourished most, the higher and lower kinds were divided by no hard and fast lines. The highest intellectual art was meant to please the eye, as the phrase goes, as well as to excite the emotions and train the intellect. It appealed to all men, and to all the faculties of a man. On the other hand, the humblest of ornamental art shared in the meaning and emotion of the intellectuals; one melted into the other by scarce perceptible gradations; in short, the best artist was a workman still, the humblest workman was an artist. (PW, 59)

Capitalism separated the two types of art, to the detriment of both.

Thus then in considering the state of art among us I have been driven to the conclusion that in its co-operative form it is extinct, and only exists in the conscious efforts of men of genius and talent, who themselves are injured, and thwarted, and deprived of due sympathy by the lack of co-operative art. (PW, 63)

In the utopia of *News from Nowhere* the intellectual and the decorative are reintegrated. This results in a great flowering of the decorative; and many of those whom Morris describes in his lecture as 'good decorative workmen spoiled by a system which compels them to ambitious individualist effort' (PW, 60), and who had become trapped into producing bad intellectual art, now find their true role and fulfilment in the co-operative, decorative arts.

Morris, in his lecture, acknowledged that pure, individualist intellectual artists did exist though 'they are very few'. The young literary man is clearly one of them in *News from Nowhere*, and the literary arts lend themselves more readily to individualist production. But in this future society, there are not many individualist artists; the individualist sculptor is, importantly, partaking in co-operative activity. She is not adding a sculpture later to a building designed and built by others; the sculptor's work is integrated with that of the structural builders.

Because of their individualist, alienated nature the literary arts are not very significant in this new world. There is, however, a lot of mention of literature in the book — Morris returns to fiction again and again, since its present and future roles both clearly troubled him. But out of all these recurrent engagements with the idea of literature, we get the continuing sense that literature is a past art form, and has little role in this future. We need to look at this theme — and see how Morris relates it to using a fictional mode for writing his vision of a future that will barely have any fiction.

The evening before the journey up-river, the Guest experiences the arts of this new world.

> We had quite a little feast that evening, partly in my honour, and partly, I suspect, though nothing was said about it, in honour of Dick and Clara coming together again. The wine was of the best; the hall was redolent of rich summer flowers; and after supper we not only had music (Annie, to my mind, surpassing all the others for sweetness and clearness of voice, as well as for feeling and meaning), but at last we even got to telling stories, and sat there listening, with no other light but that of the summer moon streaming through the beautiful traceries of the windows, as if we had belonged to time long passed, when books were scarce and the art of reading somewhat rare. Indeed, I may say here, that, though, as you will have noted, my friends had mostly something to say about books, yet they were not great readers, considering the refinement of their manners and the great amount of leisure which they obviously had. (20:326)

The pleasures of story-telling are regained without the alienations of 'literature'. The setting is a full one — there is the natural visual beauty of the 'rich summer flowers', there is wine, there is prefatory music, and then there is the story-telling. The story-telling exists in a multi-media, communal setting. It is not something to be experienced in lonely silence. The private, individual writer of a book and the private individual reader express the ultimate image of artistic alienation — seeking refuge in literature through an alienation from life, experiencing the literature in an alienated, individualistic way. Morris rejects that. But he does not want to lose the pleasures of story-telling — the germs of romance, saga, and epic as well as of the novel and story. He wants to reintegrate that experience of the story into a shared communal life. He has followed through the logic of his analysis to reveal the nature of the privatized world of the book; he now turns back 'as if we had belonged to time long passed, when books were scarce and the art of reading somewhat rare'; it is one of the many examples of his medievalism — not a return to medievalism for its own sake, but a going back to a stage in western society before society went wrong, a going back to the spot where a wrong choice was made, where a wrong set of social and artistic objectives were chosen — hoping to return to this point in time to develop from it into a different direction.

And so the arts that are shown as regularly practised and regularly enjoyed in this future society are versions of medieval entertainments and arts: the wall friezes of folk tales (16:283), the stone carvings (26:362), story-telling (20:326) and song (20:326, 22:340). And the song is song in which everyone can participate — not formalized orchestral music or any other alienated, professional high art form; the stress is on informal, spontaneous singing when the occasion occurs. So it is that Boffin is described as looking like a 'troubadour' — that is the reference at hand.

The 'high' arts or 'intellectual' arts persisting in this society, then, tend to be of a communal sort — story-telling, singing, in spontaneous groups, surrounded by visual decoration; they may have occasional ceremonial contexts — the evening the Guest describes is in honour of his visit and the reunion of Dick and Clara; but there is none of the alienated, specialized art of professional performers and passive audience. It is a marked contrast from Bellamy's projection in *Looking Backward*:

> Of course, we all sing nowadays as a matter of course in the
> training of the voice, and some learn to play instruments for the
> private amusement; but the professional music is so much grander
> and more perfect than any performance of ours, and so easily
> commanded when we wish to hear it, that we don't think of
> calling our singing or playing music at all. All the really fine
> singers and players are in the musical service, and the rest of us
> hold our peace for the main part. (11:110-11)

And later, to make the point quite unequivocally: 'I suppose it was these difficulties in the way of commanding really good music which made you endure so much playing and singing in your homes by people who had only the rudiments of the art' (11:114). Sport in Bellamy's future, however, is available to all and there are no professional players. He represents the ultimate projection of nineteenth-century bourgeois values; physical fitness, the code of amateurism in sport, gentlemen players — but art as a separate, specialized, elevated, alien activity.

But for Morris art is not a specialization; it is part of the texture of all life, its practice is available to all. Specialized art has only a small role in the society of the future — and that specialized art is generally of a communal, co-operative nature. Essentially, the artistic impulse is fulfilled by the totality of the life experience — joy in creative labour, nature, human relationships, clothes, flower arrangements, the artefacts of everyday living.

And Morris's educational theories indicate the reduced role 'intellectual' art and activities have in this society — his attitude is a mixture of disregard and hostility for literary culture. Children are not formally taught to read, nor are they ever encouraged to read. And the habit of reading is not widespread or enduring.

> As a rule, they don't do much reading, except for a few story-books, till they are about fifteen years old; we don't encourage early bookishness, though you will find some children who *will* take to books very early; which perhaps is not good for them; but it's no use thwarting them; and very often it doesn't last long with them, and they find their level before they are twenty years old. (5:210)

Indeed, not only are there no social pressures towards it, Dick is concerned to assure the Guest that the literary culture is not excessive: 'I don't think we need fear having too many book-learned men' (5:211). Morris is in that English radical tradition that reaches back to the communal socialism of Winstanley and the Diggers. 'There is traditional knowledge, which is attained by reading or by the instruction of others, and not practical but leads to an idle life; and this is not good' (364). So Winstanley wrote in his codification of the Digger vision in *The Law of Freedom in a Platform* (1651), dismissing traditional book-learning as

> an idle, lazy contemplation the scholars would call knowledge; but it is no knowledge but a show of knowledge, like a parrot

who speaks words but he knows not what he saith. This same
show of knowledge rests in reading or contemplating or hearing
others speak, and speaks so too, but will not set his hand to
work. And from this traditional knowledge and learning rise up
both clergy and lawyer, who by their cunning insinuations live
merely upon the labour of other men, and teach laws which
they themselves will not do and lays burdens upon others which
they themselves will not touch with the least of their fingers.
And from hence arises all oppressions, wars and troubles in the
world . . . . (364-5)

The other major bourgeois alienation of art that is removed in
News from Nowhere is the 'after-thought of the injustice and miser-
able toil which made my leisure' (20:326-7). In 'Art Under Plutocracy'
Morris wrote 'that any art which professes to be founded on the
special education or refinement of a limited body or class must of
necessity be unreal and shortlived' (PW, 67). Nineteenth-century
fiction was produced for a society that found its time to read, its
leisure, and its power to purchase luxury items such as books, from
the exploitation of the proletariat and the empire. And so he has
Ellen declare:

'As for your books, they were well enough for times when
intelligent people had but little else in which they could take
pleasure, and when they must needs supplement the sordid
miseries of their own lives with imaginations of the lives of
other people. But I say flatly that in spite of all their cleverness
and vigour, and capacity for story-telling, there is something
loathsome about them. Some of them, indeed, do here and
there show some feeling for those whom the history-books call
"poor", and of the misery of whose lives we have some inkling;
but presently they give it up, and towards the end of the story
we must be contented to see the hero and heroine living happily
in an island of bliss on other people's troubles; and that after a
long series of sham troubles (or mostly sham) of their own
making, illustrated by dreary introspective nonsense about their
feelings and aspirations, and all the rest of it; while the world
must even then have gone on its way, and dug and sewed and
baked and built and carpentered round about these useless —
animals.' (22:337-8)

His utopia is created to show that the sort of art produced under
the evil conditions of capitalism no longer survives, people do not

create like that any more, the products of that era are no longer valued. The Guest insists to Ellen's grandfather: 'in the land whence I come, where the competition which produced those literary works which you admire is still the rule, most people are thoroughly unhappy; here, to me at least, most people seem thoroughly happy' (22:339). But the old man, who, for all his grumbling, Morris allows to have a genuine love of literature, has the final word. 'Well, for my part I like reading a good old book with plenty of fun in it, like Thackeray's *Vanity Fair*. Why don't you write books like that now?' (22:345). The question is left unanswered, and the old man is allowed to have a case. Yet the question is answered by everything we see in *News from Nowhere*. Art is the product of the social and economic determinants of society; when that base is changed, the art will change. When life provides its full fulfilments, much of the role of art in capitalist society will be irrelevant. Its role as consolation, as the expression of conspicuous consumption, as elitist celebration of elitist life-styles, as expression of the ideology of the establishment oppressor, or of a competing elite aiming at superseding the current establishment — all these past roles for art will have vanished. No one in the new society will want an art expressing those values.

Morris deals with this theme in what Morton notes was one of his 'most popular and often repeated lectures' (PW, 86), 'Useful Work versus Useless Toil', first given at Hampstead in 1884. Starting from the assumption that art production in capitalist society is a luxury of the leisure class, and is funded by and dependent on the exploitation of the proletariat, he speculates on what will happen when that exploitation is removed and the economic base of that art has changed.

> The experiment of a civilized community living wholly without art or literature has not yet been tried. The past degradation and corruption of civilization may force this denial of pleasure upon the society which will arise from its ashes. If that must be, we will accept the passing phase of utilitarianism as a foundation for the art which is to be. If the cripple and the starveling disappear from our streets, if the earth nourish us all alike, if the sun shine for all of us alike, if to one and all of us the glorious drama of the earth — day and night, summer and winter — can be presented as a thing to understand and love, we can afford to wait awhile till we are purified from the shame of the past corruption, and till art arises again amongst people freed from the terror of the slave and shame of the robber. (PW, 105)

The removal of poverty, the sun shining on all, the 'drama' of the earth accessible to all — all this is realized in *News from Nowhere*. Possibly art will arise again after this epoch of rest; possibly intellectual art may never achieve its former role as the fulfilments of art spread through all life.

There are some pastiche nineteenth-century novels still written, but the young (the future) in the society feel these and their practitioners are somewhat ridiculous. Dick tells the Guest how Boffin

> is a capital fellow, and you can't help liking him; but he has weakness; he will spend his time in writing reactionary novels and is very proud of getting the local colour right, as he calls it; and as he thinks you come from some forgotten corner of the earth, where people are unhappy, and consequently interesting to a story-teller, he thinks he might get some information out of you. (3:201)

Morris allows that Boffin has his admirers; the weaver declares 'I think his novels are very good' (3:202); and Boffin himself is not an old man, like the old grumbler who admires Thackerary, but 'in the prime of life'. The young like Dick, however, see his work as 'reactionary', as passé. In this epoch of rest, energy has not been put into the intellectual arts — so the work that has been done in them is a minority pursuit, and imitative. Possibly the young man we encounter up-river engaged in literary activities will produce something good, a new intellectual art for the new society — but it will certainly be vastly different from nineteenth-century English fiction. It will, however, be of minority appeal. Dick tells us that: 'many people will write their books out when they make them, or get them written; I mean books of which only a few copies are needed — poems, and such like, you know' (5:209). It is like the small press movement.

Morris's debate on the role of art here is not in terms of a total rejection. He is concerned to define art; what is the nature of the art which capitalist society has produced; what is the nature of the art which a future socialist society might produce? His aesthetics are not separated from his social vision — so in essence he is one of the first sociologists of literature. His comments are not sustained or specifically 'lit.crit.' in orientation, however; he has the insights, the germs of a sociology of literature. But he clearly does not think it a worthwhile pursuit: why be an academic, professional sociologist of literature when your sociology and your literary criticism will only show that society today is a capitalist industrialist horror?

Why bother with analysing bourgeois decadence, when you could be creating a socialist future? Morris's emphasis is on the future and on activity. For all the medievalism of some of the styles of his future social organization and aesthetic, he is not antiquarian.

His distinction between 'intellectual' and 'decorative' art is not a mere abstract aesthetic; it relates to his whole social vision. In *News from Nowhere* the discussion of nineteenth-century fiction involves examining the nature of realism; but again, this is an analysis that is not merely academic, it issues in particular praxis. Morris goes on to reassert that realism is not the only fictional mode, and not the supreme mode. And from that positive argument, emerging from the discussion of realism, he expands into his own practice; and offers us in *News from Nowhere* something written in a mode other than that of realism.

Clara asks:

'How is it that though we are so interested with our life for the most part, yet when people take to writing poems or painting pictures they seldom deal with our modern life, or if they do, take good care to make their poems or pictures unlike that life? Are we not good enough to paint ourselves? How is it that we find the dreadful times of the past so interesting to us — in pictures and poetry?'

Old Hammond smiled. 'It always was so, and I suppose always will be,' said he, 'however it may be explained. It is true that in the nineteenth century, when there was so little art and so much talk about it, there was a theory that art and imaginative literature ought to deal with contemporary life; but they never did so; for, if there was any pretence of it, the author always took care (as Clara hinted just now) to disguise, or exaggerate, or idealise, and in some way or another make it strange; so that, for all the verisimilitude there was, he might just as well have dealt with the times of the Pharaohs.'

'Well,' said Dick, 'surely it is but natural to like these things strange; just as when we were children, as I said just now, we used to pretend to be so-and-so in such-and-such a place. That's what these pictures and poems do; and why shouldn't they?'

'Thou hast hit it, Dick,' quoth old Hammond; 'it is the child-like part of us that produces works of imagination. When we are children time passes so slow with us that we seem to have time for everything.' (16:285)

Morris attacks nineteenth-century realism on two grounds. First, it wasn't 'real' — its purported rationale was a false one. It might have been a stronger attack if he had gone on to examine the bases of 'realism', the ideological need for proclaiming fidelity to the 'real', while censoring out the real. But the materials for such an examination are all given in his book. He has set up the context in which to examine the bases of realism. Morris argues that all art is a fantasy art; realism may survive as another fantasy but it cannot bear any relationship to 'reality' any more than romance or fairy tale can. Although art is determined by its society Morris argues that what is determined is a fantasy structure; different societies may produce their different requirements of fantasy; the nineteenth century wanted to deny that its art was fantasy and in so doing produced one of the ultimate fantasy arts — realism; but art will always be fantasy, the product of 'the child-like part of us that produces works of imagination'. The Guest is initially surprised to see the frieze decorations in the Bloomsbury Market dining hall:

> 'I scarcely expected to find record of the Seven Swans and the King of the Golden Mountain and Faithful Henry, and such curious pleasant imaginations as Jacob Grimm got together from the childhood of the world, barely lingering even in his time: I should have thought you would have forgotten such childishness by this time.' (16:283-4)

There is something of a clash here between Morris's sense of the social determination of art, and his personal fascination with romance. It is hard to see how folk tales of kings, whether of the Golden Mountain or Fairyland, could survive in this communistic society. What enduring value would the concept of kingship have, what meaning could it purvey? The folk tales can only be a reflection of the social circumstances in which they developed. To say otherwise, to say that there is some archetypal force and worth in these folk tales, would surely lead to saying that there was some archetypal force and worth in the concept of kingship — and the hierarchical social structure that supposes, which would mean the communistic and egalitarian utopia is all wrong to archetypal forces in humankind.

Morris's determination to save some art of the past for his future society relates directly to Marx's discussion of classical Greek art in *Grundrisse*. Changed social conditions render obsolete the art which was produced under earlier conditions. It is no longer possible to produce the old forms under the new conditions. 'Certain forms of art, e.g. the epic, can no longer be produced in their world epoch-making, classical stature as soon as the production of art, as such, begins' (110). But though from the standpoint of continued production certain forms become obsolete (like the realistic novel in Morris's projected communist future), the obsolete forms of the past can still be enjoyed by the consumer. There are still people in Morris's projected future who enjoy the old, realistic novels of the nineteenth century; there are even more who enjoy the folk tales of even earlier periods. Marx tackles the problem in this way:

> The difficulty lies not in understanding that the Greek arts and epic are bound up with certain forms of social development. The difficulty is that they still afford us artistic pleasure and that in a certain respect they count as a norm and as an unattainable model.
>
> A man cannot become a child again, or he becomes childish. But does he not find joy in the child's naïveté, and must he himself not strive to reproduce its truth at a higher stage? Does not the true character of each epoch come alive in the nature of its children? Why should not the historic childhood of humanity, its most beautiful unfolding, as a stage never to return, exercise an eternal charm? There are unruly children and precocious children. Many of the old peoples belong in this category. The Greeks were normal children. The charm of their art for us is not in contradiction to the undeveloped stage of society on which it grew. [It] is its result, rather, and is inextricably bound up, rather, with the fact that the unripe social conditions under which it arose, and could alone arise, can never return. (111)

In one sense Morris has tried to capture the social conditions of a past age, and by stressing medieval art forms he is attempting to evoke a medieval note for his society. But it is a medievalism reproduced at a higher level, the kings and hierarchies will never return, the charm is the charm of 'the historic childhood of humanity'. And Marx's stress on the adult's 'joy in the child's naïveté' is something that especially relates to Morris's artistic practice. The reactions drawn on for the emotional moments of *News from Nowhere* are returns to the emotions of childhood. The Guest recalls the time 'when I was a happy child on a sunny holiday, and had everything that I could think of' (19:321). On the river 'I almost felt my youth come back to me, and as if I were on one of those water excursions which I used to enjoy so much in days when I was too happy to think that there could be much amiss anywhere' (22:330). Lindsay stresses 'how much his whole hope for the future, for a happy and

brotherly world, is linked with his childhood memories' (6). And so
Dick replies to the Guest's surprise at the survival of folk tales:

> 'What *do* you mean, guest? I think them very beautiful, I mean
> not only the pictures, but the stories; and when we were children
> we used to imagine them going on in every wood-end, by the
> bight of every stream: every house in the fields was the
> Fairyland King's House to us.' (16:184)

This child's delight in inventing imaginary worlds in familiar places
is the basis of Morris's creation of his romance. He creates a world
in which the characters are dressed like figures out of folk tale. They
even talk in the same funny words: the bight of every stream, quoth
he, to his kinsman. And in this future society in Morris's romance,
romance is recognized as the basis of art. *News from Nowhere* rejects
realism; it creates a 'nowhere' place; it creates it through a dream,
through the full surrender to the spontaneous imagination, freed
from the limiting constraints of the 'real'. The very success which
Morris achieves with his form validates his claims that for him the
true basis of art is the freed imagination. He works by the magic of
romance, the paradox of creating a future by imagining a past. He
uses a past form, the medieval dream vision, to rediscover past
values that are projected into the future, mediated by a new, nineteenth-century, marxist understanding. He awakens into a world of
the fantastic:

> Then the bridge! I had perhaps dreamed of such a bridge, but
> never seen such an one out of an illuminated manuscript; for not
> even the Ponte Vecchio at Florence came anywhere near it . . . .
> Over the parapet showed quaint and fanciful little buildings . . . .
> In short, to me a wonder of a bridge. (2:187)

It is a world of the 'quaint and fanciful', of 'wonder'.

Rejecting realism, Morris is immediately freed of a battery of
inhibiting restraints. He is able now to deal both with the current
feel of his utopian society, and with the stages by which it was
achieved, without having to write an historical chronicle novel
spanning the centuries. 'How the Change Came' (the title of chapter
17) can be told to the Guest, it does not have to be dramatized,
realized, fictionalized. Morris is immediately given the resources
of the eighteenth-century picaresque, the tale within a tale. At the
same time he does not feel constrained to provide a realistic dramatization of that tale within the tale, it can be given as report. This is

not something original with Morris. Bellamy's *Looking Backward* similarly has these recapitulatory chapters. The nature of utopian future fantasy was such that these summaries of how the society was achieved necessarily have to be given; and tend to be given in non-dramatized ways. In *Brave New World* Huxley offers a concise kaleidoscopic sequence of events (chapter 3). In *Nineteen Eighty-four* Orwell uses the excerpts from Goldstein's book for a comparable function.

Within the freedom of romance, then, Morris is able to adopt some avant-garde fictional devices. There is the witty self-consciousness of the form he is using in chapter 13, 'Concerning Politics', when the Guest asks 'How do you manage with politics?' and Hammond replies:

> 'I will answer your question briefly by saying that we are very well off as to politics — because we have none. If ever you make a book out of this conversation, put this in a chapter by itself after the model of old Horrebow's Snakes in Iceland.'
> 'I will,' said I. (13:267)

Chapter 72 of Niels Horrebow's *The Natural History of Iceland*, 'Concerning Snakes', consists of only one sentence; 'No snakes of any kind are to be met with throughout the whole island.' Happily, Morris's chapter dealing with the old superstition of politics, now revealed as the class magic mystification that politics in fact was, is chapter 13.

Rejecting realism, Morris immediately has access to these formal games that Swift and Sterne had been able to exploit. And in chapter 11, 'Concerning Politics, the disquisition that provokes the Guest's *alarm* and *dread*, Morris abandons fictional dramatization and abandons, too, any theoretical discursive essay style — fear of which perhaps caused that alarm and dread; he adopts instead a question and answer mode. It is an amazing catechism resulting in concise, devastating insights and mnemonic epigrams.

> (H.) Therefore the government really existed for the destruction of wealth?
> (I.) So it seems. And yet —
> (H.) Yet what?
> (I.) There were many rich people in those times.
>
> (H.) Yet amidst this poverty the persons for the sake of whom the government existed insisted on being rich whatever might

74

happen?

(I.) So it was.

(H.) What *must* happen if in a poor country some people insist on being rich at the expense of the others?

(I.) Unutterable poverty for the others. (13:260-1)

It is the insight we find again in Jack London's *The Iron Heel* and again in *Nineteen Eighty-four*. The system is designed to consume the surplus in a way that will ensure it is not redistributed to the labour that created it. In *The Iron Heel* the surplus is consumed in massive super-city building programmes, in the production of massive works of art by an art caste. In *Nineteen Eighty-four* it is consumed by continual war.

And in his four page catechism Morris goes on to demystify the nineteenth-century bourgeois concepts of parliament, the law courts, patriotism. He reveals the basis of these components of a liberal ideology as lying in the protection of the property interests of the rich against the unpropertied poor — protection to be exercised if ultimately tested by absolute, iron-fisted force.

Romance and dream are the basis of *News from Nowhere*. Then within those modes are the central chapters dealing with how the change came and with the nature of the organization of the new society — and here Morris uses historical summary and statement. And within this section of summary and statement — in themselves departures from the norms of nineteenth-century realistic prose fiction — we have the specific avant-gardeism of formal self-consciousness and experimentation in the two chapters 'Concerning Government' and 'Concerning Politics'.

The experimentation, the rejections of realism, are a liberation for Morris. To capture his future society he rejects limited nineteenth-century modes and looks for extensions to fictional possibility.

But why are the specifically 'experimental' chapters those concerning government and politics? The negative side of the impulse to experimentalism is revealed in the Guest's fear and dread at the prospects of a scientific disquisition on politics. Morris recoils at the prospect of political theory; his utopia has no formal politics. Yet Morris recognizes that to explain *how* it has no formal politics and government, requires political theory for the exposition. And he recoils. He adopts the quickest, the most concise modes of dealing with these matters in order to get them over with.

Similarly the crucial account of how the change came is presented as an historical survey. Rejecting realism, Morris does not have to have his protagonist — or his protagonist's father and grandfather and great-grandfather living a family chronicle of change, revolution, counter-revolution and reconstruction. And the reasons are not just a rejection of nineteenth-century fictional modes — historical fiction, family chronicle, realism. Nor is he being simply theoretically 'correct' here in choosing to stress how anonymous, co-operative group action achieved the change, rather than romantic individualism of Meredith's Nevil Beauchamp variety. He is recoiling from the material of the struggle. Morris wants his dream of the achieved utopia. 'If I could but see a day of it . . .' (1:182). It is the future happiness of the ideal associations of humanity, the unalienated relationships of the individuals to each other, to labour, to nature, that he wants to portray; not the violent struggle.

Morris's preference can be seen strikingly if we contrast him with Jack London, a very different sort of socialist writer. London's absorption of Nietzsche, Darwin and Huxley, as well as Marx, gave him the intellectual rationale for a personality stimulated by struggle, adventure, activity, even violence. London is fascinated by the struggle. *The Iron Heel* deals experientially with the socialist struggle, with the resistance to oligarchic repression: the ideal future is only noted, never presented as immediate experience. The pattern is the complete converse to Morris's.

Both of them knew their Marx. Both knew the necessities of the violent revolution, the period of repression, the phase of state socialism, and then the withering away of the state. But their imaginations were fired by different aspects of Marx's theory: London's by the struggles of the revolution, the resistance to the reaction, the class struggle. Morris, however, was more responsive to that phase of socialism when the state has withered away and organization is minimal or non-existent. So Morris's protagonist experiences this last stage, and is merely told of the preceding stages, which are got through as quickly as possible.

But was it the last stage, is there a *last* stage? When *News from Nowhere* was serialized it was subtitled *or an epoch of rest, being some chapters from a utopian romance*. The subtitle has often been ignored or omitted, but it is crucially important in introducing immediately the concept that what is presented is perhaps only a stage. The phrasing is not unambiguous; is it a final coming to rest after those centuries of toil, or is it a temporary recuperative rest on the way to further endless changes?

The dynamic nature of the dialectic distinguishes Marx's vision from other socialist visions. Other socialist visions could postulate an ideal, an end, a static society that had achieved all that was to be achieved. But can the dialectic ever stop? After the withering away of the state, what then? The stress in *News from Nowhere* is on peace, rest, stasis. Dynamic is theoretically present, though Morris implies that in actuality there is at the moment little dynamic. The Guest says to Ellen:

> 'I gathered from all I have heard that there was a great deal of
> changing of abode amongst you in this country.'
> 'Well,' she said, 'of course people are free to move about; but
> except for pleasure-parties, especially in harvest and hay-time,
> like this of ours, I don't think they do so much.' (28:379)

It is a period of peace, restfulness: 'You see, Guest, this is not an age of inventions. The last epoch did all that for us, and we are now content to use such of its inventions as we find handy, and leaving those alone which we don't want' (25:357). The phrasing is ambiguous. It is unclear whether the stress on this epoch and that age suggests that there will be other different epochs and ages to come; Morris does not presume to predict – but the phrasing allows for the possibility that there may be further change, even though his personal inclination is clearly for rest, for peace.

> I looked, and wondered indeed at the deftness and abundance of
> beauty of the work of men who had at last learned to accept
> life itself as a pleasure, and the satisfaction of the common needs
> of mankind and the preparation for them, as work fit for the
> best of the race. I mused silently; but at last I said:
> 'What is to come after this?'
> The old man laughed. 'I don't know,' said he; 'we will meet it
> when it comes.' (27:368)

It is the Guest who asks what will come next. Morris, who we can identify closely enough with the Guest, is introducing the possibility of continuing change; he is not closing off the future at this point, even if his presented future does not portray further, later stages. But the fact that it is the nineteenth-century Guest/William Morris who asks the question creates its own ambivalence.

Maybe to ask that question is to demonstrate that you are a victim of nineteenth-century uncertainties, doubts, myths of progress, protestant work-ethic compulsions that prevent you from accepting the peace of this life-style. The ambiguities are there. They are there because future change is not stressed; it is allowed, the possibilities are built into the novel – but attention is not drawn to them. That other nineteenth-century note, exhaustion, tiredness with the futility of things, the wish for the Lotos-eaters' permanent stasis, spreads strongly through this projected future.

And it is this exhaustion that is formally dominant in the romance. Nothing is prosecuted with great vigour. This is beautiful for the holiday note of the book, and the holiday note is stressed; the hay-making is a holiday experience for the people in this utopia — a version of the hop-picking holidays which the London proletariat used to take, the only way to pay for a holiday in the country; but for them still hard work. The stress here is not on the back-breaking work, but on the holiday; the Guest — who never gets to do any of the hay-making, so never strains his back — experiences 'that excited pleasure of anticipation of a holiday' (21:327). And though the boat trip is upstream, against the current, there is nothing *strenuous* about it; as we have seen, the Lotos eaters' seemingly permanent afternoon is evoked.

Morris accepted that the change from capitalism to communism would necessarily be a violent change. Old Hammond's account to the Guest stresses the violence. It is a projection from the Bloody Sunday episode, 13 November 1886. Old Hammond tells of the demonstration in which a thousand workers are massacred; the escalating violence; the bands of right-wing activists, 'Friends of Order'. 'All ideas of peace on a basis of compromise had disappeared on either side' (17:313). Civil war breaks out, the central event of the great social change.

But Morris passes by the detail of the civil war. He is not attracted to this violent conflict. Hammond announces 'The sloth, the hopelessness, and, if I may say so, the cowardice of the last century, had given place to the eager, restless heroism of a declared revolutionary period' (17:313). But this sense is never enacted in *News from Nowhere*. There is no formal reflection of this theoretical observation. Jack London structures *The Iron Heel* on violent incidents, violent confrontations, explosive narrative developments. Morris has none of that dynamic in the form of *News from Nowhere*. The mood is of a slow, languorous summer afternoon. The transitions are dream-like dissolvings, not dynamic progressions, not catalytic explosions. The movement is characteristically of evanescence, loss.

> I heard him, though my eyes were turned away from him, for that pretty girl was just disappearing through the gate with her big basket of early peas, and I felt that disappointed kind of feeling which overtakes one when one has seen an interesting or lovely face in the streets which one is never likely to see again; and I was silent a little. (4:205)

And when the movement is not to loss, then it is still a tired, weary, winding down:

> It was exceedingly pleasant in the dappled shadow, for the day
> was growing as hot as need be, and the coolness and shade
> soothed my excited mind into a condition of dreamy pleasure,
> so that I felt as if I should like to go on for ever through that
> balmy freshness. My companion seemed to share in my feelings,
> and let the horse go slower and slower as he sat inhaling the
> green forest scents, chief amongst which was the smell of the
> trodden bracken near the way-side. (5:206-7)

'Soothed', 'dreamy pleasure', 'for ever', 'balmy freshness', 'seemed', 'slower and slower' — these are the components of the characteristic languorous note.

And though the nineteenth-century reality with which the book opens dissolves into a dream of utopia, which at least is a dynamic, progressive, forward-moving transition, at the book's end it dissolves back, it relapses. The future movement is not held. And that is not because Morris is creating a ceaseless dynamic — the utopia does not turn into yet another state, but instead turns back.

Though perhaps it is not a relapsing into an identical, depressing, 'realistic' i.e. pessimistic, nineteenth-century intellectual state of insightful despair. Perhaps having been allowed to see 'a day of it', this future vision has transformed the Guest. The nineteenth-century reality has been negated by the dream vision, which is negated by a return to the nineteenth century, but a return on a higher level, a return now possessed by the conviction that the change will come, is possible, is worth struggling for. The book ends with an account of what 'Ellen's last mournful look seemed to say' — and notice Morris here has fallen into the Tennysonian 'seemed', the doubts are permeating his consciousness despite his best intentions. But his best intentions are expressed in the positive progressive message:

> 'Go back again, now you have seen us, and your outward eyes
> have learned that in spite of all the infallible maxims of your
> day there is yet a time of rest in store for the world, when
> mastery has changed into fellowship. — but not before. Go back
> again, then, and while you live you will see all round you people
> engaged in making others live lives which are not their own,
> while they themselves care nothing for their own real lives — men
> who hate life though they fear death. Go back and be the happier
> for having seen us, for having added a little hope to your struggle.

Go on living while you may, striving, with whatsoever pain and
labour needs must be, to build up little by little the new day of
fellowship, and rest, and happiness.'

Yes surely! and if others can see it as I have seen it, then it
may be called a vision rather than a dream. (32:401)

The dream becomes on this higher level a vision.

The gentle dream-like transitions certainly have their negative
aspect — an aspect of which Morris was aware. The Guest watches
things slip away, rather than seizing on to them. John Goode has
indicated the necessity of this in terms of the structure of *News
from Nowhere*: 'the narrator is dramatically powerless. He can
comfort only himself, and he can change nothing in the future with
which he holds a dialogue' (274). The Guest cannot participate in
the future. The worry is that the dream transitions, the unwilled
shrinkings and vanishings, will characterize his involvement in the
nineteenth century to which he returns.

But the positive aspects needs to be stressed too; the dream
becomes a vision which is gentle, peaceful, appropriate for this
future epoch. It is not a time of violence. The journey up-river is
inconsequential — it is not a quest with an end in view, but a journey
whose purpose is its total experience, the significance is in the
experience of the beautiful river, not a desperate search for some
mysterious grail. The pleasures of this future society are in the
rediscovery of living now, not in always striving for something else,
not in these desperate work drives, ambition drives. And the experience of the river creates the feeling of this future society — the
natural, unpolluted, realized pastoral; the poetic ideal actualized. Its
literary sources are indicated by the early introduction of Boffin,
named from Dickens's *Our Mutual Friend* (1865); and in that novel
there is a structural contrast between the filthy, polluted industrial
Thames around which the wretched dramas of a corrupted society
are played out; and the fresh pure upper reaches of the source of
the river, in which mental and physical health is restored.

Morris gives us that symbolic journey up-river, the journey to
the source for the restoration of society's health. At the same time
he shows us that in this future society, down-river is as clear and
fresh as up-river. The nineteenth-century reader needs this literary
journey of discovery; but in his future society, health has already
been restored, so the journey is inconsequential. Though inconse-
quentiality is not the same as pointlessness; just to experience and
enjoy a journey on the river is point enough in this future world,
freed from imposed drives.

So we have a gentle, natural world, freed from abrasiveness, violence, explosions; the soft transitions of streams and rivers, not the mechanical changes of explosions and machines. 'The soap-works with their smoke-vomiting chimneys were gone; the engineer's works gone; the lead-works gone; and no sound of riveting and hammering came down the west wind from Thorneycroft' (2:186-7). And salmon swim in the river Thames again.

In his lecture 'How We Live and How We Might Live' (1884) Morris spoke

of machinery being used freely for releasing people from the
mere mechanical and repulsive part of necessary labour and I
know that to some cultivated people, people of the artistic
turn of mind, machinery is particularly distasteful and they
will be apt to say you will never get your surroundings pleasant
so long as you are surrounded by machinery. I don't quite
admit that; it is the allowing machinery to be our masters and
not our servants that so injures the beauty of life nowadays.
(PW, 156-7)

Morris makes it clear that his objection to machines is not the 'artistic' one that they smell, make a lot of noise and are dirty. His objection is to the human suffering that they create under capitalism. His source is not pre-Raphaelitism but *Capital*:

Though machinery be the most potent means for increasing the
productivity of labour, that is to say for reducing the amount of
labour time necessary for the production of a commodity, in
the hands of capital it becomes the most powerful means, in
the industries on which it first establishes its grip, for
lengthening the working day far beyond the bounds imposed
by nature. (428)

In *News from Nowhere* machines are abandoned on a large scale after the revolution because they have been designed for commodity production rather than for useful creativity. They are retained for specialized uses, but no longer are the workers 'slaves to the monsters which we have created' (PW, 156). Hammond tells the Guest:

All work which would be irksome to do by hand is done by
immensely improved machinery; and in all work which it is a
pleasure to do by hand machinery is done without. There is no

difficulty finding work which suits the special turn of mind of everybody; so that no man is sacrificed to the wants of another. From time to time, when we have found out that some piece of work was too disagreeable or troublesome, we have given it up and done altogether without the thing produced by it. (15:280)

The stress is on the individual now. Machinery is there to serve the individual; unpleasant tasks are simply abandoned, not rostered and compelled as in Bellamy's world. For Bellamy's style of compulsion, though spreading out the toil equally to minimize any individual suffering from it, still makes the individual the servant of a machine or system or society — and a servant under compulsion from a democratic consensus is still as much a servant as one under compulsion from a capitalist plutocracy. Morris saw this clearly.
Hammond tells the Guest:

As to the big murky places which were once, as we know, the centres of manufacture, they have, like the brick and mortar desert of London, disappeared; only since they were centres of nothing but 'manufacture', and served no purpose but that of the gambling market, they have left less signs of their existence than London. Of course, the great change in the use of mechanical force made this an easy matter, and some approach to their break-up as centres would probably have taken place, even if we had not changed our habits so much: but they being such as they were, no sacrifice would have seemed too great a price to pay for getting rid of the 'manufacturing districts', as they used to be called. For the rest, whatever coal or mineral we need is brought to grass and sent whither it is needed with as little as possible of dirt, confusion, and the distressing of quiet people's lives. (10:250-1)

Machinery is used sparingly in this future society, because there is no need to produce for production's sake. That imperative of capitalism has ended. Machinery is used when it (1) has no polluting or environmentally disturbing and disruptive qualities; (2) is not taking away the pleasure of creative work from the individual and (3) is clearly subordinate to the individual's wishes and control, an extension of the individual's abilities, not (in Engels's phrase) an instrument for his enslavement (84). It is assumed that since individuals live harmoniously in this society, no one would ever want to use machinery as an extension of his or her power over others. Indeed, it is only at this stage of society, that it is safe to use machinery and other extensions of individual power; only now will people not use it to control and limit others. But could such a harmonious society have developed the technology to produce sophisticated machinery? Or is this developed technology the preserved heritage of capitalist industrial development? Yet can that sophisticated technology be applied and used without the continued back-up of a huge technology? Maybe it could; the ideology that implies that it couldn't is the ideology of maintaining capitalist industrialism — the propaganda of a system concerned with its own preservation.

One of the fictional problems is that though Hammond tells us machinery is used, all we ever see is one river barge powered by a 'force machine'. Rejecting the realistic novel, and personally antipathetic to technology, Morris does not feel the need to fill in the sociology of what machine work there is; he feels no need to show the ecology of a machine system; and so simply has his two or three assertions that machines exist.

We are not convinced. We still feel a need to see the infrastructure of this technology — to see it in action and in theory to be sure that it is there. Since this whole area of the novel is unrealized — whereas the personal, manual crafts and labours are detailed — we feel there is an artistic evasion somewhere. Is Morris unable to show us the use of machinery because he hasn't worked out its integration into this sort of society, because his theory is flawed or too incomplete? Our suspicions that what is absent is absent because it cannot be created damages the persuasiveness of the utopia at this point. And so the initial impression we take from reading the romance is of some Luddite anti-machine vision; this is false, as commentator after commentator points out; the machines do have a role in *News from Nowhere*; the details of this role in a socialist future are spelled out continually in his lectures. But the lectures give a much clearer impression of the machine role than the romance does; in the romance the machines get only glancing attention.

Morris avoids the details of industrial organization for the reason that he avoids the details of any other organization; organizations, systems harden and the individual becomes the servant of the system. This is one of his objections to the machine — the system of relationships that it involves can so readily become a system of tyranny, and get locked into the perpetuation of that system.

The struggle that Jack London foresees in *The Iron Heel* is the struggle for the mastery of the machines — capital v. labour. But Morris sees beyond that stage; the struggle for mastery of the machines involves too a struggle with the machines themselves. For the machines to be controlled by labour will not necessarily bring

the socialist future; state industrial socialism will produce equally
alienating conditions for the worker as industrial capitalism. Morris
realizes the trap in struggling merely for economic dominance;
once the machines are won from capital, then the whole concept of
machine civilization must be re-thought, the machines must be
relegated to positions of service, not be allowed to remain as the
social centre, as the rationale for human organization.

The reduction of the significance of the machines — by the
production of fewer objects, the abandonment of commodity
rubbish, the phasing out of certain unpleasant occupations — means
that the areas of social organization involved with machines must
get correspondingly fewer. The whole movement of Morris's future
is away from organizational structures, the lessening of their significance, so that human relationships can become direct and primary.

Decentralization is basic to this movement. The big manufacturing
centres no longer exist. The population is spread throughout the countryside. It is rare to be out of sight of a house. After the revolution:

People flocked into the country villages, and, so to say, flung
themselves upon the freed land like a wild beast upon his prey;
and in a very little time the villages of England were more
populous than they had been since the fourteenth century, and
were still growing fast. (10:253)

This, Morris stresses, was a spontaneous reaction. It is on the basis
of this spontaneous preference that 'we discourage centralisation
all we can, and we have long ago dropped the pretension to be the
market of the world' (10:249). Unlike those utopias of super-cities,
Morris envisages a society with no central governmental agencies, no
commercial system, no manufacturing of 'consumer' goods, no
imperial, economic, nationalistic or religious ambitions that demand
society should be organized. Instead the stress is on small local
communities; on the removal of bureaucratic and administrative
apparatuses. Structures, apparatuses only alienate — so the emphasis,
as with the technology, is on the minimal. The units of management
are the commune, ward, or parish 'indicating little real distinction
between them now, though time was there was a good deal' (14:270)
— the progressive abandonment of even those minimal structures is
implied in this gradual discarding of functional differentiation.
Decisions are made by the regular 'ordinary meeting of the neighbours, or Mote, as we call it' (14:271). Decisions are made by
majority vote. It is not a perfect system, but the only alternatives,
Hammond suggests, are:

First, that we should choose out, or breed, a class of superior
persons capable of judging on all matters without consulting
the neighbours; that, in short, we should get for ourselves what
used to be called an aristocracy of intellect; or secondly, that
for the purpose of safeguarding the freedom of the individual
will, we should revert to a system of private property again,
and have slaves and slave-holders once more.

The Guest proposes a third possibility, 'to wit, that every man should
be quite independent of every other, and that thus the tyranny of
society should be abolished' (14:272). Everyone laughs, and the
Guest joins in the laughter. But it is laughter not at the absurdity
of the proposal, but at the practical impossibility. It is not a contemptible wish. When Hammond 'recovered himself he nodded
at me, and said, "Yes, yes, I quite agree with you — and so we all
do" ' (14:272). The tyranny of majority rule is a real tyranny. What
Morris attempts is to get the minimum of tyranny — if such a thing
is possible. He rejects the anarchist position with laughter; it is
laughter, not argument. The argument is 'human nature' — but if
human nature can be changed so amazingly by the abandonment of
capitalism as to allow the idyllic communism of Morris's utopia —
why could it not be changed to allow anarchic individualism? Is
that an impossible stage, whereas Morris's communism is a possibility? Morris, though he rejects anarchism, recognizes the force of
the anarchist critique. It is, after all, the anarchist spirit that lies
behind the abandonment of industrial machinery, because the
industrial system tyrannizes the individual. It is his sensitivity to
the tyrannies which a socialist society can produce that caused
Morris's rejection of *Looking Backward*. Importantly it is the
Guest — the Morris figure — who raises the possibility of an anarchistic individualistic future; and the characters whom Morris
creates who reject it with laughter. The division within Morris
himself is here dramatized in the dialectic of the novel. Anarchism
has been an issue from the very beginning. The discussion 'up at
the League' that the novel takes off from, was one involving 'six
persons present, and consequently six sections of the party were
represented, four of which had strong but divergent Anarchist
opinions' (1:181). James Hulse, who is concerned to stress the
anarchist component of Morris's political thought, even speculates
that one of the six at the actual meeting that provoked the narrative might have been Kropotkin. He points out that Morris was
acquainted with Kropotkin, and that Kropotkin later praised *News
from Nowhere* as 'perhaps the most thoroughly and deeply

Anarchistic conception of future society that has ever been written' (99).

Realizing how Bellamy, in his preoccupation with the machinery of society, projected a machine society, Morris clears his mind as much as possible of structures and systems. The characteristic note of *News from Nowhere* is this minimum of apparatus – mechanical or social. He turns back to an earlier (in romantic terms readily identified as 'simpler' because it was earlier) period for some social model for his vision. And it is here, inevitably, predictably, that his future gets most limited. Morris could see Bellamy's mechanical absurdities – but cherished the archaic absurdities of calling his own village meetings the 'Mote' and giving people 'the sele of the morning' (23:341). Generally this medievalism remains merely eccentric; it does not damage the nature of the vision because in essence Morris had turned back to a medieval model since it offered a negation of the nineteenth-century hideousness; his motive is to produce a model purged of the evils of nineteenth-century industrial capitalism; he found it in this pre-capitalist dream world – a world characterized by negations – free from all the accretions of time leading to the corruptions of the nineteenth century. Out of that negation a new, free positive can emerge – something freed from the limiting vision of the nineteenth century in the way that Bellamy's vision was so patently not free. The very negativity of this aspect of Morris's return to medievalism allows for its positive future projection; projected into the future, it is not encumbered by too much predetermined rigidity of structure, either technological or social. Importantly, those structural aspects of medieval society that were unambiguously restricting and limiting, Morris excludes from his vision – the feudal aristocracy, the monarchy, the church. His is a selective medievalism, based first on a rejection of the repressive aspects of medieval society, and second on a negation of the repressive aspects of nineteenth-century industrial capitalism.

It is a vision, too, that has continuity with the radicals of the seventeenth-century English Revolution. In effect Morris revives the myth of the Norman yoke; before William the Bastard's conquest in 1066, Saxon society was democratic, egalitarian – decisions were made by open parliamentary assemblies, by the mote. Christopher Hill has explored the myth, though in looking for specific mentions of the 'yoke', 1066, and so on, he does not deal with Morris's participation in the tradition. Morris stresses the village mote – rather than a central parliamentary mote. And in this, of course, his vision is close to the radical interpretation of the myth – close to those who did not merely use it as an excuse for parliamentary rule, but who stressed traditional common rights and communalism. The spirit of Winstanley and the Diggers lies behind Morris's vision.

Morris's egalitarianism is demonstrated structurally in the Guest's experiences. There is nothing of the 'take me to your leader' technique of *Gulliver's Travels* — in which Gulliver's political discussions are always with kings or community leaders, and always deal with politics from the perspective of kings and leaders. In contrast Morris's Guest is plunged immediately into the living texture of non-elite ordinary experience. There are no elites. It is many worlds away from *Gulliver's Travels* — even the houyhnhnm with whom Gulliver stays is a member of parliament. In *News from Nowhere* there are no members of parliament, everyone is a member of parliament.

Yet some alienations remain. The stress on the individual, the personal, in this society inevitably directs us to issues of sexuality. And Morris sees sexuality as potentially socially disruptive, so that sexual disturbance, unhappiness are recurrent themes.

Again it is in keeping with the nineteenth-century weary despair of the Guest — tonally the incidents are in accord with his consciousness. And there is the belief — maybe a sad one, maybe a last lingering romantic individualism in Morris — that sexuality is something independent of society; social change will remove most causes of friction, but there will still be sexual frictions independent of the social determinants. If Morris had had a deeper, total materialism or if he had had a mystic cosmic consciousness about the unity of all things, he could not have come up with his theory of sexuality. But he had that very English consciousness, restraining him from extremes; he would always draw back from 'extremes'.

So having postulated a sexual drive independent of all social determinants, he then *worries* about his theory, and dwells on the way in which sexual drives disrupt society; as if he would *like* sexual drives to be socially determined and hence undisruptive. The stress in *News from Nowhere* is on the minimalness of this disruptiveness. The disruptiveness remains (we can hold on to our anarchic individualism) but in this society you don't feel much need to use your disruptiveness and anyway the society will always 'understand'. It is like the concept of academic freedom. You have this immense freedom and independence, government does not intrude on you to tell you what to do — but don't use that freedom to do something disturbing otherwise the academic freedom might evaporate.

We have our sexual individualism; but don't exercise it too much, don't exercise it in a way that would freak anyone out.

None the less Morris's is not at all a contemptible attempt. His sexual tolerance is way in advance of any contemporary nineteenth-century realistic novel. To begin with we are shown how Clara left Dick for someone else, and now has returned to Dick; and after their reunion, she is immediately jealous of Ellen, fearful of Dick's possible fascination with her. This incident is complemented by the implied past incidents of Ellen's life; this note of disruptiveness and sadness is constant; she tells the Guest: 'that even amongst us, where there are so many beautiful women, I have often troubled men's minds disastrously. That is one reason why I was living alone with my father in the cottage at Runnymede' (28:377). The best that Morris can offer is that with the removal of property preoccupations, most of the issues involved in nineteenth-century marriage and divorce no longer exist.

> We do not deceive ourselves, indeed, or believe that we can get rid of all the trouble that besets the dealings between the sexes. We know that we must face the unhappiness that comes of man and woman confusing the relations between natural passion, and sentiment, and the friendship which, when things go well, softens the awakening from passing illusions: but we are not so mad as to pile up degradation on that unhappiness by engaging in sordid squabbles about livelihood and position, and the power of tyrannising over the children who have been the result of love or lust. (9:238)

With these changes come changed perceptions.

The ready and easy way in which Dick accepts Clara back to him, after she had gone off with their two children for another man for a year, is in marked contrast with any other nineteenth-century English fictional treatment of such an event. For *Jude the Obscure* (1895) these are the materials of tragedy, leading out from the meanness of one society at one bad point in history to a total, cosmic despair. Morris transforms his material into an extraordinary contrast — the ease of the return, the quite natural way the separation is never even referred to on the boat journey — it just isn't an issue. In downplaying jealousy, he also plays down human sexual curiosity; but no doubt that would be something that Morris wouldn't think would exist in his utopia — it would be an alienation to get rid of, voyeurism, deviance, no doubt.

Morris has demystified himself about the property component of marriage and divorce; but his sexual morality still seems basically Christian monogamous. He clearly does not contemplate a communalism in which there is no private property in sexuality — in

which no one 'owns' another person's body, but all sexual partners
are held in common. It is not merely that Morris would reject such
an idea — more important is what seems to be Morris's failure even
to consider such a possibility, to think that such a possibility needed
refuting. Morris's treatment of sexuality is not as thought through
as other aspects of social life. And he functionally uses his unwilling-
ness to dwell too much, too deeply, on the theme. Describing a
murder that resulted from sexual passion Walter Morson tells Dick:
'I will make it short enough, though I daresay it might be spun out
into a long one, as used to be done with such subjects in the old
novels' (24:353). Sexual passion is dealt with differently in this
society; and it requires a different narration — brief, perfunctory;
the exploration of the detail of sexuality is relegated to the old
aesthetic of nineteenth-century realistic fiction, which of course
never dealt with the realities of sexuality, despite the belief in
'realism', because of the taboos on words and sexual description.
In so far as sexuality could be explored, any explicitness could
only be achieved metaphorically — contradicting the whole aesthetic
of 'realism'.

Sexuality is seen as an explosive area of human relationships.
This is admitted, accepted. And this very admission and acceptance
saves it from the lengthy nineteenth-century obsessions, moralizing,
concerns and rationalizations. What happens can be told quickly; it
does not need to dominate the texture of life or art in this society.
That seems to be Morris's sexual theory.

However, by its very recurrence, the sexual motif is dominant.
And the sexual themes of the book are tied in with the prevalent
note of sadness. The images of jealousy, of loss, of encountering
beauty yet not being able to attain or retain it, interrelate with
the Guest's similar sadness at not being able to attain the idyllic
beauty of this society in his own nineteenth-century life, not being
able to retain his experience of this future. It is a dream and will
fade — and the sadness at the inevitability of his return to the
nineteenth century after this dream vitiates his experience of the
dream future. Increasingly he sinks back into his sadness — partly
through his increasing experience of the society, partly through
his growing love for Ellen, and his inability to act upon it — his
fear of acting upon it. It is the same dread that he feels before
political action.

All along, though those friends were so real to me, I had been
feeling as if I had no business amongst them: as though the
time would come when they would reject me, and say, as Ellen's

89

last mournful look seemed to say, 'No, it will not do; you cannot be of us; you belong so entirely to the unhappiness of the past that our happiness even would weary you.' (32:401)

So that oddly, for all the beautiful future that Morris creates for us, the final note of the book is one of sadness. He has created one of the very few utopias that it would be humanly appealing to live in, and yet he has permeated it with this note of unhappiness. Even when describing the river journey at its happiest, free from any anxieties, the anxieties are introduced into his verbal structure: 'No one unburdened with very heavy anxieties could have felt otherwise than happy that morning; and it must be said that whatever anxieties might lie beneath the surface of things, we didn't seem to come across any of them' (24:349). So if everything is beautiful, why even speculate that there might be anxieties 'beneath the surface of things'? The Guest's nineteenth-century habits of thought — gloom, sadness, you're going to have to pay for any pleasure, pleasure is only transitory — permeate his consciousness, even in this so different future. He has Ellen perceptively remark: 'Do you know, I begin to suspect you of wanting to nurse a sham sorrow, like the ridiculous characters in some of those queer old novels that I have come across now and then' (30:387). Having tried to project what a future art form might be, and having liberated himself from the requirements of bourgeois realism, Morris is aware that he cannot liberate himself totally from certain nineteenth-century habits of mind. The artist is a product of his society; his consciousness is moulded by that society, and he can never totally transcend those conditions. With a brilliant effort of will and imagination, of intelligence and commitment, Morris is able to project himself forward over the centuries. But he knows that in that projection, he will have carried some of the negative, unreconstructed mental and aesthetic habits of his time.

His greatness is that ultimately he knows that he has done just that. He does not attempt to sustain a deception. He attempts the future projection; he doesn't shrink from that amazing task. But at the same time he indicates the limitations of his projection, he draws attention to those aspects of limitation that he is aware of — the tiredness, the shrinking, the sadness; then, recognized, those qualities can be correctly situated in their context so that though they permeate, they will not corrode, the future vision.

3

The Iron Heel

The two great socialist future fictions that preceded Jack London's *The Iron Heel* (1907) both concerned themselves primarily with the achieved future societies — realized, ideal. Edward Bellamy's *Looking Backward* (1887) and William Morris's *News from Nowhere* (1890) relate the difficulties of achieving utopian perfection in the course of their narratives; but they do so only partially, fragmentarily. The revolutionary process of gaining the socialist society is less their concern than the ideal that will be attained.

Despite differences of vision, both Bellamy and Morris are none the less agreed in wanting to stress the achieved ideal society rather than the wretchedness and the difficulties and the set-backs that will be encountered in the process of achieving that aim. So the details of the struggle are only sketchily present.

But in the intervening fifteen or so years, socialism seemed to have come no nearer. Set-backs had been numerous, and the failure of the 1905 Russian Revolution, followed by repression and reaction, introduced a note of gloom and pessimism into socialist groups. It was in this context that London wrote *The Iron Heel*. He looked at the negative signs and wondered whether the socialists hadn't miscalculated the historical scenario. Instead of 'the decay of self-seeking capitalism' leading rapidly to socialism, perhaps capitalism would evolve into something even more exploitive and repressive before the inevitable socialism could emerge, into

    that monstrous offshoot, the Oligarchy.

      Too late did the socialist movement of the early twentieth century divine the coming of the Oligarchy. Even as it was divined, the Oligarchy was there — a fact established in blood, a stupendous and awful reality. Nor even then, as the Everhard

Manuscript well shows, was any permanence attributed to the
Iron Heel. (3)

So Anthony Meredith writes in London's 'Foreword'. And it is this
new and unsuspected mutation, this repressive oligarchy of con-
glomerate capitalism, that is the subject of London's novel. His
narrative deals with the repression. The propagandist purpose that
Bellamy and Morris both shared is still present in London: the
fragmentary glimpses of the ultimate future indicate that socialism
will be achieved in the end; but the emphasis is on the long struggle
that has to be gone through before that end can be reached. There
were many like Bellamy who projected a future in which socialism
would painlessly evolve from the trusts, the super-conglomerates.
Indeed, Engels wrote in *Socialism: Utopian and Scientific*:

> In the trusts, free competition changes into monopoly and the
> planless production of capitalist society capitulates before the
> planned production of the invading socialist society. Of course,
> this is initially still to the benefit of the capitalists. But the
> exploitation becomes so palpable here that it must break down.
> No nation would put up with production directed by trusts,
> with such a barefaced exploitation of the community by a small
> band of coupon-clippers.
>   In one way or another, with trusts or without, the state, the
> official representative of capitalist society, is finally constrained
> to take over the direction of production. (89-90)

London is sceptical. *The Iron Heel* details the lengths to which
capitalism will go to hold off the achievement of socialism. In 1904
he had believed that the great socialist vote heralded the achievement of socialism in the USA by parliamentary means; by 1906 he
had come to realize the trusts will never simply let an elected socialist
majority take power. The ballot is tied to big business; if by some
chance the socialists win an election, despite attempts by big business to prevent that from happening, then the trusts will remove the
elected socialists from power.

The details of the Iron Heel oligarchy's repressive regime were
hailed during the 1920s and 1930s as prophetic of European fascism.
Anatole France, Leon Trotsky and George Orwell all stressed this
reading of the novel. As a result the book had a temporary revival;
but it was not the correct context, and the novel suffered as a result;
looked at in the context of fascism, it seemed to have inadequacies,
though the inadequacies resulted from this incorrect contextual

interpretation, not from the novel London wrote. The predictions of *The Iron Heel* are closer to present realities than to those of 1930s fascism. London foresaw a world of USA-based multinational corporations working in accord with and through secret agencies, like the CIA, to topple socialism and set up reactionary regimes in South America, Asia and Australia. The truth of London's predictions is now becoming chillingly revealed.

Socialism will not be achieved by peaceful, reformist means. It will be achieved only by a long and violent struggle. This was William Morris's message too. But whereas Morris's narrator is allowed to experience the achieved socialist ideal in *News from Nowhere*, and is merely told about the struggle that occurred to reach that ideal, London presents the struggle as the experience of his protagonists; the achieved socialist society seven centuries ahead is merely glimpsed – in the aspirations of his protagonists, in the impersonal annotations of some scholar of the future.

London's careful reading of Marx and Engels would have discouraged him from writing the conventional utopian novel. A hostility to utopian theorizing is one of the basic differences between Marx and the earlier socialists. Karl Mannheim remarks in *Ideology and Utopia*:

> Whereas the bourgeois theorist devoted a special chapter to setting forth his ends, and whereas this always proceeded from a normative conception of society, one of the most significant steps Marx took was to attack the utopian element in socialism. From the beginning he refused to lay down an exhaustive set of objectives. There is no norm to be achieved that is detachable from the process itself: 'Communism for us is not a condition that is to be established nor an ideal to which reality must adjust itself. We call communism the actual movement which abolishes present conditions. The conditions under which this movement proceeds result from those now existing.'
>
> If to-day we ask a communist, with a Leninist training, what the future society will actually be like, he will answer that the question is an undialectical one, since the future itself will be decided in the practical dialectical process of becoming. But what is this practical dialectical process?
>
> It signifies that we cannot calculate *a priori* what a thing should be like and what it will be like. We can influence only the general trend of the process of becoming. (112)

Fictionally, London needs to give some indication of his society of the twenty-sixth century. As a marxist he has the need to show that such a society will exist, that capitalism will inevitably collapse of its own contradictions. But as a marxist he knows the difficulties of trying to present the detail of this society, that as a writer of fiction he knows he needs to have. He does not want to divert attention from today's struggle into some future day-dream; but without the dream, can the struggle be sustained? Yet his literary predecessors had created huge problems in their future projections. As Engels put it, 'These new social systems were foredoomed to be Utopias; the more they were worked out in detail, the more inevitably they became lost in pure fantasy' (52).

Bellamy's socialist utopia in *Looking Backward* had horrified Morris; it was a disincentive to socialist commitment rather than an incentive, it was a life 'organised with a vengeance'. Images and tropes from utopian fiction had all too frequently been taken as anti-utopian horrors in other fictions. Specific details of the future society could do more harm than good for the socialist cause. Becoming your own enemy in the instant that you preach.

Marx stresses the dialectic, the process. Any utopian projection is in danger of being static — and then limiting and restrictive. Morris tries to allow for flux and change and dynamism within *News from Nowhere* — people can move around, change their jobs, alter their life-styles: but they don't do that much, and anyway it would be only a limited change within a rigidly decentralized rural society. Morris calls it 'an epoch of rest', but he doesn't show us any other epoch: the fictional stress is on the stasis of one epoch, not the continuing dialectic. H.G. Wells tries for variety in *A Modern Utopia* (1905) by having offshore islands for the social deviants — but this removes the possibility of significant social mutation within that world state. Morris advances beyond Wells's vision — Morris projects a society beyond state socialism, a society in which the state has withered away. But just because the state has withered away, does it follow that the dialectical process has ceased? There is always haunting the creation of any utopian structure the concept that Zamyatin satirizes in *We*: 'our revolution was the last one. No other revolutions may occur. Everybody knows that' (30:162).

By giving us only a fragmentary picture of the world of the twenty-sixth century, London brilliantly avoids many of these problems.

The precise form of his future society is not spelled out. The details that are given do not damage the projection by too much limiting specificity, too much intransigence of interrelationship.

He achieves this fragmentary vision by a variant of a common turn of the century literary device: the discovered manuscript, which provides us with the first person, authenticated, yet limited account of James's *The Turn of the Screw* or Wells's *The Island of Dr Moreau*. There is always the chance the narrators are mad; certainly they are biased, unobjective, from their very involvement in the materials they have described. An emotional commitment is the quality of these manuscripts. The materials they describe are unbelievable — and yet we fear they are true. They just need verifying in details to assure us that they are true. And so London has his emotional manuscript that takes us up to 1932, its detail and the hopes of its protagonists giving us a partial account of the future. And the annotations of the twenty-sixth-century editor of the discovered manuscript verify details of the manuscript, and give us glimpses of the twenty-sixth-century society which London's twentieth-century protagonists were in process of achieving. Just glimpses. The notes by the twenty-sixth-century editor tell us that both the first and the second socialist revolts were ruthlessly crushed by the united oligarchies of the world (1, nn. 3, 4:6) before the just society could be established. We are not given the name of this just, socialist society until chapter 14 when we are told that since the time of the events narrated in the manuscript 'have passed away the three centuries of the Iron Heel and the four centuries of the Brotherhood of Man' (14, n.6:143). Socialism has been finally achieved, and has endured for four centuries. Beyond that, London tells us little. The detail of the 'Brotherhood' is left for our own interpretation.

Of the sparse information, however, there is sufficient for us to see that the future includes the urban and the highly technological — though may not be totally restricted to that. There are two super-cities, Ardis completed in 1942, Asgard completed in 1984. These cities were the architectural and engineering and organizational triumphs of the totalitarian society of the Iron Heel. But they are retained when the socialist Brotherhood of Man establishes its rule — not destroyed as Morris has most of the nineteenth-century buildings destroyed in *News from Nowhere*. Jack London's socialists share the same technological enthusiasms as the plutocrats. When Avis Everhard, the author of the manuscript, hears that levies for slave workers to build these cities have been imposed, she writes:

> We of the revolution will go on with that great work, but it will not be done by the miserable serfs. The walls and towers and shafts of the fair city will arise to the sound of singing, and into

its beauty and wonder will be woven, not sighs and groans, but
music and laughter. (21:193)

Avis, the notes makes clear, was too optimistic; the building of
both cities was done by Iron Heel serfs. But the opposition between
socialists is over the alienation of labour, over the control of the
machines, over the economic uses to which the technology is put;
the socialists are not opposed to technology in itself as an inevitably
dehumanizing thing. They share with William Morris the concept
that labour is a fulfilling activity, they project an idea of building
being done to 'the sound of singing'; but unlike Morris they not
only include machine labour within this concept, they also look
forward to bigger and better technology, grandiose buildings, fast
transport. So the super-cities are retained and used in the later
socialist society.

The struggle 'for the ownership of the machines' that Ernest
Everhard predicted has been ultimately won by labour, and now
'instead of being crushed by the machines, life will be made fairer
and happier and nobler by them' (9:97). London believed with
Marx and Engels that machines were an extension and servant of
man; they did not have to be a reified technology oppressive of
man. London's future is closer to Bellamy's vision (though not
achieved in the easy gradualist peaceful way he suggests) than to
Morris's society of minimal technology.

Glimpses: on the large scale, super-cities; on the small scale,
domestic differences. From the annotator's comments on dust
problems in the nineteenth and twentieth centuries, we can deduce
that the future is furnished simply and dust free. Another of his
comments on the twentieth century allows us to deduce the nature
of twenty-sixth-century foods: 'even as late as that period, cream
and butter were still crudely extracted from cow's milk. The laboratory preparation of foods had not yet begun' (20, n.3:185). Now it
seems a lot less desirable. London's utopia of synthetic foods soon
becomes Huxley's anti-utopia in *Brave New World*, and reaches its
nadir in *Nineteen Eighty-four*. Morris's rural ideal becomes
increasingly appealing.

And that is about all we are told. Seeing how readily the ideals
can become undesirable, the tactful sketchiness of London's strategy
is now revealed as a mark of his brilliance. Orwell complained that
The Iron Heel 'shows no grasp of scientific possibilities' (CE, II:11:
46). But the novel is saved from disaster by just that avoidance of
speculation. London avoids predicting scientific possibilities and
concentrates on human economic and power motivations. When

Orwell came to write his own future projection, *Nineteen Eighty-four*, he, too, concentrated on human motivation and gave only the sketchiest indication of 'scientific possibilities'.

The explicit details of the socialist society of the Brotherhood of Man are supplemented by implicit details that we can draw and assemble from other features of the novel. The way the annotator of Avis Everhard's manuscript sees Avis and Ernest as historical leaders of the movement that led to the achievement of the Brotherhood of Man, encourages us to assume that the Brotherhood of Man fulfills what we know of Avis and Everhard's beliefs and hopes. And the way in which the annotator has to comment on evils and absurdities in twentieth-century life for his twenty-sixth-century reader, directs us to deduce that those features are mercifully absent from the world of the Brotherhood of Man. And if they are absent, that means society can exist without them, and exist better without them; and this encourages the attitude that we can remove some of those features from twentieth-century society — and thus hasten the Brotherhood of Man. The propaganda effectiveness of the mode of narration is considerable.

The future reader needs not only obsolete slang to be glossed for him in footnotes like fake, bluff, grub (22:200, 201; 23:217) but also absurd customs: like the concept of 'society' — 'to denote the gilded drones that did no labour, but only glutted themselves at the honey-vats of the workers' (4, n.4:46), or lap-dogs — 'while people starved, lap-dogs were waited upon by maids' (18, n.1:167). The annotation works at the simple propagandistic level of redefinition, or of defining things that are usually left unmentioned. The annotation is a running indictment of nineteenth- and twentieth-century capitalist society from a broad-spectrum humane point of view; though London thought as a marxist and constructed his novel in accord with his marxism, the critique mounted in the footnotes is non-doctrinaire. It is a wide, Christian-socialist, leftist, humanitarian, popular front.

Sometimes the annotator comments, giving a value judgment or an expression of amazed incomprehension; sometimes the items are left to speak for themselves. We are told about strikes, for instance, with some expressive amazement:

> These quarrels were very common in those irrational and anarchic times. Sometimes the labourers refused to work. Sometimes the capitalists refused to let the labourers work. In the violence and turbulence of such disagreements much property was destroyed and many lives lost. All this is inconceivable to us — as

inconceivable as another custom of that time, namely, the habit
the men of the lower classes had of breaking the furniture when
they quarrelled with their wives. (2, n.4:23)

We are given utterly objective figures about child employment; no
comment could be adequate: 'In the United States Census of 1900
(the last census the figures of which were made public), the number
of child labourers was placed at 1,757,187' (5, n.9:56). We are given
documentation of the Christian approval of slavery in the American
South, the theological background to the material which Twain deals
with in *Huckleberry Finn*: 'In AD 1835, the General Assembly of
the Presbyterian Church resolved that: '*slavery is recognized in both
the Old and the New Testaments, and is not condemned by the
authority of God.*' After a couple of further examples the annotator
remarks, and appends supportive evidence: 'It is not at all remarkable that this same note should have been struck by the Church a
generation or so later in relation to the defence of capitalistic
property' (2, n.8:26, 27). It is a brilliant insight, an unforgettable
illumination.

London propagandistically and brilliantly bludgeons his reader in
these devastating footnotes by stressing the continuity and similarity
between 'historical' barbarities and twentieth-century barbarities. He
confronts the twentieth-century ideology of progress by giving
examples of atrocities both from the reader's present and past. From
the perspective of seven centuries ahead, there is not much difference
between the absurd world of Louis XIV and his Swiss Guards and
the absurdities of US capitalism. There is not much difference
between African slavery, slavery in the American South, and conditions in the factories in which women and children labour. It is all
part of the same benighted historical period.

> Our only consolation is philosophic. We must accept the
> capitalistic stage in social evolution as about on a par with the
> earlier monkey age. The human had to pass through those stages
> in its rise from the mire and slime of low organic life.
> (17, n.1:159)

The analogies, the documentation, are designed to shock the reader.
The cruelties are underlined by the perspective of the future socialist
society, which does not know of such horrors, which has to have
them explained. In a similar way Swift shocks his reader by looking
at Gulliver's proud defence of English customs in the context of
the horrified reactions and (in some areas) the juster societies of the

King of Brobdingnag and the houyhnhnm master. In that Swift was writing a pessimistic account of situations for which he could offer no practical solution, he could afford to play with more complexities of irony, of level and qualification, than London. London is writing a much simpler, practical propaganda — he has a solution that he is recommending: socialism. Maxwell Geismar sees London's strategy here as 'the central device' of the novel, and suggests Thorstein Veblen's *Theory of the Leisure Class* (1899) as a source: 'The central device was that of London's stepping completely outside his own age and describing its salient characteristics as if belonging to some lost and rudimentary curiosae of primitive human behavior' (165). But the basic idea of underlining the evils of the contemporary society of the book's readership by seeing them in the context of imaginary worlds — far away in future time or in physical distance — puts London in that tradition to which Swift belongs.

So London establishes his picture of the evils of contemporary capitalist society; and simultaneously establishes his utopian vision of the future by postulating a society that finds these contemporary evils horrifying, avoidable and now firmly a feature of the historical past. The Brotherhood of Man is a negation of the details of oppression with which we are presented.

A summary of the story that Avis Everhard's manuscript tells shows clearly enough its romance features. The romance is, of course, qualified and supplemented not only by the footnotes, but by the detailed arguments and discussions that Ernest Everhard has in Avis's story. The narrative thrust of her manuscript, however, is that of romance.

Avis Cunningham is the daughter of a distinguished Berkeley professor who one evening invites Ernest Everhard to dinner. Everhard is presented in the conventional pre-First World War terms of the working-class intellectual — unruly, untamed in appearance, his masculine vigour, his virility, demonstrating itself in the way his clothes never fit him properly. The name Everhard suggests not only his steely resistance to oppression but also his sexuality, the perpetual hard on. While 'Ernest' stresses both his serious commitment and his being a foretaste, an earnest, of the future. It comes as something of a surprise to find the name is not a fictional creation.

Joan London records that after her father left Kelly's Army — the band of the unemployed marching on Washington — he stayed with the Everhards. 'Later the sand dune of this part of Lake Michigan's shore line, as well as the name of one of his cousins, Ernest Everhard, were to appear in *The Iron Heel*' (83). London was

never one to reject found materials. *The Iron Heel* drew considerably
on his own newspaper files.

Avis's first impression of Ernest is the typical ambivalence of
romance: hostility, and then being drawn, despite the social trappings separating them, by the challenge of his sexual directness. A
sexier Felix Holt.

> In the first place his clothes did not fit him. He wore a ready-
> made suit of dark cloth, that was ill adjusted to his body. In fact,
> no ready-made suit of clothes could ever fit his body. And on
> this night, as always, the cloth bulged with his muscles, while
> the coat between the shoulders, what of the heavy shoulder-
> development, was a maze of wrinkles. His neck was the neck of
> a prize-fighter, thick and strong . . . .
> And then, when he shook hands with me! His handshake was
> firm and strong, but he looked at me boldly with black eyes —
> too boldly, I thought. You see, I was a creature of environment,
> and at that time had strong class instincts . . . .
> But this boldness that I took to be presumption was a vital
> clue to the nature of Ernest Everhard. He was simple, direct,
> afraid of nothing, and he refused to waste time on conventional
> mannerisms. 'You pleased me,' he explained long afterwards;
> 'and why should I not fill my eyes with that which pleases me?'
> (1:7-8)

Ernest's directness, brusqueness, rudeness alarms Avis; but soon
she is in love because of this untrammelled force. She is won over
by the vigour of his arguments, by the way he stands up to distinguished people and points out the falsity of their ideas. 'My
eagle' she writes of him; and that's what she calls her first chapter.
She herself is a bird, too: Avis. The implicit metaphor is of their
airy romantic flight from the trammels of twentieth-century life to
a higher order of society.

The romantic hero converts her to socialism by the vigour of his
presence, by confronting her with the details of individual human
suffering, and finally by theoretical exposition.

Investigating the way Jackson, an employee of a saw-mill company, loses his arm in an industrial accident, loses his job since he
cannot work one-armed, is denied compensation and ends up having
to peddle goods from house to house, Avis sees the economic and
social base of bourgeois ethics. But this conversion of her and her
father then leads to their direct experience of the oppressions of
capitalism — no longer just observing the terrible things that happen

to others. The events that ensue are presented in the broad strokes
of romantic fiction and seem somewhat melodramatic; though to
categorize them as melodramatic is not an aesthetic judgment so
much as a commitment to bourgeois ideology. These things would
never happen, it is all too melodramatic, is our conditioned initial
reaction. Yet the things London describes have had their counter-
parts throughout this century. People have been dismissed from and
kept out of universities because of their radicalism. Radical publica-
tions have been suppressed by a combination of petty bureaucratic
harassment and ultimate force — imprisonment, forced bankruptcy,
seizure.

Having written a book, *Economics and Education*, which demonstrates the subordination of the university to business interests
(Ursula's insight in *The Rainbow* eight years later), Avis's father,
Professor Cunningham, is forced to resign from the university. The
book is suppressed. His publishers lose their nerve and withdraw all
copies from sale. No one will reprint it. Professor Cunningham tries
to publish it as a special edition of a socialist newspaper — but the
Post Office rules that special editions of newspapers are not eligible
for postal distribution; shortly afterwards they rule that the socialist
newspaper is seditious anyway and refuse to distribute it through
the mails. Finally the warehouse with the undistributed copies of
the special edition of the socialist newspaper containing the book is
burned to the ground.

Meanwhile, although Professor Cunningham owned his house
outright, a mortgage deed is forged by the plutocracy and he is
evicted for non-payment on the loan; similarly his share certificates
in Sierra Mills mysteriously disappear. Avis and her father are forced
to live in the slums, again, the typical romantic tropes; the unworldly
professor from popular romance. Archetypal scientist, Professor
Cunningham 'lived too much in the world of mind to miss the
creature comforts we were giving up ... he embarked upon the
adventure with the joy and enthusiasm of a child' (11:115). When
Ernest is later elected to congress on a socialist platform and he
and Avis move to Washington, 'father did not accompany us. He
had become enamoured of proletarian life. He looked upon our
slum neighbourhood as a great sociological laboratory, and he had
embarked upon an apparently endless orgy of investigation ...'
(16:150). Unworldly scientist; but also alienated academic finding
fulfilment in physical as well as mental work in a William Morris
socialist way. Though the unrewarding and alienated sort of 'odd
jobs' Professor Cunningham would be likely to find creates problems. Work in the socialist future can be fulfilling and enriching; for

the proletariat under capitalism, what can it offer? Professor Cunningham's intellectual excitement in exploring the sociology of the proletariat under capitalism might get him through the boring and repetitive tasks — but that isn't a solution for everyone. None the less, London stresses Professor Cunningham's enjoyment in labour, for labour is central to his marxist vision of human existence. As Marx wrote in *Capital*:

> As creator of use-values, as useful labour, labour is a necessary condition of human existence, and one that is independent of the forms of human society; it is, through all the ages, a necessity imposed by nature itself, for without it there can be no interchange of materials between man and nature — in a word, no life. (1:12)

Avis's narrative tells how the plutocracy — representing the big business super-capitalists, the trusts — becomes increasingly powerful and one by one eliminates its opposition — the farmers, then the small businessmen, then the socialists. There are large socialist gains in the 1912 elections — but the plutocracy none the less controls the Congress. Ernest makes a fiery speech; a bomb is thrown. Congressmen testify that they saw Ernest throw it; he is arrested along with the other socialist congressmen, and they are all imprisoned. The socialist movement begins to work underground — literally underground. Avis, after a spell in prison, settles in a hide-out cave near Glen Ellen on Sonoma mountain north of San Francisco — and London uses his own ranch here as another romantic archetype.

> It was quite a scramble down to the stream bed, and, once on the bed, we went down stream perhaps for a hundred feet. And then we came to the great hole. There was no warning of the existence of the hole, nor was it a hole in the common sense of the word. One crawled through tight-locked briars and branches, and found oneself on the very edge, peering out and down through a green scree. A couple of hundred feet in length and width, it was half of that depth. Possibly because of some fault that had occurred when the knolls were flung together, and certainly helped by freakish erosion, the hole had been scooped out in the course of centuries by the wash of water. Nowhere did the raw earth appear. All was garmented by vegetation, from tiny maiden-hair and gold-black ferns to mighty redwoods and Douglas spruces. These great trees even sprang out from the walls of the hole.

The Iron Heel

Some leaned over at angles as great as forty-five degrees, though the majority towered straight up from the soft and almost perpendicular earth walls.

It was a perfect hiding place. No one ever came there, not even the village boys of Glen Ellen. (18:170)

The hole in the ground opens into the cave where live the socialists who will create the land of beauty and plenty in the future. The Manson family image of a hole in the ground that led to instant satisfaction, the land with the river of milk and honey, the tree that bears twelve kinds of fruit, are part of the traditional Land of Cockaigne utopianism; London mediates it, the utopia has to be worked for, it will not happen magically, it can only happen materially; but unlike the Manson Family, he did not believe the material could happen now. So the cave holds the builders of the utopia — the founders, not the found.

The millenarian thinking that we find in London and Manson has always been a part of a tradition of radical resistance to establishment society. It can be found readily in the writings of the English Revolution of the 1640s and 1650s — Fifth Monarchists, Ranters, Seekers and so on. It is a tradition of thinking that surfaces at times of social upheaval, transition. Kermode has indicated its presence amongst the socialist groups and traditions D.H. Lawrence may have been influenced by. And the millenarianism isn't identical with socialism: from the same roots have grown right-wing activists — the Third Reich.

London would have known of this context of the turn of the century labour movement. But his rigorous commitment to rationalism, his thorough materialism, means that his millenarianism had to be expressed in materialistic forms. Hence the science-fictional stress of the book. The reified achievements of rational science serve to embody London's millenarian vision of a future. He has the impulse; but he firmly materializes it. The hole in the ground leads to utopia — eventually, seven centuries ahead.

Although his socialist aims are millenarian, London can only express his millenarianism in scientific materialism or in traditionally romantic modes. Though the village boys are mentioned as not ever coming near the cave, the mention of them sets something of the tone; this is the ideal hide-out for childhood games of bandits, outlaws, secret societies — Tom Sawyer's adventures. Now the adventures are like Huck's — real. It is an idyllic romantic adventure setting, complete with romantic revolutionary scientist Biedenbach who invents a smoke-absorbing machine so they can have fires; and with guards and passwords and lookouts.

The cave and its surrounds are also like a forest of Arden idyll. And the disguise motif of Shakespearean romance recurs: the revolutionary socialists master the art of disguise by surgical operation and by lessons in dramatic portrayal, so that they can go into the public world again as agents. With different voices, their heights stretched four or five inches or shortened by a couple, they make their way into the inner echelons of the plutocracy; they find the ultimate romantic political activity – they are employed by the unwitting plutocracy as spies and sent to work amongst the socialist underground . . . . Fantasy fiction; but so much of London's material that seemed fantasy has realized itself since he wrote. Remember the story of Kim Philby, recruited by the KGB, and then penetrating British intelligence so effectively as to be awarded the OBE from the British establishment (it was withdrawn 10 August 1965) and the Order of the Red Banner from the Soviet Union. While London's projection of a network of underground revolutionaries, fugitives moving around the country, was actualized by the weather underground and other groups that went underground in the USA after the activism and repression of the late 1960s. Jonah Raskin's novel *Underground* (1978) explores the trail of one particular fugitive, Kenny Love, alias Abby Hoffman, through this world that London foresaw.

The morning after Everhard has been rescued from Alcatraz Avis practises her disguise skills, pretends to be another woman, pours admiration over him 'and, before he could guess my intention, threw my arms around his neck and kissed him on the lips. He held me from him at arm's length and stared in annoyance and perplexity' (20:183-4). The lover not recognizing his beloved in disguise; the lover demonstrating his fidelity to his beloved all unawares; these are the materials of romance from Shakespeare's day. While the co-ordinated mass gaol break, in which over 350 socialists are sprung simultaneously from prisons throughout the USA, is the romance of the popular sensation romance, masterminded, incredible actions.

The sensation novel romance provides a major strand for *The Iron Heel*. The super-cities Asgard and Ardis come from this realm of literature. So does the romance of speed – here presented in the trip Avis takes across the USA to her Sonoma hideout on 'the Twentieth Century', 'reputed to be the fastest train in the world then' a footnote stresses (22, n.2:199). The aerial warfare of balloons carrying bombs during the Chicago riot comes from the same area. Comrade Biedenbach, the inventor, is the absent-minded scientist of popular sensation romance, a variant on the archetypal unworldly professor we have seen in Avis's father. 'He was shot by one of our lookouts at the cave-refuge at Carmel, through failure on his part to remember the secret signals' (18:172). This all shades into the romantic glorification of a technological future that we find in part in Bellamy and Wells; that we find romanticized and satirized in Zamyatin; that Swift and Huxley derided, and that Orwell rejected as both derisory and impossible; but it runs through popular fiction, the pulps, and science fiction as a major stream of twentieth-century romance.

The novel ends with the account of the Chicago Commune and its brutal repression by the plutocracy. The great political romantic act of rebellion, of attempting to overthrow the oppressor, of fighting it out with the oppressor in direct combat, is here presented as the culminating episode of the manuscript narrative. And the emphasis is on the battle. Despite London's calling chapter 22 'The Chicago Commune', as Walter Rideout points out, 'there is no description of the kind of government ("the better world", so to speak) that the Socialists would supposedly, judging by the chapter title, attempt to set up' (44). The emphasis is all on the thrill, the horror, the violence of the street-fighting — the romance.

And romance is the central theme of Avis's narrative — the romantic love interest of the popular 'romance' novel. Avis writes of the night Ernest was freed from Alcatraz: 'Not more impatiently do I await the flame of tomorrow's revolt than did I that night await the coming of Ernest' (20:182). The sexuality of her waiting for Ernest — the phallic flame, the coming — is stressed. And it is stressed as in accord with the political: the flame of revolution, the coming of the deliverer. (The incorrectness of her optimism and of her individual worship is indicated by the annotator.) *The Iron Heel* is one of the few political novels in which sexuality is not in conflict with political impulse (as with Somers and Harriet in *Kangaroo*) or in which the political lovers do not finally betray each other (as in *We*, *Darkness at Noon*, and *Nineteen Eighty-four*). In *Nineteen Eighty-four* sexuality has been distorted and effectively destroyed — sex is totally and only a political activity. With London, the sexual and political are *in accord*, but independent of each other. Sexuality has its own validity; it is the vigour of Everhard's political harangues that turns Avis on to him. Avis's politicization is a combination of her decision to develop interests that would make her appealing to him, and of her developing his interests as their love develops. Just a little chauvinistically it is the woman who reaches political understanding through romantic-sexual love (though in the ensuing narrative London stresses that women socialist activists are as significant as male activists). Zamyatin offered it the other way round — the male D-503 becomes caught up with the revolutionaries through his sexual fascination with the female I-330.

In *We* there is always the nagging possibility that I-330 used sex as a way of drawing D-503 into the revolution so the revolutionaries can seize his space-ship. There is no such suggestion of manipulation in *The Iron Heel*. Everhard's sexual attractiveness is quite uncalculated, he is not playing a part to lure Avis. However, it equally needs to be stressed that Everhard responds sexually to Avis. He is not one of those political leaders who is all commitment, thought and mind, utterly disregarding the body. London allows that some people may prefer it like that and make that their choice; one of them is occasionally referred to in the footnotes as a major activist, 'The Red Virgin' (19, n.1:175). London allows for a range of individual behaviours; while making it clear that his own protagonist is the fully rounded man: intellectual, courageous, strong, hard-working, not a monastic celibate or a recluse or a sexless fanatic. London is concerned to make politics sexy and excitingly active — as he liked and wanted and tried to live his own life. To give Avis the final words on Everhard's sexuality, 'there was never such a lover as he':

> His arms were around me before I knew. His lips were on mine
> before I could protest or resist. Before his earnestness
> conventional maiden dignity was ridiculous. He swept me off
> my feet by the splendid invincible rush of him. He did not
> propose. He put his arms around me and kissed me and took
> it for granted that we should be married. There was no
> discussion about it. The only discussion — and that arose
> afterwards — was when we should be married. (5:48)

Avis's conversion to socialism is in part emotional, romantic. But the other aspect of political commitment is the intellectual, the rational, the scientific. And this is equally stressed in *The Iron Heel*, not only by the objective, statistical tone and content of the footnotes glossing the romantic narrative, but by Ernest Everhard's expositions of Marx within the narrative.

George Orwell complained of *The Iron Heel* that 'the hero is the kind of human gramophone who is now disappearing even from Socialist tracts' (CE II:11:46). He complained similarly that Gletkin in Koestler's *Darkness at Noon* was 'a thinking gramophone' (CE III:68:277). Orwell represents here that predominant body of literary commentators who have been brought up in the aesthetic of

106

liberal bourgeois realism, and can't handle anything that isn't realism; never really understanding that realism is the way bourgeois capitalism sees things, it isn't the only way or the best way or the absolute way or even objectively a very good way. For all his attacks on the totalitarian left, Orwell was basically in agreement with their aesthetics: a reduced version of nineteenth-century bourgeois realism.

But certain information has to be communicated in a political novel, and it is usually material that seems recalcitrant for the form of conventional romance or art fiction or bourgeois realism. D.H. Lawrence encountered the same same problem in writing *Kangaroo*, and he used the same dismissive term that Orwell had used to describe Ernest Everhard. Writing of his own protagonist, Somers, Lawrence says, 'He preached, and the record was taken down for this gramophone of a novel' (14:309). London, like Lawrence, chose to face the problem head on. If the novel is going seriously to deal with political ideas, then they have to be expressed. The form of the novel can be changed to accommodate them — in preference to changing the ideas to suit the form of the novel. So both London and Lawrence let their protagonists hold forth like gramophone records. Their ideas are the core of the novel. And if this results in a clumsiness, a lack of 'style', a certain uncouthness in the eyes of some critics, so much the better. The political realities that way impinge on the fragile form of the bourgeois novel and the delicate sensibilities of the bourgeois literary critics. A new style is born.

The uncouthness of Everhard's holding forth is featured in *The Iron Heel*. Rather than hide and conceal the ideas that have to be expressed, London pushes them into the forefront and stresses their very intrusiveness. The elegantly comfortable dining-room of Professor Cunningham is disrupted by Everhard's presence. 'It was "preacher's night", as my father privately called it, and Ernest was certainly out of place in the midst of the churchmen' (1:7). Socially he is out of place in his ill-fitting clothes. Yet one irony is that he should be fully in place; Everhard, the new secular preacher of socialism, is just as much a preacher as the clergy. The genial liberal intellectual's laughter at preachers is presented in Professor Cunningham's attitude, stressing the social uncouthness of preachers, ranters and ravers anyway. As Lawrence does with Somers, so London with Everhard stresses the preaching quality. The further irony is that the socialism which Everhard preaches should be in accord with the views of those preaching clergy — except that the established church has sold out on the values of early Christianity. The story of Bishop Morehouse, one of the novel's strands, tells how he gives up his wealth and tries to live as a primitive Christian, a practising socialist. It serves to stress the betrayal by the established churches of true Christian values. Philip Foner records that in the Oakland Socialist Labour Party, to which London belonged, there were 'several ministers who saw in socialism a means of reviving the spirit of early Christianity' (1964, p.26).

Since Everhard is to expound his views, London features his argumentative verbal assertiveness. Avis recalls that first encounter:

> How the scene comes back to me! I can hear him now, with that war-note in his voice, flaying them with his facts, each fact a lash that stung and stung again. And he was merciless. He took no quarter and gave none. I can never forget the flaying he gave them in the end. (1:16)

Similarly at the address he delivers to the Philomath club: 'Sometimes he exchanged the rapier for the club and went smashing amongst their thoughts right and left. And always he demanded facts and refused to discuss theories. And his facts made for them a Waterloo' (5:62). His verbal encounters are described in the images of battle. The opposition that occurs often enough in political fiction between words and deeds does not exist in this novel; here thought and idea are unified by the language; and the action of the novel demonstrates the validity of the metaphors. Everhard the preacher, the debater, the verbal expounder of socialism becomes Everhard the activist, the revolutionary, the street fighter when the class struggle issues into open battle.

The words of the human gramophone, the ideas that are delivered with such pugnacious metaphors — these are important too. Here London propagandizes the basic aspects of marxist theory. Here is the theoretical intellectual centre of the book — the theory which the narrative and multiple visions and other fictional modes have expressed, enacted in fictional terms. London avoids the utopian fantasies of the pre-marxist and non-marxist left and follows the 'scientific' procedure laid down in Engels's *Socialism: Utopian and Scientific*:

> Henceforward socialism no longer appeared as an accidental discovery by this or that intellect of genius, but as the necessary outcome of the struggle between two classes produced by history — the proletariat and the bourgeoisie. Its task was no longer to manufacture as perfect a system of society as possible, but to examine the historico-economic process from which these classes

and their antagonism had of necessity sprung and to discover
in the economic situation thus created the means of ending
the conflict. (72)

So the 'utopian' future is only glimpsed; instead the focus is on the
forces that are leading to the inevitable confrontation of capital and
labour. The basic materials of London's projection are the materials
of marxist analysis of historical and contemporary capitalism; the
facts of analysis not the fantasies of fiction.

Central to the novel is the theory of surplus value. It is from an
acceptance of this theory that London projects his future. Everhard
explains it in detail in his encounter with the small businessmen. 'It
was the first time I had ever heard Karl Marx's doctrine of surplus
value elaborated, and Ernest had done it so simply that I, too, sat
puzzled and dumbfounded' (9:102).

Technological utopias have looked forward to a time when the
mechanics of production have become so sophisticated that the
whole community shares in the prosperity. But London's vision of
the next three centuries is one in which the capitalists continue to
retain the surplus for themselves and monopolize the nation's
wealth. He sees the immediate development of industry as one in
which the super-capitalists, the trusts, dominate and proceed to
eliminate the small businessmen:

The ownership of the world, along with the machines, lies
between the trusts and labour. That is the battle alignment.
Neither side wants the destruction of the machines. But each side
wants to possess the machines. In this battle the middle class
has no place. The middle class is a pygmy between two giants.
Don't you see, you poor perishing middle class, you are caught
between the upper and nether millstones, and even now the
grinding has begun. (9:103)

This is the process that is occurring in the course of the novel. And
London presents the long-term inevitable conclusion, the breakdown
of capitalism from its own contradictions. Everhard gives the
scenario:

'I have demonstrated to you mathematically the inevitable
breakdown of the capitalist system. When every country stands
with an unconsumed and unsaleable surplus on its hands, the
capitalist system will breakdown under the terrific structure of
profits that it itself has reared. And in that day there won't be

any destruction of the machines. The struggle then will be for the ownership of the machines. If labour wins, your way will be easy. The United States, and the whole world for that matter, will enter upon a new and tremendous era. Instead of being crushed by the machines, life will be made fairer, and happier and nobler by them. You of the destroyed middle class, along with labour — there will be nothing but labour then; so you, and all the rest of labour, will participate in the equitable distribution of the products of the wonderful machines. And we, all of us, will make new and more wonderful machines. And there won't be any unconsumed surplus, because there won't be any profits.'

'But suppose the trusts win in this battle over the ownership of the machines and the world?' Mr Kowalt asked.

'Then,' Ernest answered, 'you, and labour, and all of us, will be crushed under the iron heel of a despotism as relentless and terrible as any despotism that has blackened the pages of the history of man. That will be a good name for that despotism, the Iron Heel.' (9:97-8)

The annotation from the twenty-sixth-century narrator assures us that the collapse of capitalism and the triumph of labour did indeed ultimately occur. The process was inevitable. Orwell is quite wrong when he claims that:

> the book is chiefly notable for maintaining that capitalist society would not perish of its 'contradictions', but that the possessing class would be able to form itself into a vast corporation and even evolve a sort of perverted Socialism, sacrificing many of its privileges in order to preserve its superior status. (CE, IV:7:42)

London's whole point is that capitalism *will* perish of its contradictions; but it will survive for a long, long time, before the collapse occurs. And his other point is that the period of corporate-capitalist oligarchy will be a period of hideous repression — except for those who join or do deals with the oligarchy. In no way does London see that as even a *perverted* Socialism; it is the period of the Iron Heel. And it is this interim period that London is basically concerned with. This is the substance of his novel. His concern is with exploring the techniques of the Iron Heel, the trusts, the plutocracy, the super-capitalists, in their attempts to retain power; which for three centuries they successfully do.

Like Morris's *News from Nowhere*, the emphasis of the manuscript is on socialism in one country, on trying to turn one capitalist society into a socialist society, not on world revolution. But London provides a wider perspective on the revolution than Morris offered in *News from Nowhere*. The annotator's comments fill in the detail. The way in which the USA-based super-capitalists, the multi-nationals, destroy socialism throughout not only the USA but the rest of the world, is eerily predictive.

> The Second Revolt was truly international. It was a colossal plan
> — too colossal to be wrought by the genius of one man alone.
> Labour, in all the oligarchies of the world, was prepared to rise at
> the signal. Germany, Italy, France and all Australasia were labour
> countries — socialist states. They were ready to lend aid to the
> revolution. Gallantly they did; and it was for this reason, when
> the Second Revolt was crushed, that they, too, were crushed by
> the united oligarchies of the world, their socialist governments
> being replaced by oligarchical governments. (1, n.4:6)

London has a model for the future global changes. However, it is only sketched in. His main concern is with repression in the USA.

The world of the Iron Heel is a world of brutal repression, political murders, imprisonment, hired mercenaries, private armies for intimidation, destruction of property and life, public executions, agents provocateurs, spies, counter-spies. The repression is direct and explicit. Elected politicians are removed from office and gaoled if their views are counter to the plutocracy's. Resistant areas of the country are starved. But as well as all these direct, explicit, brutal expressions of repressive power, the oligarchy is flexible enough to try more subtle approaches.

It does a deal with the unions and selectively buys off crucial sections. This fragments the labour movement by introducing castes and separatist hostilities. It is in the short-term interests of the selected labour unions who are getting special treatment to identify with the plutocracy; that way their privileges are preserved. 'Wages are going to be advanced and hours shortened in the railroad unions, the iron and steel workers' unions, and the engineer and machinist unions. In these unions more favourable conditions will continue to prevail' (14:140). By buying off these crucial unions who 'do all of the vitally essential work in our machine civilisation' (14:140) 'the Iron Heel can snap its fingers at all the rest of labour.' The rest of labour is further and further oppressed, and plunged into slave conditions. The privileged crucial unions become a privileged caste who, for their own safety, soon begin to live in protected compounds, educating their children at schools which only the children of families in these unions attend.

With the crucial unions bought off, production is guaranteed for the trusts. With the labour movement divided, the trusts have destroyed their opposition. And this is all done without giving away too much of the surplus, without redistributing and sharing equally the wealth made by labour in this capitalist situation. The surplus is now consumed in splendid works of art, huge cities built by a proletariat living in slave or serf conditions. Everhard predicts the future scenario:

> These things the oligarchs will do because they cannot help doing them. These great works will be the form their expenditure of the surplus will take, and in the same way that the ruling classes of Egypt of long ago expended the surplus they robbed from the people by the building of temples and pyramids. Under the oligarchs will flourish, not a priest class, but an artist class. And in place of the merchant class of bourgeoisie will be the labour castes. And beneath will be the abyss, wherein will fester and starve and rot, and ever renew itself, the common people, the great bulk of the population. And in the end, who knows in what day, the common people will rise out of the abyss; the labour castes and the Oligarchy will crumble away; and then, at last, after the travail of the centuries, will it be the day of the common man. I had thought to see that day; but now I know that I shall never see it. (14:143)

But in the end the Brotherhood of Man will triumph. A confidence in the inevitable emergence of socialism was one of the basic tenets of London's beliefs. And this historical inevitability is another of the basic marxist doctrines that London expounds in *The Iron Heel*. 'You cannot escape us', Ernest tells the Philomath club:

> Just as your class dragged down the old feudal nobility, so shall it be dragged down by my class, the working class. If you will read your biology and your sociology as clearly as you do your history, you will see that this end I have described is inevitable. It does not matter whether it is in one year, ten, or a thousand — your class shall be dragged down. (5:64)

With his amalgam of Marx and Darwin, London expounds the 'social evolution' of humanity from 'mire and slime' via capitalism to socialism, stressing the slowness of the process as much as the inevitability. Avis's manuscript opens hailing the new dawn of 'an international revolution wide as the world is wide' (1:6). But the annotator indicates how she was mistaken, and the revolution at that stage was repressed. Nevertheless, in the end, socialism will be achieved.

The role of ideology in capitalist society is another important theme in *The Iron Heel*, and one on which London is particularly insightful. Comparing *The Iron Heel* with Huxley's *Brave New World*, Orwell attacked the latter on grounds that

> no society of that kind would last more than a couple of
> generations, because a ruling class which thought principally
> in terms of a 'good time' would soon lose its vitality. A ruling
> class has got to have a strict morality, a quasi-religious belief
> in itself, a mystique. London was aware of this, and though he
> describes the caste of plutocrats who rule the world for seven
> [*sic*] centuries as inhuman monsters, he does not describe them
> as idlers or sensualists. They can only maintain their position
> while they honestly believe that civilization depends on
> themselves alone, and therefore in a different way they are just
> as brave, able and devoted as the revolutionists who oppose
> them. (CE, II:11:46)

Orwell's English public school-colonial police worries about 'idlers' and sensualists and good times have somewhat distorted his reading here. He correctly points to London's presentation of the Iron Heel's ethical code. But London is concerned to expose that code for the ideology that it is — the way it presents to the ruling class the rationale for its activities in ethical terms, and diverts attention from the realities of that class's position. London correctly saw that 'high ethical righteousness' as the ruling class's strength: they persuaded themselves of it, they persuaded their exploited of it. It was an ideological position necessary to maintain their control, though the material realities of the Iron Heel's maintenance of power always did and always will reside in their economic domination, and in their determination to preserve power and privilege for themselves.

London was not impressed by the 'high ethical righteousness' — unlike Orwell, who found this aspect the strength of the book. Orwell continued:

> In an intellectual way London accepted the conclusions of
> Marxism, and he imagined that the 'contradictions' of capitalism,
> the unconsumable surplus and so forth, would persist even after
> the capitalist class had organized themselves into a single

corporate body. But temperamentally he was very different from the majority of Marxists. With his love of violence and physical strength, his belief in 'natural aristocracy', his animal-worship and exaltation of the primitive, he had in him what one might fairly call a Fascist strain. This probably helped him to understand just how the possessing class would behave when once they were seriously menaced. (CE, II:11:47)

But in describing the Iron Heel oligarchy, it is Orwell who refers to them as 'brave, able and devoted', it is Orwell who rejects 'idlers and sensualists' — the fascination with fascism is all in Orwell at this point, not London. It is Orwell who is looking for the admirable in the oligarchs — and who then detects a fascist strain in London. And this is more than a classic example of projection. It moves beyond Orwell's personal problems and the complexities of his psyche, into a public, political discrediting of London's marxist vision by these charges of fascism. Robert Barltrop's account of *The Iron Heel* is similarly distorted in this way — and Barltrop like so many commentators draws on Orwell for his approach to the book. And no matter how Barltrop and others disagree in detail with Orwell, they go along all the way with Orwell's glib characterization of 'what one might fairly call a Fascist strain' in London. Raymond Williams has drawn attention in *Culture and Society* to the political implications and class bias in Orwell's use of the word 'little' as a pejorative tic (279). His use of the word 'fairly' merits similar investigation.

London's naked statement of the true base of the 'high ethical righteousness' of the Iron Heel oligarchy comes very early in the novel, when Everhard predicts a socialist future. Mr Wickson, a minor plutocrat, is provoked to reveal the true values of the plutocracy:

This, then, is our answer. We have no words to waste on you. When you reach out your vaunted strong hands for our palaces and purpled ease, we will show you what strength is. In roar of shell and shrapnel and in whine of machine-guns will our answer be couched. We will grind you revolutionists down under our heel, and we shall walk upon your faces. The world is ours, we are its lords, and ours it shall remain. As for the host of labour, it has been in the dirt since history began, and I read history aright. And in the dirt it shall remain so long as I and mine and those that come after us have the power. There is the word. It is the king of words — Power. Not God, not Mammon, but Power. Pour it over your tongue till it tingles with it. Power. (5:63)

It is with this angry revelation in mind that the account of the ethical beliefs of the plutocracy is to be read; in this way the nature of ideology is revealed. Avis tells us how the plutocracy

> as a class, believed that they alone maintained civilisation. It was their belief that if ever they weakened, the great beast would engulf them and everything of beauty and wonder and joy and good in its cavernous and slime-dripping maw. (21:190)

'I cannot lay too great stress upon this high ethical righteousness of the whole oligarch class', she continues.

> Prisons, banishment and degradation, honours and palaces and wonder-cities, are all incidental. The great driving force of the oligarchs is the belief that they are doing right. Never mind the exceptions, and never mind the oppression and injustice in which the Iron Heel was conceived. All is granted. The point is that the strength of the Oligarchy today lies in its satisfied conception of its own Righteousness.
>   For that matter, the strength of the Revolution, during these frightful twenty years, has resided in nothing else than the sense of righteousness. (21:191)

Both the Iron Heel and the revolutionaries can survive only as long as they believe in the right of their own position. London's point is important, not only as political insight but as propaganda; he is urging his readers not to underestimate the strength of the oppressors, not to think they are simply corrupt, pleasure seeking, selfish. They are all that; but the strength of their position lies in their religious commitment to their ideology. Without that commitment, the whole apparatus of power and repression would be ineffective. But that it is an ideology, that the true rationale for the Iron Heel is the preservation of power and privileges, we know from Wickson's outburst. That is the basis of the high ethical superstructure the Iron Heel presents.

London extends his explorations of ideology into examining the way the proletariat are ideologically manipulated by language and literature. In his address to the Philomaths, Ernest discusses the *Seaside Library* novels that he used to read as a child:

> in which, with the exception of the villains and adventuresses, all men and women thought beautiful thoughts, spoke a beautiful tongue, and performed glorious deeds. In short, as I

accepted the rising of the sun, I accepted that up above me was
all that was fine and noble and gracious, all that gave decency
and dignity to life, all that made life worth living and that
remunerated one for his travail and misery. (5:52)

The annotator comments on the *Seaside Library*: 'A curious and
amazing literature that served to make the working class utterly
misapprehend the nature of the leisure class' (5, n.3:52). Allied with
this deliberate production of disinformation, there is the suppression of realities — something Avis discovers when she tries to get the
press to tell the true story of Jackson's Arm. There is no way the
truth can be published.

> We're all solid with the corporations . . . . If you paid advertising
> rates, you couldn't get any such matter into the paper. A man
> who tried to smuggle it in would lose his job. You couldn't get
> it in if you paid ten times the regular advertising rates. (4:44)

There is a comparable conspiracy of suppression over Professor
Cunningham's book.

In manipulation by language, London has insights into an area in
which Swift and Orwell are usually thought to be pre-eminent. His
observations are not as extensive as theirs, but the footnote that the
annotator gives to the word *utopian* encapsulates a wealth of social
observation:

> The people of that age were phrase slaves. The abjectness of their
> servitude is incomprehensible to us. There was a magic in words
> greater than the conjurer's art. So befuddled and chaotic were
> their minds that the utterance of a single word could negative
> the generalisations of a lifetime of serious research and thought.
> Such a word was the adjective *Utopian*. The mere utterance
> of it could damn any scheme, no matter how sanely conceived,
> of economic amelioration or regeneration. Vast populations
> grew frenzied over such phrases as 'an honest dollar', and 'a full
> dinner pail.' The coinage of such phrases was considered strokes
> of genius. (5, n.4:53)

The marxist theories of surplus value, historical inevitability and
of ideology are the materials of *The Iron Heel*. But in themselves
they are not necessarily dramatic. They are theories that can inform
London's social thinking, but they are not necessarily expressed by
action. And one of the problems for the political novelist is finding a

central theoretical issue that is innately dramatic, so that the action of the novel expresses that issue. Ideally there will be a unity between the political theories and the rationales of action. To create an action for the novel that revolves primarily around some non-political events, activities, dramas, leaving the political theories as simply so much filling for the dialogue, is to fail to deal satisfactorily with the particular problems of the political novel. And it is from these sorts of failures that the critical hostility towards long political discussions in fiction in part arises. Long political, theoretical discussions inevitably seem excrescent, intrusive and inept when the action of the novel is not integrated with or meaningfully related to those political issues.

London, however, does integrate theory and action. The long discussions and debates are effective since the issues they raise are the issues that give the dynamic to the novel's action. The dynamic of the novel is the theory of the class struggle. 'The history of all hitherto existing society is the history of class struggles', the *Manifesto of the Communist Party* declares (40). That it is a scientific concept of the same order as surplus value or historical inevitability or ideology, Ernest makes quite clear:

> We say that the class struggle is a law of social development. We are not responsible for it. We do not make the class struggle. We merely explain it, as Newton explained gravitation. We explain the nature of the conflict of interest that produces the class struggle. (2:21-2)

And we see the struggle in its various phases. We see the initial encounter of bourgeois and proletarian positions between Ernest and Avis, her father and the clergy. Ernest ultimately wins this struggle, converting Avis, her father and Bishop Morehouse from their bourgeois ideology to socialism. We see the class struggle in the story of Jackson's arm — how Jackson is defeated by his capitalist employers and their lackeys (foreman, lawyer, etc.) in his attempt to get compensation for an industrial accident. We see the struggle in the details of the repression of labour by the plutocracy; we see it take a different form in the plutocracy's buying off selected crucial unions; we see it in the culminating episode of the Chicago Commune, where the plutocracy selectively picks off one whole section of the proletariat, foments an insurrection through agents provocateurs, and then engages in genocidal mass slaughter.

The struggle is not only between capital and labour; that is its ultimate form, but its earlier variants include the elimination by the plutocracy of its closest rivals, the small capitalists and farmers, before beginning its major confrontation with labour.

And London stresses the bitterness of the class struggle. Capitalism will never simply surrender to the forces of labour. Ernest's arguments are described in images of fighting, aggression, struggle — because the struggle will be an aggressive, violent combat, not a peaceable transfer of power, not a polite reformist process. The theory of the class struggle is a theory that, though it can be expressed in intellectual, theoretical terms, can only issue and be resolved in violent action. And London presents both theory and inevitable expression in cataclysmic action.

In the course of examining the individual components of London's political vision — romance, theory, analysis, action — various problems of form in political fictions have been raised. It is a mark of the greatness of *The Iron Heel* that discussion of its political materials inevitably leads to discussion of its form. London succeeded in integrating his political vision with an appropriate form. The subtleties and the experimentalism of London's fictional method need to be stressed, however, since they have been missed even by his sympathetic critics. Leftist critics have not been generally receptive or responsive to formal innovation; even when they expound the dialectic of history with its constant change and progress, they have wanted to freeze the dialectic of art back in some safe nineteenth-century position — as if art could be separated from the historical circumstances of its creation. Joan London quotes Trotsky who, though he admired *The Iron Heel*, felt its strength arose despite its literary form, 'its artistic qualities': He wrote in 1937:

> The book produced upon me — I speak without exaggeration —
> a deep impression. Not because of its artistic qualities; the form
> of the novel here represents only an armour for social analysis
> and prognosis. The author is intentionally sparing in his use of
> artistic means. He is himself interested not so much in the
> individual fate of his heroes as in the fate of mankind. By this,
> however, I don't want at all to belittle the artistic value of the
> work, especially in its last chapters beginning with the Chicago
> commune. The pictures of civil war develop in powerful frescoes.
> Nevertheless, this is not the main feature. The book surprised me
> with the audacity and independence of its historical foresight.
> (313)

Orwell is even more explicitly dismissive about its formal qualities; he calls it 'a crude book' (CE, II:25:172), 'hugely inferior' to H.G.

Wells's *The Sleeper Awakes*, and 'clumsily written' (CE, II:11:46). And these extraordinarily perverse judgments of the work have been perpetuated in Alan Swingewood's *The Novel and Revolution*: he repeats Orwell's formulations, describing it as 'a crudely written, badly constructed novel seriously lacking in genuine characters' (145). And he concludes that

> although London's grasp of the structural basis of social conflict and change was sociologically superior to contemporary utopian and anti-utopian novelists, he was unable to create a genuine novel. *The Iron Heel* is of interest solely for its sociology, not for its characters or its insights into the human condition. (149)

We can see where this is all at, with the worries about 'the genuine novel' ('is this a genuine novel or did you make it up yourself?'), 'genuine characters', and the 'clumsily written'. The experimental, innovative nature of *The Iron Heel* has been largely misunderstood.

London's formal innovations express the traditional opposition in political fiction of romantic individualism and realistic documentation. At the beginning of her manuscript Avis looks forward to the impending Second Revolt of the socialists planned by her husband. It is the splendid note of romance — committed, enthusiastic, unqualified by doubt:

> I cannot sit idly by and wait the great event that is his making, though he is not here to see. He devoted all the years of his manhood to it, and for it he gave his life. It is his handiwork.

> When the word goes forth, the labour hosts of all the world shall rise. There has been nothing like it in the history of the world. The solidarity of labour is assured, and for the first time will there be an international revolution wide as the world is wide. (1:5-6)

An appended footnote situates this romantic assertion with some objective, realistic qualification:

> With all respect to Avis Everhard, it must be pointed out that Everhard was but one of many able leaders who planned the Second Revolt. And we, today, looking back across the centuries, can safely say that even had he lived, the Second Revolt would not have been less calamitous in its outcome than it was. (1, n.2:6)

Avis celebrates Ernest's glorious individual force and commemorates the life he sacrificed for the cause. The annotator points out that the revolution was guided by other leaders, too — it was not a single individual's plan but a communal effort; and that in the short term it was a failure. Yet in the long term, Everhard and his comrades were working towards the finally established Brotherhood of Man. The manuscript celebrates the romantic revolutionary; the notes objectively qualify the individualism, and yet do not undercut it; they show how the individualism was part of a group movement, how the particular historical battles that mean so much to the participants are, from the perspective of seven centuries ahead, seen in perspective: just part of an on-going historical progress. Yet this placing never dismisses the value of the individual in the way the individual is seen as worthless by the societies portrayed in *We*, *Darkness at Noon* or *Nineteen Eighty-four*.

The unique tone of *The Iron Heel* is achieved by this union of romantic narrative and objective footnote. The two values — opposed and alternating in *Beauchamp's Career* and *Kangaroo* — are here presented as near to simultaneity as a literary work can achieve. Both aspects simultaneously on the page.

The romantic nature of Avis's narrative has already been looked at in its various manifestations. The footnotes are an equally important strand in the novel — though to see them as '*the* central device' of the novel as Maxwell Geismar does is to ignore the equally important device of the romantic narrative.

The footnotes fill a multiplicity of roles — visual, typographical, formal, aesthetic, documentary, informational. The very idea of the footnote suggests a stress on fact, an objective qualification and supplementation. Avis recalls Ernest 'flaying them with his facts, each fact a lash that stung' (1:16). 'Facts' are important to London, they are the bricks of his materialism. He has the annotator actually correct an inaccuracy in the manuscript narrative. Avis reports Ernest as saying that the militia legislation was introduced into the USA House of Representatives on 30 July 1902. A footnote remarks: 'Everhard was right in the essential particulars, though his date of the introduction of the bill is in error. The bill was introduced on June 30, and not on July 30' (8, n.5:90). It is a trivial, unimportant correction in terms of content. But it is important for London's purposes; not so much to show the fallibility of Ernest, whose supersocialist qualities are eulogized in his wife's memoir; but to create an impression of utter objective accuracy; even with so trivial a point the annotator makes sure the facts are given correctly. So our faith in the objective accuracy of the annotation —

and of Avis's manuscript narrative everywhere else that it isn't corrected — is given this justification, this strengthening.

Scholarly accuracy is the other impression created. The annotation gives us the statistics, supporting quotations, analogies. This is appropriate since Ernest when we first meet him 'was earning a meagre living by translating scientific and philosophical works for a struggling socialist publishing house' (2:19), and Avis's father is a professor at Berkeley. The annotations support this scholarly, scientific ambience. Objective statistical evidence is provided by the footnotes; that is what they are there for and aesthetically, that is the tone they are there to suggest.

Though the notes are not merely objective. They are often powerfully emotional and evaluative: 'There is no more horrible page in history than the treatment of the child and women slaves in the English factories' (2, n.7:25). Although there is a basic formal structure of romantic narrative and objective statistical notes, and of coherent romantic narrative and fragmented annotation of past and future detail, narrative and notes do not remain schematically circumscribed to these specific areas. Ernest, after all, cites much objective factual material in his arguments reported in the narrative. The story of Jackson's arm is an actual, contemporary case — it might have been cited in a note, but London uses it as part of his narrative. The notes themselves contain other narratives.

The class struggle provides the dynamic for the action of the manuscript narrative. But the action of *The Iron Heel* does not only consist of dramatic action. Too readily it is assumed that dramatic, sustained narrative action is the only possibility for fiction. But fiction has forms of action that are not available to the drama; it has a much wider scope — which London here exploits. In the footnotes, we find summarized fictions, in which a whole field of action is touched on but not dramatized. We are given concise, pregnant episodes in a few lines.

> Despite continual and almost inconceivable hazards, Anna Roylston lived to the royal age of ninety-one. As the Pococks defied the executioners of the Fighting Groups, so she defied the executioners of the Iron Heel. She bore a charmed life, and prospered amid dangers and alarms. She herself was an executioner for the Fighting Groups, and, known as the Red Virgin, she became one of the inspired figures of the Revolution. When she was an old woman of sixty-nine she shot 'Bloody' Halcliffe down in the midst of his armed escort and got away unscathed. In the end she died peaceably of old age in a secret

refuge of the revolutionists in the Ozark mountains.
(18, n.3:167-8)

Here are the materials of another novel, summarized, encapsulated, realized, evoked in concise detail in a footnote. Compressed fiction. Matchbox novels. Similarly those brief footnotes on the building of Asgard and Ardis create the scope of a novel in their future projections.

The action of *The Iron Heel*, then, is created not only by dramatic event (bomb-throwing in congress; Chicago street-fighting) but through annotation — vignettes, summaries, indications of action. This conceptual fiction is even more apparent in the speculative future predictions. Here the focus is on the model, on the generative idea. The whole scenario of the developing crisis of the unconsumable surplus under capitalism that results in the artistic programme of building super-cities and the plutocracy's subsidization of artists, is not dramatized but presented in answer to a question from Avis. Ernest replies with a prophetic vision that sees the whole process, and its ultimate collapse from its own contradictions.

The avant-garde nature of these novels-in-brief was recognized later in the century in the work of Jorge Luis Borges. In the Prologue to *Fictions* Borges explained his procedure:

The composition of vast books is a laborious and impoverishing extravagance. To go on for five hundred pages developing an idea whose perfect oral exposition is possible in a few minutes! A better course of procedure is to pretend that these books already exist, and then to offer a résumé, a commentary. Thus proceeded Carlyle in *Sartor Resartus*. Thus Butler in *The Fair Haven*. These are works which suffer the imperfection of being themselves books, and of being no less tautological than the others. More reasonable, more inept, more indolent, I have preferred to write notes upon imaginary books. (13)

London's invented books (like Ernest Everhard's *Working Class Philosophy*), his summarized narratives, and his footnotes properly belong in this context of literary experimentation, of formal innovation and avant-gardeism.

Ultimately the fragmentary form of annotation increasingly becomes the appropriate mode for the social realities being narrated. The Second Revolution that Avis looks forward to, we learn of only through the notes. Her manuscript takes us up to the failure of the First Revolution, the bloodbath of the suppression of the Chicago

Commune. Then the narrative abruptly ends. The romantic action is abruptly terminated. Reality cuts across romantic hopes.

Yet because of the future perspective afforded us by the footnotes, we know that ultimately the romantic dream will come true, even if the immediate current action will not lead to it. And formally, the sudden curtailment of the manuscript, leaving its loose ends and unsolved mysteries (like the arrest of Ernest that led to his execution) appropriately enacts the conditions in that society. The narrative details have been becoming increasingly fragmented, as the ordered pattern of life in the academic community of Berkeley, where Avis begins her story, has been shattered, and she moves to the slums, and ultimately to the hide-out in the hills. Material crowds in and she finds it increasingly difficult to keep all the threads running separately and simultaneously. She follows through particular sequences of idea or action that result in the disruption of simple chronology; they involve her in having to go back to pick up earlier threads; and as the Iron Heel plutocracy becomes more repressive and freedom of movement is curtailed, passes have to be carried, communications become increasingly difficult, the narrative becomes more fragmentary. Characters who appeared earlier in the less nightmarish parts of the novel are often glimpsed again — but only glimpsed; that is the only contact now. People disappear; and the sudden curtailment of the manuscript in mid-sentence as Avis's hiding place is discovered (so the annotator speculates) results in the disappearance of all our characters. Earlier the narrator had commented on the way people continually disappeared in the society of the Iron Heel:

> Disappearance was one of the horrors of the time. As a *motif*, in song and story, it constantly crops up. It was an inevitable concomitant of the subterranean warfare that raged through those three centuries. This phenomenon was almost as common in the oligarch class and the labour castes as it was in the ranks of the revolutionists. Without warning, without trace, men and women, and even children, disappeared and were seen no more, their ends shrouded in mystery. (19, n.2:175)

Orwell remarks:

> An underground struggle against dictatorship was the kind of thing that London could imagine, and he foresaw certain of the details with surprising accuracy; he foresaw, for instance, that

peculiar horror of totaliarian society, the way in which
suspected enemies of the régime *simply disappear*. (CE, IV:7:42)

It is a chilling feature of the society, and London makes full fictional
use of the chill it creates. Having drawn attention to it in his note, he
then functionally uses disappearance in his narrative — and for the
climax of his narrative, when everyone disappears as the manuscript
breaks off.

He was not a naive but a very self-aware, conscious, innovative
artist. And he had too the intuitive novelistic sense of having a
sudden break at this point. He wrote to his editor at Macmillans,
George P. Brett: 'I originally told you that *The Iron Heel* would be
100,000 words long. You will find that it is only 90,000 words long.
I didn't dare an anticlimax after The Chicago Commune. So I cut it
short right there' (15 December 1906) (*Letters from Jack London*,
p.235). Against the flowing movements of nineteenth-century
romance, London juxtaposes the fragmentary forms of a new
twentieth-century aesthetic, the collapsing, crumbling narrative,
the separated detail of footnoting.

As for setting the climax of the novel in Chicago, London had
good historical reasons. On 3 May 1886 police had fired on a peaceful demonstration of strikers in Chicago, killing six and wounding
several more. A protest meeting the following day was again attacked
by police, a bomb was thrown, and a policeman was killed while
several others were wounded. Several leading anarchists were arrested,
though no serious attempt was made to implicate them in the
bomb-throwing, and five were condemned to death. Later that same
year similar violence erupted in London when police and soldiers
attacked a peaceful demonstration in Trafalgar Square and killed
three demonstrators and wounded 200 more. That was Bloody
Sunday, 13 November 1886. On the day before, *The Times* had
praised the judicial murder of the Chicago anarchists. The following
week another English radical was run down and killed by police.

Lindsay has related the impact of these incidents on Morris's
News from Nowhere in *William Morris: His Life and Work* (324-5).
Jack London naturally situates his climax in Chicago in commemora-
tion of the earlier massacre. And as with so many aspects of London's
projections, Chicago fulfilled his predictions in being the site of the
major confrontation of the police-military-establishment power and
the anti-war, radical and alternative groups on 26-9 August 1968.
That particular violence is recorded in Norman Mailer's *Miami and
the Siege of Chicago* (1968) and in Ed Sanders's novel, *Shards of
God* (1970).

The conscious and deliberate complementing of popular romance narrative with the documentary tone of the footnotes and the theoretical discussions within the body of the novel, the juxtaposition of narrative flow with fragmentation, produce the unique tone of *The Iron Heel*. London is writing about revolution, and produces a revolutionary experiment in form. In comparison Orwell's form in *Nineteen Eighty-four* is ultimately unimaginative — revealingly appropriate for the conservative message. Orwell has his notes, his appendix and his documentary intrusions from Goldstein's book — but these are only a small part of his novel; essentially it is a simple conventional narrative.

London didn't have many resources of modernism at hand — he doesn't use them, anyway. The experimentalism of *The Iron Heel* consequently can seem somewhat inert in comparison with the modernism of Zamyatin's mode in *We*. London's experimentation is closer to Lawrence's in *Kangaroo*: the attempt to create a new totality out of the components that bourgeois culture has separated — romance, realism, documentation, theorizing. To try to reintegrate these separated aspects, to try to evolve a new formal solution for their expression, was something preoccupying both London and Lawrence. Fragmentation was the solution which both adopted. Neither could see a coherent, well-rounded traditionally realized whole as being a feasible possibility. Both chose fragmentation as the way of getting specific attention directed to each of the component aspects of the novel. So that finally *The Iron Heel* and *Kangaroo* are gesturing towards a totality that neither achieves.

The tragic is an important, major component. In one context the death of Everhard and the failure of the Second Revolution is the material of tragedy. And a lot of the novel's force comes from this inclusion of the tragic — something continually problematic for socialist art. London recognizes the problem — so includes and then subsumes the tragic into an overall optimistic, positive framework. But he does this not by reducing the tragic; in no way does he undercut it. The individual tragedy of Everhard and the revolution is clear enough; but the wider time-span places the tragic into a finally positive scheme. In this same context, the positive hero so beloved of socialist criticism is presented by London in a novelistically satisfying way. The positive aspects of Everhard are dominant, and would satisfy any socialist realist; but the problems associated with the positive hero, the tiresomeness that seems a recurrent concomitant, are here mitigated and qualified by London's broader dimension — putting the positive hero in a tragic situation, placing the positiveness in an historical period that is unreceptive and inappropriate to such positiveness. Hence the simplicities that the positive hero so readily embodies are given the qualification and complication of being placed in a resistant historical period. London is able to fuse together the positive socialist hero, the hero out of key with his time from bourgeois tragedy, the tragic destruction of the individual by capitalist bourgeois society, and the optimistic resolution of the socialist novel in a society of peace and egalitarianism. The dual time perspective and the differing modes of narration combine for the unique novelistic vision.

And the final distinction of *The Iron Heel* is this positive note that subsumes the tragic. It is not a naive positiveness. The details of the three centuries of repression are spelled out fully enough. But what the novel so persuasively asserts, is that ultimately the Brotherhood of Man will triumph; that the period of repression is inevitably doomed. The force of will of the plutocracy may be able to extend it — even as long as three centuries. But in the end socialism will eventually emerge.

4

The Rainbow:
'smashing the great machine'

The accepted leftist judgment of D.H. Lawrence as a novelist is one that was formulated some forty years ago by Christopher Caudwell. It is expressed in his essay 'D.H. Lawrence: a study of the bourgeois artist', collected in his posthumous *Studies in a Dying Culture*:

> It is Lawrence's importance as an artist that he was well aware of the fact that the pure artist cannot exist to-day, and that the artist must inevitably be a man hating cash-relationships and the market, and profoundly interested in the relations between persons. Moreover, he must be a man not merely profoundly interested in the relations between persons as they are, but interested in changing them, dissatisfied with them as they are, and wanting newer and fuller value in personal relationships.
>
> But it is Lawrence's final tragedy that his solution was ultimately Fascist and not Communist. It was regressive. Lawrence wanted us to return to the past, to the 'Mother'. He sees human discontent as the yearning of the solar plexus for the umbilical connexion, and he demands the substitution for sharp sexual love of the unconscious fleshy identification of foetus with mother. All this was symbolic of regression, of neurosis, of the return to the primitive. (56-7)

But because Lawrence did not offer a conventional radical critique of society, it does not follow that he was a fascist. And because he is sceptical of a dependence on pure rational intellect, it does not follow that he advocated regressive modes of consciousness or social organization, or a return to the primitive. Yet this is the simplified and distorted view of his thinking that has passed into common

127

acceptance. Thirty years after Caudwell, Laurenson and Swingewood tell us in *The Sociology of Literature* that Lawrence's

> novels are rarely political or even social in the sense that milieu is concretely realized, and in his important works, *Sons and Lovers*, *The Rainbow*, *Women in Love*, he writes almost to the exclusion of extrapersonalized themes. (83)

> Lawrence is a reactionary thinker; he has a distinct ideology which results in depicting love relations, that is, social relationships in non-social terms. There is no totality in his novels: the foreground is wholly taken up with the basic problem of the blood and sexual polarity; human relationships develop within this field . . . . (86)

But Lawrence's work is much more radical than his leftist commentators have been able to comprehend. *The Rainbow* (1915) offers an acute analysis of the failures of capitalist industrial society and of the conventional ways of criticizing that society. And it contains the first sketches of the political approach he was to evolve more fully in his later work.

In *The Politics of Twentieth-Century Novelists* V. de Sola Pinto expresses the simplistic view of *The Rainbow*:

> In *The Rainbow*, working on an epic scale, Lawrence shows the traditional culture in the farming Brangwens, based on the rhythm of the seasons and the old hierarchy of the English village, disintegrating in the later generations under influence of the modern industrialism which produces such horrors as the mining village of Wiggiston. (35)

But the novel is much more complex than that. We can see the destructive nature of industrialism symbolically expressed in the drowning of Tom Brangwen by the bursting of the canal-bank, as Arnold Kettle and Jack Lindsay both do. But if we do that then we should see the death of Tom's father by falling off a hay-rick as symbolically expressing the destructive nature of the old rural life. F.R. Leavis has claimed in *D.H. Lawrence: Novelist* that: 'The book might have been written to show what, in the concrete, a living tradition is, and what it is to be brought up in the environment of one' (108). And Raymond Williams writes in *The English Novel* that the form of *The Rainbow* 'is the experience of community . . . and then of its breakdown'; the novel shows how 'a social system, industrialism, has destroyed given reality by forcing people into systematic roles' (144).

The 'living tradition', however, the 'experience of community', Lawrence shows to have always been something ambiguous. The strength of the rural tradition which the Brangwens thrived on was the existence of neighbouring industrial markets for their farm produce. 'The Brangwens received a fair sum of money' from having the canal built across their land; and later when the colliery and the railway were opened, 'the town grew rapidly, the Brangwens were kept busy producing supplies, they became richer, they were almost tradesmen' (1:12). The 'organic community', the comfortable rural life are dependent on the industrial towns since the towns supply their prosperity.

Lawrence does not present a simple confrontation of country versus city, there is not a simple degeneration from country to city. The developing prosperity of the country life of the Brangwens is shown to require a developing industrial society to which to sell. The country and the city are interdependent; and the country has its destructive and deadening qualities as strikingly as does the city. This is stressed from the very beginning:

> But the woman wanted another form of life than this, something
> that was not blood-intimacy. Her house faced out from the farm
> — buildings and fields, looked out to the road and the village with
> church and Hall and the world beyond. She stood to see the
> far-off world of cities and governments and active scope of man,
> the magic land to her, whose secrets were made known and
> desires fulfilled. She faced outwards to where men moved
> dominant and creative, having turned their back on the pulsing
> heat of creation . . . . (1:9)

The novel follows this course of the woman, moving away from the limitations of the country, dissatisfied with the Brangwen men's dependency on 'the teeming life of creation', seeking that wider world in which men had set out 'to enlarge their own scope and range and freedom' (1:9). And whatever deadening and disintegrating qualities industrialism is shown to possess later in the novel, they are possessed simultaneously with other qualities which the country cannot offer — a wider scope, range and freedom, a political world of complex social organization and interaction — cities and governments. It is important to stress that the worlds of Tom and Lydia and of Will and Anna are extremely circumscribed, limited worlds. The usual version of the myth of the ideal organic country life was that though it might be limited, it contained all that man required. In *Middlemarch* various moral dilemmas occur yet they are never resolved in any positive *urban* way; although George Eliot is writing about the urban society of the 1830s — and writing, more-over, from the perspective of the 1870s — she doesn't see that urban life offers any solutions, any real possibilities for human fulfilment. Fred Vincy reforms his ways and begins farming — the return to the land marking his moral and psychological improvement; whereas Lydgate's degeneration is indicated by his becoming a fashionable London doctor. It wasn't possible when George Eliot wrote *Middlemarch* (1871-2), for everyone to take up the rural life again; yet in literature, the rural life continued to be represented as the moral ideal. Lawrence, however, is sceptical of the values of the rural life; and however hideous he finds modern urban life, it is only through this wider, urban, political world of cities and governments and active scope of man that the possibility of a better life is to be reached; and if that means blowing up the cities, fine; but that is not an idea that could ever be thought out and carried through from the country, without ever having the experience of urban life.

Ursula escapes from the unrewarding life of her parents. Whatever tranquillity Will, her father, achieved, 'he was aware of some limit of himself . . . He was unready for fulfilment. Something undeveloped in him limited him, there was a darkness in him which he *could* not unfold, which would never unfold in him' (7:210). Ursula, unwilling to accept these limitations, escapes to the city. She doesn't escape in one single movement; it isn't as easy as that to get away. She has to make a series of different attempts. And with each encounter with this wider world, we are presented with a further analysis of indus-trial capitalist society. But Lawrence is not presenting a case for a withdrawal back to the country: a retreat is historically impossible, and would be a retreat merely to other limitations; rather, he drama-tizes through Ursula the search for a breakthrough into something else, some other form of social possibility.

Ursula's first encounter with the industrial world is her visit to Wiggiston, where her uncle, Tom Brangwen, is a mine manager:

Wiggiston was only seven years old. It had been a hamlet of
eleven houses on the edge of heathy, half-agricultural country.
Then the great seam of coal had been opened. In a year
Wiggiston appeared, a great mass of pinkish rows of thin, unreal
dwellings of five rooms each. The streets were like visions of pure
ugliness; a grey-black macadamized road, asphalt causeways,
held in between a flat succession of wall, window, and door,

a new-brick channel that began nowhere, and ended nowhere.
Everything was amorphous, yet everything repeated itself
endlessly. (12:345)

It is not simply the ugly appearance that Lawrence is attacking. The
ugliness is the product of and the visual symbol of the mechanical,
uncaring industry that has developed here; the utterly utilitarian,
capitalist approach of maximizing profit and providing the minimum
conditions for the workers who are viewed as simply part of the
mechanical process — not as individual humans at all. Lawrence
follows William Morris here; this sort of capitalist industrial society
can only produce ugliness; ugliness is its inevitable and necessary
aesthetic expression. The ugliness of the surroundings contributes to
the emptiness of human existence there, it is one of the causes of
and the expression of that alienation:

> The place had the strange desolation of a ruin. Colliers hanging
> about in gangs and groups, or passing along the asphalt pavements
> heavily to work, seemed not like living people, but like spectres.
> The rigidity of the blank streets, the homogeneous amorphous
> sterility of the whole suggested death rather than life. There was
> no meeting place, no centre, no artery, no organic formation.
> There it lay, like the new foundations of a red-brick confusion
> rapidly spreading, like a skin-disease. (12:345)

The consequence of this mechanical, rigid, inorganic, unnatural way
of human organization that the industry imposes on its employees is
an existence of sterility, of death in life. The passage is remarkably
reminiscent of Conrad's description of the exploited black workers
in *Heart of Darkness* (1902):

> Black shapes crouched, lay, sat between the trees, leaning against
> the trunks, clinging to the earth, half coming out, half effaced
> within the dim light, in all the attitudes of pain, abandonment,
> and despair. Another mine on the cliff went off, followed by a
> slight shudder of the soil under my feet. The work was going on.
> The work! And this was the place where some of the helpers
> had withdrawn to die.
>   They were dying slowly — it was very clear. They were not
> enemies, they were not criminals, they were nothing earthly now
> — nothing but black shadows of disease and starvation, lying
> confusedly in the greenish gloom. (1:17)

But Lawrence's concern is not with the condition of the mine workers in this book. He has just dealt with that in *Sons and Lovers* (1913), the novel that immediately preceded *The Rainbow*. He simply alludes to it here, and refers to Zola's *Germinal* in passing as a reference for those who want to read further in these materials. He presents the condition of the miners clearly enough, but that is not the focus of his attention. Like Conrad, his primary concern is with the managerial class of this system, specifically with Tom Brangwen, the colliery manager.

For Tom himself is part of the machine. Economically well-off, he is still not a free man. He is manager of the colliery, not the capitalist, not the owner drawing off the profits or the rentier living on the dividends. Tom is in the position of Marlow or Mr Kurtz or the Manager in *Heart of Darkness* — one of the technocratic or managerial middle-rank employees of the organization. He is not physically oppressed like the workers; he has sufficient leisure to develop his mental capacity; he is not too exhausted to think. And he does think; he is able and intelligent enough to manage the colliery, so that he is intelligent enough to see what is really happening.

> 'But is this place as awful as it looks?' the young girl asked, a strain in her eyes.
> 'It is just what it looks,' he said. 'It hides nothing.'
> 'Why are the men so sad?'
> 'Are they sad?' he replied.
> 'They seem unutterably, unutterably sad,' said Ursula, out of a passionate throat.
> 'I don't think they are that. They just take it for granted.'
> 'What do they take for granted?'
> 'This — the pits and the place altogether.'
> 'Why don't they alter it?' she passionately protested.
> 'They believe they must alter themselves to fit the pits and the place, rather than alter the pits and the place to fit themselves. It is easier,' he said. (12:347)

It is this destruction of human individuality to fit the industrial system that Lawrence so hates and so powerfully indicts. But his emphasis here is on Tom's acceptance of this as a fit procedure. And Tom, of course, has accepted the dominance of the industry. Though not suffering the same physical dangers or engaged in the same physically hard work as the miners, he is as spiritually destroyed; like them, he accepts the priority of the industrial system. He adjusts himself to conform to the system.

Lawrence's interest is in *how* Tom accepts the system. And he
explores the guise of intellectual realism which Tom adopts. ' "It is
just what it looks", he said. "It hides nothing." ' Tom's implication
is that Ursula wants some romantic further meaning — while he
offers the plain, realistic, rational, sensible, undeluded intelligent
view. 'It is just what it looks.' But this no-nonsense, undeluded view
is of course the huge delusion: the acceptance of the system as some
sort of absolute imperative, the belief that the system — industry or
society — is more important than the individuals involved in it. And
what is worse is that Tom recognizes and admits to the toll the
system takes in human life and human spirit. He knows its destruc-
tiveness, and accepts it. Winifred Inger tries to support him against
Ursula:

> 'I suppose their lives are not really so bad,' said Winifred Inger,
> superior to the Zolaesque tragedy. He turned with his polite,
> distant attention.
> 'Yes, they are pretty bad. The pits are very deep, and hot, and
> in some places wet. The men die of consumption fairly often.
> But they earn good wages.'
> 'How gruesome!' said Winifred Inger.
> 'Yes,' he replied gravely. It was his grave, solid, self-contained
> manner which made him so respected as a colliery manager.
> (12:348)

It is Tom's ready, open acceptance of a system he knows is corrupt,
destructive, alienating, evil, that provokes Ursula's passion. Tom
talks of the sexual behaviour of the mine workers.

> 'They go dragging along what is left from the pits. They're not
> interested enough to be very immoral, it all amounts to the
> same thing, moral or immoral — just a question of pit-wages.
> The most moral duke in England makes two hundred thousand
> a year out of these pits. He keeps the morality end up.' (12:349)

But Lawrence doesn't dwell — as another novelist might have — on
the socio-political issue of the most 'moral' duke making his fortune
from this exploitation. Just as the condition of the miners was dealt
with in *Sons and Lovers*, so the condition of the mineowners and
industrialists is given a novel to itself: *Women in Love*, not published
till 1921, but part of it already written by the time *The Rainbow*
was published. *Sons and Lovers*, *The Rainbow* and *Women in Love*

comprise a trilogy on English industrial capitalism. What concerns Lawrence in the middle volume is the middle classes, the way Tom can accept and tolerate and continue to work in the system which he intellectually knows is corrupt.

The key, as Lawrence presents it, is an opposition between intellect and passion. Unlike the earlier Brangwens immersed in the activities of the farm, this younger Tom has his 'large library, with one end devoted to his science' (12:346). Intelligent, rational, Tom perceives and analyses the evils of the industrial capitalist system of the mine. But in this very analysis he — and Winifred — accept it. 'Ursula sat black-souled and very bitter, hearing the two of them talk. There seemed something ghoulish even in their very deploring the state of things. They seemed to take a ghoulish satisfaction in it' (12:349). Tom and Winifred offer an intellectual critique of the system — but their very intellectuality makes them respond to and depend on the very system they are criticizing. The industrial system is a product of the intellect, of rationality; the structures of industrial technology and capitalist financing are worked out by intellect, not passion. And though the intellect can perceive the evils of the system, it can never tackle them — because the intellectual procedures that lead to the critique are the same intellectual procedures that created the system. Tom and Winifred are fascinated by their realistic, intellectual critique of the system: but the system, created by those same intellectual procedures, inevitably exercises a similar fascination over them. Not only will they never experience the passion (without which the perceptions of their intellect will never be acted on), but they positively like the passionless mechanicalness of the system. Hearing Tom talk to Winifred, Ursula realizes he is

> cynically reviling the monstrous state and yet adhering to it, like a man who reviles his mistress, yet who is in love with her. She knew her Uncle Tom perceived what was going on. But she knew moreover that in spite of his criticism and condemnation, he still wanted the great machine. His only happy moments, his only moments of pure freedom were when he was serving the machine. Then, and only then, when the machine caught him up, was he free from the hatred of himself, could he act wholly, without cynicism and unreality.
>
> His real mistress was the machine, and the real mistress of Winifred was the machine. She too, Winifred, worshipped the impure abstraction, the mechanisms of matter. (12:350)

Ursula's reaction is an extreme one; and it is one that seems to be supported by Lawrence:

> Hatred sprang up in Ursula's heart. If she could she would smash the machine. Her soul's action should be the smashing of the great machine. If she could destroy the colliery, and make all the men of Wiggiston out of work, she would do it. Let them starve and grub in the earth for roots, rather than serve such a Moloch as this. (12:350)

Ursula's reaction is one of *heart* and *soul* against the intellectual and mechanical nature of the system. And the system, Lawrence stresses, is capitalism: it is an industry organized according to a system of economic exploitation, a Moloch to whom hideous sacrifices are made, not simply a Mammon of greed. Now to destroy the colliery so that the miners have to starve and grub in the soil may seem an irrational and impractical response to the problems of industrial capitalism. But Lawrence's point is that the practical, intellectual responses will achieve nothing either. Since rational, mechanical, clear, hard-headed thinking created the system, those sorts of approaches will never destroy it. Ursula's reaction is not, nor is Lawrence's, bourgeois taste horror: oh the horrid houses these poor people live in, oh what ugly names they have (remember Matthew Arnold's play with 'poor Wragg'). It is a revolutionary perception — a quality that can best be brought out by putting it against this passage from Marx and Engels's *The Holy Family*:

> In the conditions of existence of the proletariat are condensed, in their most inhuman form, all the conditions of existence of present-day society. Man has lost himself, but he has not only acquired, at the same time, a theoretical consciousness of his loss, he has been forced, by an ineluctable, irremediable, and imperious *distress* — by practical *necessity* — to revolt against this inhumanity. It is for these reasons that the proletariat can and must emancipate itself. But it can only emancipate itself by destroying its own conditions of existence. It can only destroy its own conditions of existence by destroying *all* the inhuman conditions of present-day society, conditions which are epitomized in its situation. (Bottomore and Rubel, p.237)

From this passionate response to her vision of the conditions of the mining proletariat, Ursula moves through the novel to an ever-widening conspectus of capitalist society, that leads to the book's

135

culminating vision of the destruction of 'all the inhuman conditions' so that a new humanity can emerge. And that destruction begins in the miners' cottages of Wiggiston, begins amongst the proletariat.

The explicitly political implications of Tom and Winifred's attitudes are drawn out in Ursula's confrontations with Skrebensky. Skrebensky is an officer in the army — in the same middle rank of a system as Tom; and like Tom he accepts the priorities of the structure. Ursula asks him:

> 'But what would you be doing it you went to war?'
> 'I would be making railways or bridges, working like a nigger.'
> 'But you'd only make them to be pulled down again when the armies had done with them.' (11:310)

Ursula cannot accept his sense of the importance of all this to the individual life. She insists on testing the slogans against her own immediate, personal response.

> 'But the results matter,' he said. 'It matters whether we settle the Mahdi or not.'
> 'Not to you — nor me — we don't care about Khartoum.'
> 'You want to have room to live in; and somebody has to make room.'
> 'But I don't want to live in the desert of Sahara — do you?' she replied, laughing with antagonism.
> '*I* don't — but we've got to back up those who do.' (11:310)

Khartoum means nothing to Ursula. Skrebensky defends the official line, his commitment to the imperialist position, by invoking the idea of the nation, in whose name Khartoum must be fought for.

> 'Where is the nation if we don't?'
> 'But we aren't the nation. There are heaps of other people who are the nation.'
> 'They might say *they* weren't either.'
> 'Well, if everybody said it, there wouldn't be a nation. But I should still be myself,' she asserted brilliantly. (11:310-1)

Skrebensky cannot accept Ursula's spontaneous anarchism, her stress on the primacy of the individual — because he cannot accept his own individuality. Like Will, there is something unfulfilled in him, like Tom Brangwen his ambitions 'had all ended in a disintegrated lifelessness of soul ... a stability of nullification' (12:344).

Will surrendered himself to a sort of religious mysticism, Tom to a worship of the machine of industrialism, Skrebensky surrenders to the imperialist army and the belief in the 'nation'.

> He went about at his duties, giving himself up to them. At the bottom of his heart his self, the soul that aspired and had true hope of self-effectuation lay as dead, still-born, a dead weight in his womb. Who was he, to hold important his personal connection? What did a man matter personally? He was just a brick in the whole great social fabric, the nation, modern humanity . . . .

> The good of the greatest number was all that mattered. That which was the greatest good for them all, collectively, was the greatest good for the individual. And so, every man must give himself to support the state, and so labour for the greatest good of all. One might make improvements in the state, perhaps, but always with a view to preserving it intact. (11:328)

Commitment to the perpetuation of a system – religion, industrial capitalism, military imperialism – means a surrender of the individual. Those systems can only thrive if individuals surrender or are deprived of the major part of their individuality.

Lawrence's critique of these systems is based not on the way they oppress and subjugate in the obvious economic and social ways; the exploitation of the mine workers by industrial capitalism, or the Indian people by imperialism he takes as read and not needing to be demonstrated further. What he concentrates on in *The Rainbow* is the destruction exercised on the administrators of those systems, on the managerial and intellectual members of the oppressive class who ought to be able to offer an effective critique of the systems they operate, but who are destroyed, made mute and powerless. So Ursula's attack on Skrebensky's going out to India is mounted not in the usual terms of economic exploitation or authoritarian repression; her case is that he will be imposing the deadness of English society onto India, making another society as dead and mechanical as industrial England:

> 'You think the Indians are simpler than us, and so you'll enjoy being near them and being a lord over them,' she said. 'And you'll feel so righteous, governing them for their own good. Who are you, to feel righteous? What are you righteous about, in your governing? Your governing stinks. What do you govern

for, but to make things there as dead and mean as they are
here!' (15:462)

Ursula's description of Skrebensky is validated by the novel; her
view is Lawrence's own view. The imperial transportation of death
into new worlds is the theme of *Heart of Darkness* too, that is what
the imagery and the brutal realities show. And Skrebensky's rationale
for his life is the same as Marlow's. The Victorian capitalist imperialist
mystification about 'work' as an end in itself, as a spiritual good —
no matter what end it is applied to. Lawrence attacks the cult of
work in his study of Thomas Hardy. Work is bad unless it extends
human consciousness. Skrebensky and Marlow work, however, to
close off their consciousnesses from seeing the full context of things;
they do not want to see how the work is imperialist economic
exploitation of another people, and how seeing it as an end in itself
blocks off any active critical inquiry and activity that might lead to
change in the system. When Ursula asks Skrebensky if he will like
being in India he says:

> 'I think so — there's a good deal of social life, and plenty going
> on — hunting, polo — always a good horse — and plenty of
> work, any amount of work.'
>   He was always side-tracking, always side-tracking his own soul.
> She could see him so well out there, in India — one of the
> governing class, superimposed upon an old civilization, lord and
> master of a clumsier civilization than his own. It was his choice.
> He would become again an aristocrat, invested with authority
> and responsibility, having a great helpless populace beneath him.
> One of the ruling class, his whole being would be given over to
> the fulfilling and the executing of the better idea of the state.
> And in India, there would be real work to do. The country did
> need the civilization which he himself represented: it did need
> his roads and bridges, and the enlightenment of which he was
> part. (15:443-4)

Notice the 'enlightenment', the same imagery of imperial 'civilization' as in *Heart of Darkness*. And what it means is 'rule' and 'work'.
Ursula may be temporarily mystified about India's 'need' for that
sort of enlightenment: but what it comes down to is the exercise of
power over the subject race, power called 'authority', 'authority'
exercised for its own sake, for its demonstration of power, to give
the Skrebenskys an identity; and work for its own sake, to avoid
thinking, to side track the soul, an ideology for the realities of

imperialist economic exploitation. Skrebensky is as mystified in his situation as Tom Brangwen was in his love for the industrial machine; no change in the system can come from either of them.

In Ursula's view democracy is just another such system that stunts the individual, that denies the individual. 'Only the greedy and ugly people come to the top in a democracy', she said, 'because they're the only people who will push themselves there. Only degenerate races are democratic' (15:461). Skrebensky tries to defend the official ideology.

'The people elect the government,' he said
'I know they do. But what are the people? Each of them is a money interest. I hate it, that anybody is my equal who has the same amount of money as I have. I *know* I am better than all of them. I hate them. They are not my equals. I hate equality on a money basis. It is the equality of dirt.' (15:461)

This important outburst is obviously readily susceptible to the traditional interpretation of Lawrence as fascist. Arnold Kettle comments:

It is a very subtle passage. The indictment of Skrebensky could scarcely be more shrewd or more profound from any point of view, psychological or social. And in Ursula's anger the whole of Lawrence's hatred and contempt of bourgeois society comes through. Yet there is also something very deep in Ursula's own attitude which prevents her from being able to cope adequately with Skrebensky. Her identification of the people with 'a money interest' disarms her. That it should disarm her as a debater doesn't of course matter (no one need demand that Ursula must, in a theoretical sense, be 'right'). What does matter is that it disarms her as an active agent in the novel and hands her over to an orgy of mystical clap-trap. Since Ursula is at this point carrying on her shoulders all of the positives of the novel — it is she who is about to achieve the vision of the rainbow — it matters intensely that these positives should be given no coherent, concrete expression. (II:137)

It is certainly true that Ursula comes up with no social programme. But what she does stress is the priority of the individual on which any social programme must be based. She is expressing her refusal to submerge an identity beneath the mechanical, artificial pressures of society, beneath the abstract concept of 'the nation'. Her opposition to democracy is certainly not a fascist opposition; indeed she attacks Skrebensky for taking on a servile, obedient role to the idea of the state, for pigeonholing himself into a position in a hierarchical structure, instead of fulfilling himself. She sees 'democracy' as advocated in Britain as an intellectualized, mechanical theory that moulded people to it — just as the mine forced people to mould themselves to it. The ideal society would be formed and shaped by the individuality of its members.

This stress on the primacy of the individual is crucial to Lawrence's social and political thinking. But it is often misunderstood by commentators on his work. Raymond Williams in *Culture and Society*, for instance, remarks:

> Lawrence was so involved with the business of getting free of the industrial system that he never came seriously to the problem of changing it, although he knew that since the problem was common an individual solution was only a cry in the wind. It would be absurd to blame him on these grounds. It is not so much that he was an artist, and thus supposedly condemned, by romantic theory, to individual solutions. In fact, as we know, Lawrence spent a good deal of time trying to generalize about the necessary common change; he was deeply committed, all his life, to the idea of re-forming society. But his main energy went, and had to go, to the business of personal liberation from the system. (203)

For Lawrence, there can be no 'social' freedom until there is individual freedom. Until there is personal liberation there can be no other liberation: but Williams is worried by the individualism of Lawrence's search for liberation. For Williams, this concentration of effort on achieving personal liberation from the industrial system, is an avoidance of seriously coming to the problem of changing that system. Lawrence's point, of course, is that those attempts to change the system that do not in themselves already embody the freed individualism of the participants, are simply further systems of restriction and oppression. Williams goes on to quote from Lawrence's essay 'Democracy':

> So, we know the first great purpose of Democracy: that each man shall be spontaneously himself — each man himself, each woman herself, without any question of equality or inequality entering in at all; and that no man shall try to determine the being of any other man, or of any other woman. (*Phoenix*, p.716)

'At first sight, this looks like, not democracy, but a kind of romantic anarchism' (208), Williams remarks; but he goes on to say that 'Lawrence is very close to the socialism of a man like Morris, and there can be little doubt that he and Morris would have felt alike about much that has subsequently passed for socialism' (209).

It is important to see Lawrence's stress on the individual in the context of a socialist critique of industrial capitalism. This is his orientation, his base. Less sympathetic commentators, like Christopher Caudwell, have stressed the 'bourgeois individualist' interpretation: but this is a distortion of his position. What gets continually missed is Lawrence's emphasis that the only worthwhile social revolution will be one that is built on the primacy of the individual: not the individual of the old society, either, he emphasizes, but a new individual. The new individual that Marx and Engels envisaged as participating in the 'community of revolutionary proletarians', as *The German Ideology* puts it:

> It follows from the whole preceding analysis that the communal relationship into which the individuals of a class entered, and which was determined by their common interests over against a third party, was always a community to which these individuals belonged only as average individuals, only in so far as they lived within the conditions of existence of their class. It was a relationship in which they participated not as individuals but as members of a class. But with the community of revolutionary proletarians, who establish their control over the conditions of existence of themselves and the other members of society, it is just the reverse: the individuals participate as individuals. It is just this combination of individuals (assuming, of course, the advanced level of modern productive forces) which brings the conditions for the free development and activity of individuals under their own control, conditions which were formerly abandoned to chance and which had acquired an independent existence over against the separate individuals. This independence resulted from the separation of individuals, and from the forced character of their combination, which was determined by the division of labour, and which had become an alien constraint. (Bottomore and Rubel, pp. 253-4)

But Ursula comes up with nothing as coherent as this in her reaction against Skrebensky. She can merely identify Skrebensky as representing a past system, a system that has had its day and is now dead. 'I'm against you, and all your old, dead things' she says to him (15:462).

Few critics have recognized the revolutionary force behind Ursula's rage and rejection of Skrebensky. Caudwell's complaint about Lawrence's rejection of intellectual analyses has been a focus of orthodoxy:

> Bourgeois defects are implicit in bourgeois civilisation and therefore in bourgeois consciousness. Hence man wants to turn against the intellect, for it seems that the intellect is his enemy, and indeed it is, if by intellect we mean the bourgeois intellect. But it can only be fought with intellect. To deny intellect is to assist the forces of conservatism. In hundreds of diverse forms we see to-day the useless European revolt against intellectualism. (66)

But what Lawrence denies is the bourgeois idea that intellect 'can only be fought with intellect'. Caudwell's old left stance here cannot comprehend the alternative consciousness that Lawrence is exploring.

Lawrence devotes a large part of his work to demonstrating the limitations of the position which Caudwell holds in regard to intellect, rationality. In *The Rainbow* Ursula's escape from the Brangwen farming world into the wider urban world might theoretically have been expected to have offered her a wider range and scope of life opportunities, experience, understanding. Ursula has moved from the unthinking rural life into the life of intellectual possibility. The intellectual component of this new life is stressed — in the sorts of discussions she has with Skrebensky about ideas, in the categorization of young Tom Brangwen and Winifred Inger as intellectuals, and in the setting of two major episodes of her experience in places of learning.

However, the places of learning are shown to offer little or nothing of value; and they are shown to be crucially and intimately connected with the capitalist industrial system. It is shown to be bourgeois intellect that is offered; and a very shoddy version of that product, the cheap mass-produced grade. That is the commonest version of it around, after all.

The mechanical deadness of the educational processes reflects the mechanical deadness of the intellectual approach. Mr Harby, the headmaster of the school at which Ursula teaches,

> was imprisoned in a task too small and petty for him, which yet, in a servile acquiescence, he would fulfil, because he had to earn his living. He had no finer control over himself, only this blind, dogged, wholesale will. He would keep the job going, since he

must. And his job was to make the children spell the word
'caution' correctly, and put a capital letter after a full-stop. So
at this he hammered with his suppressed hatred, always
suppressing himself, till he was beside himself. (13:387)

The analogies with the other servants of imperialism and industrialism are clear. Like Skrebensky he has a 'servile acquiescence' to
the system in which he operates, like Tom he is 'always suppressing
himself'; his teaching is not any romantic vocation but a way 'to
earn his living', a 'job', at which he 'hammered' — like any other
exploited employee of the industrial system. 'The whole situation
was wrong and ugly' (13:388) Ursula concludes — ugly just as the
houses of Wiggiston are ugly. Ursula tries to be different. 'Ursula
thought she was going to become the first wise teacher by making
the whole business personal, and using no compulsion' (13:383);
she fails. The necessary impersonality of the teaching situation is
directly analogous to the alienated impersonal relationships in the
capitalist industrial system.

In terms of any over-all argument about urban life or about
education, however, it would be easy enough to try to discount this
powerful episode. The usual argument is, we all know schools are
bad and there are survivals of outmoded systems still operating,
but the ideal education offers more, and that ideal education can
progressively be spread through society. So for those suffering from
that delusion, Lawrence shows us the university. And at first Ursula
is full of ideals and illusions again, just as when she began teaching.
But during her second year:

> The life went out of her studies, why, she did not know. But the
> whole thing seemed sham, spurious; spurious Gothic arches,
> spurious peace, spurious Latinity, spurious dignity of France,
> spurious naïveté of Chaucer. It was a second-hand dealer's shop,
> and one bought an equipment for an examination. This was only
> a little side-show to the factories of the town. Gradually the
> perception stole into her. This was no religious retreat, no
> seclusion of pure learning. It was a little apprentice-shop where
> one was further equipped for making money. The college itself
> was a little, slovenly laboratory for the factory. (15:434-5)

The university is part of the industrial capitalist world, it is the prop
of that world; it is intimately connected with it in economic terms.
This is the discovery Professor Cunningham makes in Jack London's
avowedly revolutionary marxist novel, *The Iron Heel*. Lawrence

continues, 'Everywhere, everything was debased to the same service. Everything went to produce vulgar things, to encumber material life' (15:435). It is the insight of Morris in the avowedly revolutionary marxist romance, *News from Nowhere*. Lawrence's insight into education, and into the 'intellect' celebrated by that education, is delivered here as a revolutionary exposé. No wonder the book was banned in Britain and 1,200 copies burned; the publishers offered no defence to the charges of obscenity. It was not reissued till 1926.

The intellect that formal education cultivates is the intellect that created and that maintains the system — intellectual inquiry turns out to have the same arid, rational, mechanical nature as the structures of the commercial, technological world of industrial capitalism.

> 'No, really,' Dr Frankstone had said, 'I don't see why we should attribute some special mystery to life — do you? We don't understand it as we understand electricity, even, but that doesn't warrant our saying it is something special, something different in kind and distinct from everything else in the universe — do you think it does? May it not be that life consists in a complexity of physical and chemical activities, of the same order as the activities we already know in science? I don't see really, why we should imagine there is a special order of life, and life alone —' (15:440)

Dr Frankstone expresses the belief of the twentieth-century intellectual, the rationalist freed from religious superstition; indeed one of the themes of *The Rainbow* is the lessening significance of the church, the way in which, as Arnold Kettle observes, the church diminishes in importance and is no longer seen to 'embrace the whole of the universe; its pretensions are ultimately bogus' (II:128). But Lawrence is also claiming that the ideology of the rationalist, narrowly materialist intellectual is likewise bogus, for it is an ideology that in fact expresses the needs of industrial capitalism. It is an ideology that rejects the individual, that denies personal relationships; it is an ideology that sees all relationships as merely mechanical or electrical or chemical — as versions of the machine, of technology; it is the ideology that allows capitalism to see relationships as only cash relationships.

Ursula rejects the ideology of rational, materialist intellectualism as put forward by Doctor Frankstone.

> Electricity had no soul, light and heat had no soul. Was she herself an impersonal force, or conjunction of forces, like one of these? She looked still at the unicellular shadow that lay

within the field of light, under her microscope. It was alive. She saw it move — she saw the bright mist of its ciliary activity, she saw the gleam of its nucleus, as it slid across the plane of light. What then was its will? If it was a conjunction of forces, physical and chemical, what held these forces unified, and for what purpose were they unified?

It intended to be itself. But what self? Suddenly in her mind the world gleamed strangely, with an intense light, like the nucleus of the creature under the microscope. Suddenly she had passed away into an intensely-gleaming light of knowledge. She could not understand what it all was. She only knew that it was not limited mechanical energy, nor mere purpose of self-preservation and self-assertion. It was a consummation, a being infinite. Self was a oneness with the infinite. To be oneself was a supreme, gleaming triumph of infinity.

Ursula sat abstracted over her microscope, in suspense. Her soul was busy, infinitely busy, in the new world. (15:441)

Ursula's rejection of Dr Frankstone's position is, of course, utterly intuitive. There is no evidence, no theory, no argument, because theory and argument are the things she is rejecting. Lawrence has to assert, because he cannot use intellectual, logical arguments to reject the structure that logic and intellect have assembled. That mode of perception is locked into those sorts of structures. The only way to avoid the structures, to replace them, is to perceive in different ways — in Ursula's case at this point, by intuition. And what Lawrence asserts through Ursula here is the interrelatedness of the educational-intellectual-rationalist positions and their function as an ideology that maintains — that supports and provides validation for — the imperialist capitalist industrial system. It is the ideology of a system that denies the individual, the self.

Ursula rejects intellectual analysis for the soul. 'Her soul was busy, infinitely busy, in the new world.' And it is a *new* world she seeks out, she is not making a return to an old world. Similarly in *Kangaroo* Somers is looking for 'a new show' of political possibilities. There is no suggestion that the old forms of life offer any answer. Ursula does not return to the farming world; that is never put up as a possibility. As Raymond Williams stresses about Lawrence in *The Country and the City*,

industrialism and its forms of property and possession are seen as the signs of death. Yet what is opposed to them is not, in the

run of his work, a farming community; it is rather a primitivism,
at times given some social or historical base, as in the Indians of
New Mexico, but more often and more significantly accessible
as a form of direct living in contact with natural processes —
animals and birds and flowers and trees but also the human body,
the naked exploration and relationship. (319)

The alternative to urban intellectualism is to turn to other resources
of the human psyche, to non-intellectual perceptions. In 1913, the
year he began working on the first version of *The Rainbow*, Lawrence
wrote his now well-known letter to Ernest Collings:

> My great religion is a belief in the blood, the flesh, as being wiser
> than the intellect. We can go wrong in our minds. But what our
> blood feels and believes and says, is always true. The intellect is
> only a bit and a bridle. What do I care about knowledge? All I
> want is to answer to my blood, direct, without fribbling
> intervention of mind, or moral, or what not . . . . (17 January
> 1913) (*The Collected Letters*, I:180)

This is the sort of thing, of course, that Kettle and Caudwell see
as clap-trap, as the regressive, and as leading to certain fascist positions. But there is nothing necessarily fascist in what Lawrence is
saying. He is saying that there are other modes of perception than
the intellectual-logical; and that other societies have had different
sorts of perceptions. He elaborates this in *Kangaroo*:

> the Christian-democratic world prescribes certain motions, and
> men proceed to repeat these motions, till they conceive there
> are no other motions but these. And that is pure automatism.
> When scientists describe savages, or ancient Egyptians, or Aztecs,
> they assume that these far-off peoples acted, but in a crude,
> clumsy way, from the same motives which move us. 'Too much
> ego in his cosmos.' Men have had strange, inconceivable motives
> and impulses, which were just as 'right' as ours are. And our
> 'right' motives will cease to activate, even as the lost motives of
> the Assyrians have ceased. Our 'right' and our righteousness will
> go pop, and there will be another sort of right and righteousness.
> (16:235)

Caudwell argues that 'Civilization cannot be cured by going back
along the path to the primitive, it can only become at a lower level
more unconscious of its decay' (67). But Lawrence was never

advocating a return to the primitive. His position was like William Morris's: somewhere society had taken a wrong turning. We need to seek out where that turning was made, and then resume our course from there in the correct direction. It was not a regression he advocated, but getting back on the correct course. If it was a return, it was a return on a higher level in the spiral. 'We must make a great swerve in our onward-going life-course now, to gather up again the savage mysteries. But this does not mean going back on ourselves', he wrote in *Studies in Classic American Literature* (130-1). And the future he looks to is not a fascist future. Caudwell complains: 'He saw the march of events as a bourgeois tragedy, which is true but unimportant. The important thing, which was absolutely closed to him, was that it was also a proletarian renaissance' (71). Yet in *The Rainbow* Ursula's intuitive, irrational, non-intellectual grasp of the sources of strength for the new society are manifestly proletarian. The intellectual bourgeoisie is shown as unable to reform itself, trapped in its aridity and self-doubt and self-hatred, subordinating itself to the system. The argument with Skrebensky over imperialism, culminates with a devastating indictment from Ursula. ' "It seems to me," she answered, "as if you weren't anybody — as if there weren't anybody there, where you are. Are you anybody, really? You seem like nothing to me" ' (11:311).

And immediately after this comes the encounter with the man on the barge. He embodies a proletarian vitality, a spontaneous life that hasn't been crushed by education, by intellectualization or by factory depersonalization, industrial alienation. And his job allows him a certain freedom, a degree of self-determination. He is an individual, not someone reduced to just a job. Lawrence calls him a 'man', a 'father'; revealingly the few commentators who realize the significance of this passage enough to refer to it refer to him as the 'bargeman' (Eagleton in *Exiles and Emigrés*, 205, 212) or as the 'bargee' (Leavis in *D.H. Lawrence: Novelist*, 145). Bargee is even more clearly a middle-class depersonalizing term than 'bargeman', removing the claim to humanity of the '-man', making him a mere appendage to a commercial carrier.

Lawrence does not call him 'barge-man' until the end of the scene, after Ursula and Skrebensky have left. 'The barge-man watched them go' (11:316). Then there is a deliberate aesthetic distancing, the end of the scene. And the hyphenation stresses that the word denotes a compression — man-on-a-barge — rather than a denotation of his job on analogy with milkman, coalman and other unhyphenated categories. The whole point of the episode is to show the vitality and individuality of this member of the proletariat.

> She went hastening on, gladdened by having met the grimy, lean man with the ragged moustache. He gave her a pleasant warm feeling. He made her feel the richness of her own life. Skrebensky, somehow, had created a deadness round her, a sterility, as if the world were ashes. (11:316)

And if a new world is to rise from the ashes, it will be from the vitality and individuality of such men.

The final vision of the novel shows such men *en masse*, a proletariat rising to cast off the chains of the machine civilization. Ursula sees the mine workers, in their living death: 'She saw the stiffened bodies of the colliers, which seemed already enclosed in a coffin, she saw their unchanging eyes, the eyes of those who are buried alive, she saw the hard cutting edges of the new houses.' And as she looks across this vision of death in life, this landscape of the mining villages, the rainbow appears.

> And the rainbow stood on the earth. She knew that the sordid people who crept hard-scaled and separate on the face of the world's corruption were living still, that the rainbow was arched in their blood and would quiver to life in their spirit, that they would cast off their horny covering of disintegration, that new, clean, naked bodies would issue to a new germination, to a new growth, rising to the light and the wind and the clean rain of heaven. She saw in the rainbow the earth's new architecture, the old, brittle corruption of houses and factories swept away, the world built up in a living fabric of Truth, fitting to the over-arching heaven. (16:495-6)

The rainbow, notice, is living within the proletariat already; the social change will come from them as they 'issue to a new germination'. How it will come Lawrence does not say; he shows us how it will *not* come — from the intellectual bourgeoisie. He suggests that it will come — as this final vision of Ursula's comes — from non-intellectual forces. It is an expression of faith in the possibility of a new society.

It is certainly not a regressive, or reactionary ending. That, no doubt, is why Dr Leavis disliked it so much: 'No real conclusion of the book, only a breaking-off, is possible .... There is something oddly desperate about that closing page and a half ... that confident note of prophetic hope in the final paragraph — a note wholly unprepared and unsupported, defying the preceding pages' (148).

Of course this last chapter breaks all the 'conventions' and 'rules' of the novel. All the habits of the English novel of society up to this date are affronted by Lawrence·here — by his rejection of argument, intellect and ideas, and by his commitment to this assertion, this unargued and unsubstantiated assertion expressed by the quasi-religious image of the rainbow. And yet, of course, it works. It does establish this marvellous and rare positive note. The possibilities for the ending of an English socio-political novel traditionally were: one, the individual destroyed by society, or forced to moderate his or her ambitions to fit in with society — the case of *Middlemarch*; two, the tragic destruction of the hero, possibly futilely, for the good of the cause — but, whether futilely or not, he is still destroyed — as in *Beauchamp's Career*; three, the accommodation of the individual to the ways of society, seeing the error of his or her romantic or individualistic ways and settling down into conformity — as in *Emma*; or fourth, the ultimate alienation of the hero who at the end has to reject society, like Huckleberry Finn having to light out for the territory. But in *The Rainbow* we have none of these downbeat endings; we have instead an assertion of hope, a pledge of the future, a symbolic vision of a new world. It is certainly a retreat from conventional political programmes and solutions; but it is not a retreat that in any conceivable way implies a hostility to social change. It is a vision of revolution. It is a vision that rejects currently accepted means of change (progress, reformism), alongside an apocalyptic assurance that change is necessary and change will come — and a reassertion that the seeds of change are alive within the oppressed, the proletariat.

5

Kangaroo: 'a new show'

D.H. Lawrence's *Kangaroo* (1923) is a strange, inconclusive book. Its very inconclusiveness is part of its fascination as a political novel. It resists enlistment into any ideology. Richard Lovat Somers, the protagonist, rejects the appeals of both right and left, yet his rejection does not amount to a rejection of the idea of all political involvement. It would not be correct to style *Kangaroo* as anti-political; its interest comes from Lawrence's exploration of the impulse towards political commitment, and of a certain set of appeals towards political action; though the restricted nature of this set of appeals pushes *Kangaroo* near to the anti-political. Its lack of concern with many of the conventional materials of political fiction is striking: but it makes connections, not common in most political fiction, between sexual and domestic concerns and the political. It places political engagement in an important emotional-sexual-marital context, an engagement not isolated from other human commitments. And it explores the impulse to and the temptations of 'pure' power.

Nothing positive in the way of programme or policy emerges from *Kangaroo*. This is another aspect of its inconclusiveness. It has no suggestions, no solutions. But it does explore a range of possibilities of position, of action, of sorts of commitment. Its inconclusiveness is a result of its resistance to simplifying or propagandizing. Where there are simplifications, these are part of an over-all qualifying flux of attitude that places them in a complex context. It is an important political novel from its very obliqueness, its non-partisan, sceptical, questioning stance. It is a stance torn within itself: an impulse to a rejection of the political − of people, parties and apparatus; in tension with an impulse to engagement and participation − and leadership. It is a choice of the moral leadership of the writer who rejects practical power, or the political leadership of the activist. The former gets the power of a guru, a prophet, a philosopher, without having to push people around — fantasies of leadership without actually compromising the moral purity of the idea by enacting it. And the dubiousness of that 'moral' superiority is a dubiousness which Lawrence clearly sees.

It has, hence, alongside its inadequacies of analysis of the political and social context, resulting from Lawrence's holding back from the political and social, an invaluable awareness of the complexities of attitude of the partially engaged or non-engaged, an invaluable critique of the sacrifices of independence and freedom and power that commitment requires.

The title of *Kangaroo* refers not to the Australian marsupial, but to the leader of a returned soldiers' organization (the action takes place about five years after the First World War) that is planning to take over Australia. There were numerous such returned soldiers' organizations in Australia at that time, and many of them were ultra-right. It seems increasingly likely that Lawrence was aware of such activity, and that his novel is based upon contemporary Australian realities. 'Do you think the Australian Govt. or the Diggers might resent anything?', Lawrence wrote to his American publisher Thomas Seltzer on 7 October 1922 (*Letters to Seltzer*, 43). He writes as if his political materials might offend the Australian government — which could imply the government knew of or was involved in either Kangaroo's or Willie Struthers's activities. And he writes of the Diggers as of a known, formal group. In the manuscript of *Kangaroo*, now at the University of Texas at Austin, the Digger clubs are at their first mention called 'Returned Soldiers'; this is crossed out and 'Diggers' substituted. This again suggests a specific identification with one of the various returned soldiers organizations. The fact that Lawrence airs his worries that the 'Diggers' might resent what he has written, is strong evidence that he was drawing on an actual organization of returned soldiers for his novel. But beyond that there is no specific evidence of Lawrence's associations with or knowledge of such a group; none of his published letters from Australia mention the *content* of *Kangaroo*. He writes often about its *form*; but he says nothing either way about the source of his materials. The very absence of comment is significant. He never once says, 'I'm projecting material from the rise of fascism in Italy into Australia' — which is the argument of a number of critics. He never says, 'I've found out about these right-wing clubs organizing for a coup.' He never says, 'I'm totally fantasizing the material and placing it in an Australian setting.' The fact that he never mentions the *content* of *Kangaroo*, could suggest he has something to conceal about it. He is saying nothing, rather than telling what he doesn't want known or telling a false account of its origins.

It is significant that Lawrence should title his political novel by the nickname of a political leader. The concern of the novel is not with political beliefs, social classes, economic forces, party structures. The emphasis is on the personal, on individuals; not only on Kangaroo, but also on the socialist leader Willie Struthers, and, most important of all, on the protagonist, Richard Lovat Somers. Somers is a scarcely concealed representation of Lawrence, and the novel's concern is with the attempted conversion of him to political commitment — a conversion attempted by Kangaroo, by Struthers, and by Somers himself. In *Beauchamp's Career* Meredith placed the emphasis on the attempt by Nevil Beauchamp to convert a class, the attempt by the protagonist to commit others to radical politics. Lawrence's inversion of this structure indicates a major shift in thinking during the intervening fifty years. The new hero is not shown committing himself to society and trying to lead it or improve it; instead he is shown trying to preserve his individuality against fragments of a fragmented society wooing him to join them. There has been a shift from a belief in the primary values of social organization and political belief, to a belief in the primary value of the individual, a suspicion of ideologies and social values. The protagonist is now the resistant individual. Caudwell recognized this stance:

> Lawrence remained to the end a man incapable of that
> subordination of self to others, of co-operation, of solidarity as
> a class, which is the characteristic of the proletariat. He
> remained the individualist, the bourgeois revolutionary angrily
> working out his own salvation, critical of all, alone in possession
> of grace. He rid himself of every bourgeois illusion but the
> important one. (71)

Kangaroo is not a novel about democratic reforms nor about revolution nor about the structures or recruiting of democratic or revolutionary groups. It is about the attempted conversion of an individual. And the conversion is attempted by individuals. Somers does not observe the structures of Australian society, of its colonial exploitation, of its capitalist industry, or anything else, nor does he read political theory. We are told that he has written essays on democracy before arriving in Australia, but theoretical concepts are not shown as important. The attempted conversion is all by individual contact, by discussions with Kangaroo and Struthers and Jack Callcott; and they are discussions depending on argument and on emotional rapport — no one ever takes Somers on tours of factories or slums or schools or meetings of the returned soldiers' groups. Neither theory nor empirical substantiation has a place in the attempted conversion of Somers.

The emphasis on a few individuals in *Kangaroo* has resulted in the book's being classed as a 'leadership' novel. John Harrison in *The Reactionaries* claims that 'what Lawrence became increasingly certain about in writing *Kangaroo* was the need for aristocracy, authority, rule based on the natural superiority of certain individuals' (183):

> Bertrand Russell, who knew him well, said that Lawrence imagined that he would be the supreme leader when a dictatorship had been established. Russell also said that Lawrence had developed the whole philosophy of fascism before the politicians had thought of it, that Lawrence was 'an exponent of the cult of insanity' of the between-wars period, of which nazism was the most emphatic expression. (189)

Certainly the theme of leadership is present in the novel, but it is not a concept which the novel is concerned to advocate in the simple way Harrison would imply. The emphasis is on the preservation of individuality, and political beliefs are seen in terms of individuals. That for his representative individuals he selects two leaders indicates something of his elitist, anti-democratic thinking; it was a convenient shorthand that is also revelatory of his thinking, the drift into hierarchical schemes. None the less Jack Callcott is equally important in the attempted conversion of Somers, and he is simply one of Kangaroo's followers with no especially high status. As for Somers — Lawrence himself wanting to be a leader — this possibility is included in *Kangaroo* in a way that mocks the idea. When Jack Callcott first talks about the Diggers, Somers asks, ' "But who are your leaders?" ... thinking of course that it was his own high destiny to be a leader' (5:104). The self-mockery at this delusory temptation is explicit — not that this denies that it *was* a temptation.

Leadership is present sometimes comically, sometimes seriously, as one of the temptations put to Somers to draw him into political commitment. He is offered some sort of leadership in the Diggers by Kangaroo, and Struthers offers the bait of 'come and take charge of a true People's paper for us'. It is a very naturalistic temptation, and draws on an accurate depiction of the Australian left's complaints and hopes, the same today as in 1922. Struthers says, 'We want a voice. Think of it, we've got no real Labour newspaper in Sydney – or in Australia. How *can* we be united? We've no voice to call us all together' (11:222). But leadership is also presented as an instrument of the infringement of individual liberty – in the people the leadership power is exercised over, and in the demands it would make on Somers himself if he chose leadership. Certainly Lawrence recognized the appeal. Norman Mailer remarks in *The Prisoner of Sex* on 'such unread tracts as *Aaron's Rod* and *Kangaroo*, when the uneasy feeling arrives that perhaps it was just as well Lawrence died when he did, for he could have been the literary adviser to Oswald Mosley about the time Hitler came in . . .' (136-7). But to recognize and to attempt to create the appeal of the charismatic leader figure in fiction, is not to endorse the idea of totalitarian or dictatorial political systems. As Mailer realizes:

> For if we can feel how consumed he was by the dictatorial
> pressure to ram his sentiments into each idiot throat, he never
> forgets that he is writing novels, and so his ideas cannot simply
> triumph, they have to be tried and heated and forged, and finally
> be beaten into shapelessness against the anvil of his profound
> British skepticism which would not buy his ideas, not outright,
> for even his own characters seem to wear out in them . . . .
> Lawrence was not only trying to sell dictatorial theorems, he
> was also trying to rid himself of them. (138-9)

It is the fascist quality, the imposition of authority, the use of violence, the disregard of human individuality, that causes Somers's final rejection of Struthers and Kangaroo. He maintains his individuality against them, just as in the presentation of his marriage with Harriet, he is shown fighting a running battle to resist domination.

In a novel so much concerned with the individual, the political conclusions will be closely related to the nature of the individual who is the protagonist. The political themes will derive largely from the individual's preconceived political attitudes, or from the inter-action between him and the socio-political environment. In *Kangaroo* such interaction is almost entirely absent – except for the meetings and discussions with Jack, Kangaroo and Struthers. His contact with other people is minimal. But Somers's preconceived political views are strongly present. His recoil from social contacts, from social connections, is apparent in the opening chapter, implicitly in his fleeing from Europe, and explicitly in his anger at Harriet's making contact with the next door neighbours in their Sydney suburb. 'He started with a rabid desire not to see anything and not to speak one single word to any single body' (1:24). Balanced against this, though, is a curiosity. In his initial avoidance of their neighbours, Somers none the less wants to know what is going on:

> He left off sweeping the little yard, which was the job he had set himself for the moment, and walked across the brown grass to where Harriet stood peeping through the rift in the dead hedge, her head tied in a yellow, red-spotted duster. And of course, as Somers was peeping beside her, the neighbour who belonged to the garden must come . . . . (1:21)

Similarly, for all Somers's stance of isolation, the political is implicitly present from the beginning. The novel opens in Macquarie Street, Sydney — site of the New South Wales State Parliament. The workman watching Somers speculates about him, 'Perhaps a Bolshy' (1:11).

As the novel proceeds, the anti-social aspect of Somers is linked closely with a racism and a hostility to democracy. He says to Jack: 'The real sense of liberty only goes with white blood. And the ideal democratic liberty is an exploded ideal. You've got to have wisdom and authority somewhere, and you can't get it out of any further democracy' (5:102). Australia represents the extreme of democracy Somers recognizes straightaway.

> Somers for the first time felt himself immersed in real democracy — in spite of all disparity in wealth. The instinct of the place was absolutely and flatly democratic, *à terre* democratic. Demos was here his own master, undisputed, and therefore quite calm about it. No need to get the wind up at all over it; it was a granted condition of Australia, that Demos was his own master.
>
> And this was what Richard Lovat Somers could not stand. You may be the most liberal Englishman, and yet you cannot fail to see the categorical difference between the responsible and the irresponsible classes. You cannot fail to admit the necessity for *rule*. Either you admit yourself an anarchist, or you admit the necessity for *rule* — in England. (1:27)

It is with this English prejudice for rule, this distaste for democracy, that Somers encounters his further political experiences. His views are not necessarily endorsed by Lawrence. Critics have too readily assumed that statements made at a particular time by Somers can represent Lawrence's considered position. But Lawrence is at pains to show the flux of Somers's attitudes, his constantly shifting views.

And at the very end of chapter 1 he explicitly states the wrongness of Somers's position here.

> But Richard *was* wrong. Given a good temper and a genuinely tolerant nature — both of which the Australians seem to have in high degree — you can get on for quite a long time without 'rule'. For quite a long time the thing just goes by itself.
>   Is it merely running down, however, like a machine running on but gradually running down?
>   Ah, questions! (1:28)

Although Australia represents for Somers the extreme of democracy, his revulsion from democracy is not something that is a response to Australia. Australia may serve to remind him of his attitudes; but their cause lies in his experience in England during the First World War. Not until chapter 12, 'The Nightmare', are we shown these events and his responses. And when we are finally shown the demagogue-led democracy, the mass hysteria, the civilian abuses, this is to parallel the situation that Somers has now come to see would be created if Kangaroo seized power in Australia. The revelation of the roots of Somers's political attitudes is delayed until it serves, when it is given, to underline the nature of Kangaroo's Digger groups.

'The Nightmare' is based closely on Lawrence's own experiences as a civilian in the war. Crucial experiences for him, he sees them as crucial for a political novel. This is what 'democracy' could easily get like with a bit of manipulation: this is maybe what democracy is always like. Lawrence rejected the suggestion of Robert Mountsier, his literary agent in the USA, 'to cut out my own long "war" experience, condense it to a couple of pages for Kangaroo, & publish the "experience" apart, perhaps with "Democracy"'; 'I want to *keep in* the war-experience piece' he insisted in letters to Seltzer, his USA publisher (7 October, 16 October 1922; *Letters to Seltzer*, 43, 44). The war experience chapter had to stay in. It firmly established the harassment by civilian and military authorities, the summoning before conscription boards, the pressures to accept and get caught up in the war hysteria, the actions of a repressive bureaucracy acting for the 'common good'. The theme of the chapter is how:

> From 1916 to 1919 a wave of criminal lust rose and possessed England, there was a reign of terror, under a set of indecent bullies like Bottomley of *John Bull* and other bottom-dog members of the House of Commons. Then Somers had known

what it was to live in a perpetual state of semi-fear: the fear of
the criminal public and the criminal government. The torture was
steadily applied, during those years after Asquith fell, to break
the independent soul in any man who would not hunt with the
criminal mob. A man must identify himself with the criminal
mob, sink his sense of truth, of justice, and of human honour,
and bay like some horrible unclean hound, bay with a loud
sound, from slavering, unclean jaws. (12:235-6)

It is a chapter that has received much critical commentary, though
little understanding of its role in the novel. Graham Hough's complaints in *The Dark Sun* are representative of frequent objections
to it:

The horrors of war cannot be indicted by hysterical sulking and
screaming. There is no moral basis for Somers' indignation. His
objection is to the upsetting of his domestic privacy. He is not
a pacifist or a conscientious objector — he simply wants to be
medically rejected and to run home to his own wife and
cottage. He will not make his protest on any grounds that are
fit to be stated or fit to be heard, as Russell and the other
objectors did. The Somers who insists on the virtues of
authority and obedience is horrified at the mildest
regimentations of barrack life, and pathologically horrified
by medical examination. (138)

The 'pathological horror' at the medical examination is society's,
not Lawrence's. Lawrence wrote about doctors looking up con-
scripts' arses, and then had to censor what he wrote for the English
edition — the 'pathological horror' lies all with the publishers and
public.

What Hough finds it hard to accept is that Lawrence does not
object to warfare as such, he is not making a pacifist objection. The
horrors of war are not relevant to the concerns of *Kangaroo*. War is
self-evidentally horrible — except to the naïve middle-class ideo-
logues, the public-school poets who leapt into the war as a great
adventure. Lawrence had no illusions. Lawrence's objections to
England in 'The Nightmare' are objections to the political consequences of the war, not to the horrors of the trenches. His critics
argue that in the context of the slaughter of the First World War,
Lawrence's objection to compulsory medical examination is selfish
and trivial. But to make such an objection is to assume that only
the physically violent is significant; and to assume that the war is an

accidental cataclysm visited on us from outside — not something generated by the conditions and nature of the society we live in. What Lawrence realized was that the physically violent derives and grows from the acceptance of the quieter moral violence, the intrusions on civil liberties, the restrictions on the individual's private existence. Once these are accepted, then it is an easy step to condoning physical violence. And physical violence is the way in which those intrusions on the individual's liberties are maintained. A bourgeois ethic allows an objection to the horrors of war, but denies that there is a direct connection between those horrors and the nature of bourgeois society. Lawrence objects to the domestic violences resulting from, or 'justified' by, war — from the First World War through to Vietnam — conscription, imprisonment of those who refuse to register for conscription, censorship, police surveillance of groups opposing the war. War in the name of democracy, freedom, provides the excuse and occasion for the restrictions on freedom and democracy within the nation.

Remembering this in Australia, Lawrence makes connections with the demagogy of Bottomley and of Kangaroo, associating the intrusive regimentation of life in England then with the regimentation and the repressive aims of Kangaroo's paramilitary organization. In the authority structures of the socialists he senses similar intrusions on individual liberties: 'Richard was thankful to get out of Canberra Hall. It was like escaping from one of the medical-examination rooms in the war' (11:225). Having escaped once, he has no intention of getting caught up again. He repudiates those authoritarian systems he has given momentary assent to. He recognizes their intrusiveness on the individual, their totalitarian leanings.

The crucial nightmare chapter is a flashback memory to events that took place before the beginning of the novel, to pre-Australian experiences. Somers's political views are not based on observations of Australian life, but were formed earlier. Kangaroo is the 'thought-adventure' of Somers. The political experience is internal and has few correlatives of action. There is no exploration of Australian society here comparable with the accounts of the miners and hosiery workers in *Sons and Lovers*, no consideration of the machine-like nature of capitalist industry and its destructive effect on both employees and employer, as in the portrayal of Gerald Crich and his workmen in *Women in Love*.

Neither the detailed naturalistic careful account of bourgeois society in *The Rainbow*, nor the caricature-symbol of the paralysed establishment class, Sir Clifford in *Lady Chatterley's Lover* (1928), find any place in *Kangaroo*. Although aspects of the nature of

Australian democracy are mentioned, this is not to show the ripeness
of the country for takeover by Kangaroo or Struthers, or its unripe-
ness. Nor is there a dramatic presentation of the nature of Australian
democracy: it is presented through Somers's thoughts and observations on Australia. At the end of the first chapter he meditates on
these themes, and he continues to watch and meditate throughout
the novel. He forms a relationship with the Callcotts, but the Callcotts
are never seen in contact with or as representative of any larger
social group. They seem as isolated, as alien, as the Somerses.
Kangaroo and Struthers are likely enough political leaders for
Australian society. But the relationships of interactions between
society and the political figures are never shown. We see the society
through Somers's eyes; we hear the political leaders speak. We see
the way Somers reacts to what he sees of the society (though without any involvement); we see the way Somers reacts to the political
leaders — and here there is some interaction. But between society
and the politicians there are no connections; we never see them in
their economic and power and party-machinery context. The closely
observed social mores are not used in the expected way for a political novel; they remain static observations, they are given no political
implications.

Nor is there any political action. We never see Kangaroo in relationships with his followers, his disciples, his clubs. We see him only
in relation to Somers. We are told of the Digger clubs and their
organization, but Somers never visits them; they are never present
in the action. Struthers is visited in his office, but he is never seen
in the context of his party or followers. The exception to this exclusion of political events from the action is the final débâcle, the
political meeting which Struthers addresses, at which a bomb is
thrown, and at which Kangaroo is mortally wounded. This, the sole
incident of politics in action, is the episode that convinces Somers
that he was right to avoid political engagement. The chapter is
given the unglorified title of 'A Row in Town', degrading any appeal
which political engagement might make. As the only representative
of political activity in the novel, it carries considerable weight. It
puts the struggle between the socialists and the Diggers firmly in the
area of revolutionary politics and agents provocateurs. But it remains
unclear how representative of Australian politics the incident is to be
seen. Is this an untypical, aberrant event in a context of parliamentary democracy? Or is this a foretaste of the struggle between
left and right, a struggle that is now moving out of the parliamentary
forum and being fought in the streets, as it soon was to be fought in
Europe. Lawrence had seen the beginnings of that, and had left

Europe. Now Somers-Lawrence rapidly leaves Australia. And Somers's rejection of revolutionary political involvement, a rejection confirmed by this event, spreads outward to a rejection of all political involvement.

Lawrence is not dealing with political machinery or even with political action. His theme is the commitment of one man to political action. But his emphasis results in a peculiar sense of the isolation, the irrelevance, of what remains as 'political'. Politics in all their wealth of social, economic, public implications, are reduced here to the thought-adventure of one man. In *Beauchamp's Career* Meredith's manner of procedure allowed us to see not only the theme of conversion, commitment, but also a whole anatomy of the establishment, which Nevil was trying to convert. But in *Kangaroo* there is none of this social amplitude. Not only has Lawrence focused his political examination on the attitudes of one man, but this one man is an alien. He is not a citizen, not a national, none of the political issues of representation, responsibility, participation are to be found in him in any representative way. He is alienated, he is in exile. This is underlined in the first chapter when Jack wonders if Somers is a German, certainly realizes he is a foreigner. And later, when Somers makes it clear that he will not become involved, and is leaving Australia, Jack says, 'You come out from the old countries very cocksure, with a lot of criticism to you. But when it comes to doing anything, you sort of fade out, you're nowhere' (15:320). Because he is an alien, the political conversion or rejection in Somers can tell us little about the political structure of Australia. The specific issues that might make sense or nonsense of a particular programme or position in a specific context, can mean little to Somers. Lawrence is dealing with political conversion in a vacuum. Australia is chosen as the setting because it is a new country, a clean-slate society; and into this an alienated non-committed observer is dropped. But even this *tabula rasa* setting and image is not developed in any expected way; Lawrence is not interested in what institutions and attitudes might develop in the new country and in the new man.

Politics for Somers is not a matter of particular practical aims, but of some general emotional, religious, sexual commitment. The lack of political detail in the novel is the direct result of this initial assumption of Somers-Lawrence. Lukács objected to this assumption in Lawrence and other modernist writers of the 1930s in *The Meaning of Contemporary Realism*:

A new feature in the later stages of this process is the increasing exclusiveness, the radical, almost brutal elimination of social significance. Take, for instance, D.H. Lawrence's reduction of erotic relations to phallic sexuality, or the even more extreme version of this reduction in Henry Miller. (74)

But Lawrence is not retreating from the socio-political for the private-sexual-emotional. For him the two are intimately connected, overlapping, even identical.

The focus of political attention is Somers's consciousness. Lawrence's interest is in the political 'thought-adventure', in Somers considering commitment. The choices offered to him are between Kangaroo and Struthers — but before a choice can be made the political positions need to be understood. The nature of the appeal of Kangaroo, what he offers and why Somers responds to him, has always been a point of debate — and deliberately so. The nature of Kangaroo's politics is as obscure and mysterious to Somers as to the reader, and the novel follows the process of Somers's demystification.

Struthers serves as a recognizable touchstone. The conventionalities of Struthers's case serve to indicate the apparent originality of what Kangaroo offers. Struthers presents a conventional left-wing socialist programme and makes a conventional class loyalty appeal. 'Now Mr Somers, you're the son of a working man. You were born of the People. You haven't turned your back on them, have you, now that you're a well-known gentleman?' (11:222). And Somers hasn't. He recognizes the force of the socialist case; 'perhaps better Struthers than Kangaroo', he meditates (13:293). Eighteen months earlier Lawrence had written to Eleanor Farjeon from Sicily:

> If I knew how to, I'd really join myself to the revolutionary socialists now. I think the time has come for a real struggle. That's the only thing I care for: the death struggle. I don't care for politics. But I know there *must* and *should* be a deadly revolution very soon, and I would take part in it if I knew how. (20 January 1921) (*The Collected Letters*, II:639-40)

The inclination to revolutionary socialism is still there; but becoming strangely mutated; it is the 'death struggle' that appeals in theory, and the political theory that repels. These ambiguities persist through *Kangaroo*. When Kangaroo on his death-bed (victim of the actualized death struggle Lawrence had earlier merely theorized about) asks Somers what he thought of Struthers's speech, Somers replies, 'It seemed to me logical' and remarks later, 'I don't feel I belong to any class. But as far as I *do* belong — it is to the working classes. I know that. I can't change' (17:356, 357).

161

That intuitive, innate, emotional commitment to proletarian revolution remains, even when the details of leftist politics repel. Struthers's socialism, moreover, is logically correct. But it is that very logicality of Struthers that in part causes Somers's rejection of him. For Somers is looking for something new, something transcending the conventionally accepted, the merely logical; he is looking for something outside the traditional polarities. Lawrence's radical perspective that we saw in *The Rainbow* still survives: but it is still a radicalism that rejects party politics. And one, moreover, that shows a not very thorough understanding of socialist theory. None the less Lawrence is not simply rejecting socialism from a right-wing stance. At no time does he consider industrial capitalism as worth supporting. In 'The Nightmare' chapter, capitalists are paralleled with German militarism, and both are equally rejected. Orwell, recalling his early reactions to Lawrence's work, remarked how 'Both "The Prussian Officer" and "The Thorn in the Flesh" impressed me deeply. What struck me was not so much Lawrence's horror and hatred of military discipline, as his understanding of its nature' (CE, IV:9:50). Lawrence's identification of Germanic militarism with industrial capitalism is not a top of the head analogy, but a deeply felt political insight into the nature of the capitalist-industrialist-imperialist-militarist system. He knew the interconnections, the nature of the organism.

> He had been in Germany enough times to know *how* much he
> detested the German military creatures: mechanical bullies
> they were. They had once threatened to arrest him as a spy,
> and had insulted him more than once. Oh, he would never
> forgive *them*, in his inward soul. But then the industrialism and
> commercialism of England, with which patriotism and
> democracy became identified: did not these insult a man and
> hit him pleasantly across the mouth? How much humiliation
> had Richard suffered, trying to earn his living! How had they
> tried, with their beastly industrial self-righteousness, to
> humiliate him as a separate, single man? They wanted to bring
> him to heel more than the German militarist did. And if a man
> is to be brought to any heel, better a spurred heel than the
> heel of a Jewish financier. (12:237)

In Lawrence's view, socialism is only the opposite polarity to capitalism. Somers finally rejects Struthers because the principle of organization of socialism, in his view, is the same principle as that of capitalism — money:

162

But his heart was big within him, swollen in his breast. Because
in truth he did love the working people, he did know them
capable of a great, generous love for one another. And he did
also believe, in a way, that they were capable of building up this
great Church of Christ, the great beauty of a People, upon the
generous passion of mate-love. All this theoretical socialism
started by Jews like Marx, and appealing only to the will-to-
power in the masses, making money the whole crux, this has
cruelly injured the working people of Europe. For the
working people of Europe were generous by nature, and money
was not their prime passion. All this political socialism — all
politics, in fact — has conspired to make money the only god.
It has been a great treacherous conspiracy against the generous
heart of the people. And that heart is betrayed: and knows it.

Then can't the injury be remedied? Can't the working men
be called back, man to man, to a generous opening of the heart
to one another, money forgotten? Can't a new great inspiration
of belief in the love of mates be breathed into the white Peoples
of the world, and a new day be built on this belief? (11:223)

The racism, the misunderstanding of Marx, provide problems enough.
And Lawrence does not stop here. Somers has already rejected the
love-bond because

human love, human trust are always perilous, because they break
down. The greater the love, the greater the trust, and the greater
the peril, the greater the disaster . . . . Since man has been trying
absolutely to love women, and women to love man, the human
species has almost wrecked itself. If now we start a still further
campaign of men loving and absolutely trusting each other,
comrades or mates, heaven knows the horror we are laying up.
(11:220)

The result, of course, is a rejection of any known sort of society
and any known political stance. At the end of the Struthers discussion, Somers puts his faith in his dark god, not in love for fellow
men.

Love bonds, the dark god, the Lord Almighty. The concepts are
made even more elusive by Lawrence's manner of presenting the
flux of Somers's views. All is flux and change, and to seize on
anything as firm evidence is to run the risk of distortion, in the
very moment of fixing it and examining it. Its protean movement
is part of its nature.

Rejecting the merely logical and intellectual, Lawrence resists analytical explication. But having seen the grounds for Somers's rejecting Struthers, perhaps we can now see the grounds for his attraction towards Kangaroo. First, having left Europe, Somers is looking for something other than the bourgeois democratic to believe in. Keith Sagar remarked that 'Somers is likely to be taken in, not because of the real merits of Kangaroo and his Diggers, but because of the pressure from within to find some body of men with whom to associate himself, through whose organisation to channel his energies' (134). This is partially true, but if it were the whole truth it would leave Somers an absurdly blinkered figure — in his eagerness for some commitment avoiding any recognition of the nature of what was before him. Leavis remarks in *D.H. Lawrence: Novelist* that 'we are not, however, asked to suppose Somers ever in imminent danger of committing himself to the "revolution"; his disbelief in mere political movements is too profound. The attraction for him of the Diggers' movement is that it offers to be more than political' (67). But Leavis goes on to discuss the conversation with Struthers, not Kangaroo's 'more than political' appeal.

What is this 'more than political' appeal? Somers is initially attracted to the Diggers because they seem to be outside the conventional and traditional political alignments, are bringing a new dimension into political possibilities. This is indicated by the fact that whereas we can call Struthers the socialist leader, we cannot call Kangaroo anything comparable. Indeed the fact that Kangaroo is rarely called by his name, Ben Cooley, is significant. He is presented at first as outside the traditional political spectrum of right to left, his name is outside the everyday human social world. The newspaper reports on the bomb incident

> gave a large space to the disturbance, but used the wisest
> language. 'Brawl between Communists and Nationalists at
> Canberra Hall. Unknown anarchist throws a bomb. Three persons
> killed and several injured. Ben Cooley, the well-known barrister,
> receives bullets in the abdomen, but is expected to recover.
> Police, aided by Diggers, soon restored order.'
> This was the tone of all the newspapers. (16:352)

The 'wisest language' is the language the establishment uses to defuse and blur the issue. Kangaroo is called Ben Cooley here and identified as a figure of public establishment life, a barrister (which he is) and in no way identified as a figure of political life, and in no way linked with the Diggers. It is left deliberately vague whether the Diggers are also the Nationalists involved in the incident, or whether they helped the police 'restore order' as an independent third party. The ever convenient 'unknown anarchist' serves to deflect inquiries. The press, the police, and the Diggers combine to cover up the incident.

By the end of the novel the contradictions between Kangaroo's professed love and his violent methods, his paramilitary base, becomes clear. And his movement is seen to fall readily enough into the usual and predictable patterns of political violence, into a fascist category. But at the novel's beginning the point is that the movement cannot be categorized, it does seem separate from the traditional political stances. 'We stand for Australia, not for any of your parties', Jack says. 'Somers at once felt the idea was a good one . . . . The only thing he mistrusted was the dryness of Jack's voice: a sort of that's-how-it's-got-to-be dryness, sharp and authoritative' (5:106). The supra-party appeal, the new dimension, is what appeals to Somers. The rigid authoritarian note he detects and is immediately suspicious of.

In so far as Kangaroo's political programme is outlined, it is not very significant. It is the idea of a supra-political association of men that appeals to Somers. Details of political programmes drag the movement down into the practical, the conventionally political. They also quite clearly associate Kangaroo with authoritarian systems. Kangaroo's policies involve soup kitchens for the children of the poor, and letting the people have full lives (while believing that education for 90 per cent of those people is useless); he believes 'the secret of all life is in obedience', and he believes that 'man needs a quiet, gentle father who uses his authority in the name of living life, and who is absolutely stern against anti-life' (6:126), to take responsibility on his patriarchal, papal shoulders. Importantly, Somers gives no intellectual reaction to these proposals. He listens, admires Kangaroo's voice, and is emotionally and sexually attracted to Kangaroo. But he offers neither endorsement nor rejection of the political policy, such as it is.

And in the final conversation before the bomb incident, the refusal by Somers to support Kangaroo is based not on any intellectual renunciation of the muddle that is Kangaroo's thought, but on an emotional recoil. There is hardly any conventionally political discussion. Somers puts forward to Kangaroo the view earlier outlined by William James Trewellah, that Kangaroo should co-operate with the 'reds', with Struthers: 'Let him proclaim the rule of the People: let him nationalize all industries and resources, and confiscate property above a certain amount: and bring the world about his ears. Then you step in like a saviour' (11:230). But there is no reason why Somers takes over these views here — unless to suggest he does not care either way now, that none of the politicians interests him. The political element in this conversation is unimportant. Most of the episode is emotional, sexual, Kangaroo 'pressing the slight body of the lesser man against his own big breast and body', declaring, 'I love you so' (11:231). ' "I want to hear," said Kangaroo, "your case against me." "It's not a case, Kangaroo," said Richard, "it's a sort of instinct" ' (11:232).

In showing the flux of Somers's reactions to Jack Callcott, to Kangaroo and to Struthers, a striking feature of Lawrence's treatment emerges. The reactions are all emotional, intuitive. It is the emotional dialectic that is presented. The arguments, the directly presented information or opinions, remain strangely inert. Somers reacts not to them, but from a sort of blood-empathy with Kangaroo. It is a characteristic theme of Lawrence's work; and it is not out of place in a political novel. For political commitments are not purely rational or intellectual; the irrational, instinctive, emotional, and sexual are important. And Lawrence is examining what happens when the various aspects do not gell; the intellectual decision may not parallel the emotional commitment. Somers can find Struthers's socialism 'logical' but there is none of the live emotional bond between them that there has momentarily been between him and Kangaroo, so he is never really drawn to commit himself to Struthers. Strikingly, although Lawrence is more concerned with the appeal of Kangaroo, he is more successful in presenting the logical case for Struthers's position. He insists on Kangaroo's mystique, he tells us of Somers's reactions, but the irrational, emotional bond between Somers and Kangaroo scarcely comes alive. It remains inert, asserted, unrealized. By presenting the political world as mere talk, without action, without social connections, Lawrence has devitalized Kangaroo. He is given no context in which to show his asserted personal charm, his aura, his power.

One of the odd aspects of Somers's attraction towards the Diggers is that the Diggers are a returned soldiers' organization. To ally himself with such a group is strange for a man who during the war 'would not enter the army, because his profoundest instinct was against it' (12:236). Psychologically, we see his allying himself now with returned soldiers as an effort to demonstrate that he is not a coward. Hence the appeal of the violence implicit in their organization. But the violence, the military-style coup planned, is also something appealing to him against Harriet's power. During the war he chose to stay with Harriet rather than fight. Now to assert his dominance, to prove he is not dependent on her, he will ally himself with the paramilitary.

And so Somers's insistence that his activity must be with men, asserting his manhood, readily becomes a homosexual camaraderie. And the homosexual is stressed. Talking to Somers about the Diggers, Jack clasps Somers's hand 'drawing the smaller man to him and putting his arm round his shoulders and holding him near to him' (5:103). 'Jack's eager, conspirator voice seemed very close to his ear, and it had a kind of caress, a sort of embrace' (5:104). When Jack and Somers quarrel, Harriet mocks, 'They might be man and wife' (15:316). A similar intimacy develops between Somers and Kangaroo. Whereas one of the reasons for the rejection of Struthers is clearly that Somers does not find him physically attractive; he tells Kangaroo:

> 'I don't like him physically — something thin and hairy and spiderish. I didn't want to touch him. But he's a force, he's *something*.'
> Kangaroo looked puzzled, and his face took a heavy, stupid look.
> 'He wouldn't want you to touch him,' he barked. 'He didn't offer to shake hands, did he?'
> 'No, thank goodness,' said Somers, thinking of the red, dry, thin-skinned hand. (11:228)

Like Birkin in *Women in Love*, Somers feels the need for a relationship with a man as well as with a woman; this is a necessity for fulfilment. And it is a mark of the failure for Somers of Kangaroo's promise that such a fulfilment is not forthcoming. Though the withdrawal is on Somers's part, not Kangaroo's. And it is unclear whether Somers withdraws because he is ultimately unable to commit himself to a homosexual relationship; whether he finds Kangaroo, as Struthers, not physically attractive enough (the insistence on Kangaroo's physical appearance supports this possibility); or whether he sees through the ideological confusions of Kangaroo, professing love but using violence.

Love is a recurrent term in *Kangaroo*. It relates the sexual and the marital directly to the political, since it is a key term in the ideologies of both Struthers and Kangaroo.

> Now Richard knew what Struthers wanted. He wanted this love, this mate-trust called into consciousness and highest honour.
> He wanted to set it where Whitman tried to set his Love of Comrades. It was to be the new tie between men, in the new

167

democracy. It was to be the new passional bond in the new society. The trusting love of a man for his mate. (11:219)

And after seeing Struthers, Somers is offered Kangaroo's variant on the love theme:

> the greatest danger to the world today is anarchy, not bolshevism. It is anarchy and unrule that are coming on us — and that is what I, as an order-loving Jew and one of the half-chosen people, do not want. I want one central principle in the world: the principle of love, the maximum of individual liberty, the minimum of human distress. (11:230)

Lawrence rejects both of them from a mistrust of the concept of love — and a mistrust of what it means in both of their vocabularies. In the first of his Talks at the Yenan Conference, 2 May 1942, Mao Tse-Tung provided a critical context in which to see the love slogan:

> a fundamental Marxist viewpoint is that existence determines consciousness, that is, the objective reality of class struggle and national struggle determines our thoughts and feelings. Some of our comrades, however, reverse the proper order of things and maintain that everything ought to start from love. Now as for love, in a class society there can be only class love; but these comrades are seeking a love that transcends the classes, love in the abstract as well as freedom in the abstract, truth in the abstract, human nature in the abstract, and so on. This shows that these comrades have been deeply influenced by the bourgeoisie. (82-3)

But Lawrence's exposures of the contradictions in Kangaroo's Digger ideology are made in the *sexual* area that 'love' relates to, not in the *class* area. Somers rejects Kangaroo as a political possibility not from a class analysis, not from a socio-political analysis, but from an analysis of his sexual nature and notation. The final revulsion from Jack and the Kangaroo-Digger ethic is one provoked by the sexual implications, not the political implications, of the bomb episode. For Lawrence the two are not separable. The sexual *is* the political.

From the beginning there have been clues about Jack: the bullet mounted on his mantelpiece — extracted from his throat — might hint at a certain glorification of military violence; at the very least it indicates an acceptance of it. Somers claims that Jack represents a new political feeling but Harriet replies, 'I very much doubt it. He's a returned war hero, and he wants a chance of keeping on being a hero — or something like that' (5:111). This indicates the military aspect of Jack; but more important is the effect on Jack of political discussion — he 'seemed as if he were a little bit drunk . . . . Strange, he seemed as if in a slight ecstasy' (3:53). And at the end of that particular discussion, Jack offends the Lawrentian taboos about sexual display, when Victoria comes into the room.

> Harriet started at the sudden revelation of palpitating intimacy. She wanted to go away, quick. So did Somers. But neither Jack nor Victoria wanted them to go.
> Jack was looking up at Victoria with a curious smile, touched with a leer. (3:55)

The sexuality — whether uninhibited or exhibitionism or an invitation to an orgy — frightens Somers and Harriet into bourgeois property-ownership anxieties. It is the hierarchical aspects of the Diggers that has fascinated Somers, not the mateship egalitarianism: the male bond, not the wife-swapping; suddenly it is all as promiscuous and libertarian as the intellectuals of *Women in Love*. In Lawrence's denotation, this episode clearly indicates there is something sexually amiss about Jack and the Diggers. Metaphors, fantastic speculations are suddenly offered as if actual modes of behaviour. The same pattern is repeated in the military-violence component of Jack's thought. His war-hero aspect, the excited response he feels to political discussion, give the hint to the way in which Jack can become a potentially frightening figure. His various aspects all find release after the bomb incident, when Lawrence's political speculations have to encounter the actualities of military-style coups, revolutionary violence. Jack works himself into a frenzy of killing.

> 'Tell you what, boy,' he said in a hoarse whisper, 'I settled *three* of 'em — three!' There was an indescribable gloating joy in his tones, like a man telling of the good time he has had with a strange mistress — 'Gawr, but I was lucky. I got one of them iron bars from the windows, and I stirred the brains of a couple of them with it, and I broke the neck of a third. Why it was as good as a sword to defend yourself with, see —'
> He reached his face towards Somers with weird, gruesome exultation, and continued in a hoarse, secret voice:
> 'Cripes, there's *nothing* bucks you up sometimes like killing a man — *nothing*. You feel a perfect *angel* after it.'

Richard felt the same torn feeling in his abdomen, and his eyes watched the other man.

'When it comes over you, you know, there's nothing else like it. *I* never knew, till the war. And I wouldn't believe it then, not for many a while. But it's *there*. Cripes, it's there right enough. Having a woman's something, isn't it? But it's a flea-bite, nothing, compared to killing your man when your blood comes up.'

And his eyes glowed with exultant satisfaction.

'And the best of it is,' he said, 'you feel a perfect *angel* after it. You don't feel you've done any harm. Feel as gentle as a lamb all round. I can go to Victoria, now, and be as gentle —' He jerked his head in the direction of Victoria's room. 'And you bet she'll like me.'

His eyes glowed with a sort of exaltation.

'Killing's natural to a man, you know,' he said. 'It is just as natural as lying with a woman. Don't you think?'

And still Richard did not answer. (16:351-2)

The sexual identity of murder for Jack — the phallic image of the iron bar like a sword, the blood coming up — suggest the final truth about the 'love' of Kangaroo's movement. Returned soldiers, military ethics, and 'love' combine for this hideous climax.

Lawrence's vision of, perhaps, some pure, Spartan, male-only intellectual and physical rule suddenly looks different in practice. Jack is suddenly the brutal soldier, off for a fuck after a good day's killing — not the abstract blood brother. For Jack the height of sexual ecstasy comes from, results from, killing. Kangaroo's reign of love is to come after the killing by Jack and the Diggers of opponents of the regime. The corruption is stressed not so much in the taking of life, as in the distortion of the sexual impulse; this is how Lawrence makes his emphasis; this provides confirmation for Somers of his rightness in not fighting in the war, and the determination to avoid revolutionary politics, to avoid all political involvements.

It has been a false apocalypse, the millennium has not begun. The parallels with Lawrence's commentary on *Apocalypse* are clear. In his commentary Lawrence pointed out

the division of the book into two halves, with two rather discordant intentions. The first half, before the birth of the baby Messiah, seems to have the intention of salvation and renewal, leaving the world to go on renewed. But the second half, when the Beasts rouse up, develops a weird and mystic hate of the world, of worldly power, and of everything and everybody who does not submit to the Messiah out and out. The second half of the Apocalypse is flamboyant hate and simple lust, lust is the only word, for the end of the world. (6:33)

Jack's sexual excitement at murder is the lust of Apocalypse, the lust for the end of the world, the slaughter to usher in the millennium. And the lamb sacrificed 'for the sake of a greater Resurrection,' that Lawrence discusses in his commentary (9:58), is the dying Kangaroo, already described in the novel as 'the lamb of God grown into a sheep' (6:127). But Jack Callcott is a false prophet, not a John the Baptist nor a John of Patmos, but plain Jack. And Kangaroo is not the Messiah.

Somers's rejection of any involvement with Jack and the Diggers is confirmed as the correct decision by these final events. The apocalypse does not occur: all that remains is the bestial killing, and the bathetic, futile bomb incident, irrelevant to the political situation. The message seems to be similar to that offered in *Nostromo* by Decoud: political commitment leads to disaster. But this is a message only for the immediate political possibilities. As Leavis comments, 'Harriet (or Frieda) is, in a sense, proved right about the particular political project, but Richard Lovat remains convinced that the impulsion that led him to contemplate it seriously represents something profoundly valid' (56). Lawrence arrived in New Mexico in September 1923, and then wrote the final chapter of *Kangaroo*. The novel ended on the note of a conclusive rejection of England and English systems as a political possibility. Britain, the British empire, are given the last farewell.

So, it was time to take out handkerchiefs and wave across space. Few people wept. Somers waved and waved his orange silk kerchief in the blue air. Farewell! Farewell! Farewell Victoria and Jaz's wife, farewell Australia, farewell Britain and the great Empire. Farewell! Farewell! The last streamers blowing away, like broken attachments, broken . . . . (18:393)

The novel originally ended at this point, but at the last moment Lawrence added a final page. It takes Harriet and Somers conclusively out of Sydney harbour and into the open ocean. They have left the political arena firmly behind and are now together; but they travel 'over a cold, dark inhospitable sea'. It is not an affirmative ending. Despite his return to the marital domestic world, Somers remains unfulfilled.

171

What has Lawrence-Somers rejected English-style politics and society in favour of? 'What Richard wanted was some sort of a new show: a new recognition of the life-mystery, a departure from the dreariness of money-making, money-having, and money spending' (16:334). The negation of bourgeois capitalist 'democracy' is clear enough. The positive aspects of the 'new show' are more ambiguous: Lawrence is playing with possibilities here — and some of the possibilities are those more dubious aspects of Lawrence's beliefs: the categorizations 'of one man meet for service and another man clean with glory, having majesty in himself'. We know which one Lawrence will be. The mockery about his leadership fantasies is dropped here.

It is easy to see these utterances as associating Lawrence with the fascist, the elitist, the authoritarian. That aspect is undeniable. But it is not the total aspect. It is also possible to see the radical component of his thinking. He refuses to accept the offered political possibilities as the only possibilities, he is determined to keep his mind open for new possibilities, to look for ways out of the political impasse. He refuses to commit himself to the inadequate, the false, the distorting political immediacies. He rejects Struthers and Kangaroo, both of them.

His disquisition on telepathic communication is central to his political vision.

This vertebral telepathy is the true means of communication between animals. It is perhaps most highly developed where the brain, the mental consciousness, is smallest. Indeed the two forms of consciousness, mental and vertebral, are mutually exclusive. The highest form of vertebral telepathy seems to exist in the great sperm whales. Communication between these herds of roving monsters is of marvellous rapidity and perfection. They are lounging, feeding lazily, individually, in mid-ocean, with no cohesion. Suddenly, a quick thought-wave from the leader-bull, and as quick as answering thoughts the cows and young bulls are ranged, the herd is taking its direction with a precision little short of miraculous. Perhaps water acts as a most perfect transmitter of vertebral telepathy. (16:329)

The last sentence indicates the determinedly *practical* nature of his speculations. Years later the US Navy was to experiment with telepathic communication in porpoises as a possible military weapon; if man shared that telepathic capacity, a new mode of communication could be evolved.

Development, evolution of this quality is what Lawrence considers. Why assume our existing modes of social-political communication are the only ones. Thought has not stopped, evolution of consciousness has not stopped. 'A rabbit might evolve into something which is still rabbit, and yet different from that which a rabbit now is' (16:324). He stresses that there are possibilities of thought, possibilities of social structuring, possibilities of communication, other than those few which we acknowledge. He refuses to accept the *logic* of Struthers's position as the final possibility. He insists on our remembering that new forms can evolve or be developed, history has shown that they have done.

> Well now. There is the dark god knocking afresh at the door. The vast mass hear nothing, but say: 'We know all about the universe. Our job it to make a real smart place of it.' So they make more aeroplanes and old-age pensions and are furious when Kaiser William interrupts them. The more sensitive hear something, feel a new urge and are uneasy . . . .

> And still, all the time, even in the vulgar uneducated — perhaps more in them than in the hearty money-makes of the lower middle classes — throb-throb-throb goes the god-urge deep in their souls, driving them almost mad. They are quite stone-deaf to any new meaning. They would jeer an attempt at a new interpretation, jeer it to death. So there they are, between the rocky Scylla of the fixed, established ideal, and the whirling Charybdis of the conservative opposition to this ideal. Between these two perils they must pass. For behind them drives the unknown current of the God-urge, on, on through the straits. (16:326-7)

He develops the Scylla and Charybdis image:

> the monster of humanity with a Scylla of an ideal of equality for the head, and a Charybdis of industrialism and possessive conservatism for the tail, howls with frenzy, and lashes the straits till every boat goes down, that tries to make a passage. (16:327)

It was applied in the previous chapter to the two conventional possibilities for the novel — romance and realism. Lawrence is trying to steer between them, through to a new undiscovered ocean for a new novel form for the new political forms.

As in *The Rainbow*, Lawrence is speculating on revolution. And he relates revolution to the emergence of a new consciousness breaking through the existing limited possibilities.

Break the balance of the two great controlling influences, and you get, not a simple preponderance of the one influence, but a third state, the mob-state. This is the state when the society, tribe, or herd degenerates into a mob. In man, the mind runs on with a sort of terrible automatism, which has no true connexion with the *vertebral* consciousness. The vertebral inter-communication gradually gathers force, apart from all mental expression. Its vibration steadily increases till there comes a sudden click! And then you have the strange phenomenon of revolution, like the Russian and the French revolutions. It is a great disruptive outburst. It is a great eruption against the classes in authority. And it is, finally, a passionate, mindless vengeance taken by the collective, vertebral psyche upon the authority of orthodox *mind*. In the Russian revolution it was the *educated* classes that were the enemy really: the deepest inspiration the hatred of the conscious classes. But revolution is not a mob-movement. Revolution has direction, and leadership, however temporary. There is point to its destructive frenzy.
In the end, it is a question with us today whether the masses will degenerate into mobs, or whether they will still keep a spark of direction. (16:331)

Both Kangaroo and Struthers represent limited, superimposed mental forms, restrictive and distortive of the full consciousness of man.

'Now, Kangaroo,' said Richard, 'is in a false position. He wants to save property for the property owners, and he wants to save Labour from itself and from the capitalist and the politician and all. In fact, he wants to save everything as we have it, and it can't be done. You can't eat your cake and have it, and I prefer Willie Struthers. Bolshevism is at least not sentimental. It's a last step towards an end, a hopeless end. But better disaster than an equivocal nothingness, like the present.' (16:334)

Again the Lawrentian apocalyptic note, the preference for a ritual, violent purgation, disaster, over the alienations of the present. At least disaster might release the vertebral consciousness; and a new show might be born. After the dictatorship of state socialism, then the withering away of the state. Lawrence's dynamic thinking is not incompatible with marxian dialectic; it is the conservatism of Kangaroo that Somers rejects, Kangaroo futilely trying to 'save everything as we have it, and it can't be done.'

Kangaroo moves away from specific political commitment; Somers refuses commitment, unlike the protagonists of those great nineteenth-century political novels like *Beauchamp's Career* or *Felix Holt*. But it does not share *Nostromo*'s total repudiation of politics. *Kangaroo* is concerned with abstaining from immediate commitments in order to make a commitment the new revolution when the time comes — the revolution in consciousness outside existing structures. It may not be possible in western industrial society — the surface structures of habits of thought, limited mental consciousness, may be too rigid for the vertebral consciousness to break through. But possibly non-industrialized societies, without a history of alienation, of repression by the capitalist machine, will be readier for the apocalyptic moment.

And then will burst out the new revolution, the destruction of old forms, the respect for the primacy of individual values — without which any social organization is valueless.

Form was a huge problem facing Lawrence in writing *Kangaroo*. *The Rainbow* within itself had formally superseded the old George Eliot-Thomas Hardy novel. Eliot and Hardy had been able to assume a scope and range and knowledgeability that by the early twentieth century seemed impossible. Lawrence had shown he could do it in the opening chapters of *The Rainbow*; but the mode is superseded within the book and the new mode of the Ursula materials emerges for the ending.

The mode of the opening of *The Rainbow* is a past mode used to describe a past era. It is beautiful, somewhat overblown, pastiche. With the continuation of *The Sisters* material in *Women in Love* Lawrence opened up the fictional possibilities considerably; yet that very opening up leads to a fragmentation. How can you write a novel of politics or society when your new mode is one of fragmentation. you can capture the alienations and fragmentations but you need more than that, you need some organic form to hold the materials in place; and if society is so fragmented as to have no organic form, where will it be found for fiction?

Lawrence plunges into the freedoms, the fragmentations. There is no point in faking past forms. He plunges into the new and works from two principles: affront and spontaneity. 'All great mass uprisings,' Somers meditates,

175

are really acts of vengeance against the dominant consciousness
of the day. It is the dynamic, vertebral consciousness in man
bursting up and smashing through the fixed, superimposed
mental consciousness of mankind, which mental consciousness
has degenerated and become automatic. (16:331)

It is the note of dada and surrealism. Revolution and revolutionary
art must be an affront on the dominant consciousness of the day,
the educated classes, on the bourgeoisie. By confronting the negation you might break straight through into a new form.

And this celebration of the subconscious, or the vertebral psyche,
is in literary terms the celebration of automatic writing, found
objects, collage, accident, spontaneous writing. You take up whatever is at hand; you use the random and unexpected and unplanned
materials. You sit down each day and write 3,000 words a day for
six weeks, not knowing what will come next, knowing you want
to write your views and feelings and meditations on political possibility, not knowing anything much about the country you are living
in, but incorporating whatever you find out whenever you happen to
find it out. The novel had to be finished in time to catch a boat from
Sydney to San Francisco. It is like the experiments in automatic
writing which Malcolm Cowley describes in *Exile's Return*: you
work to a set time-scale — three hours — and write continually
through that, and then stop. Lawrence had his political theme, his
daily ration of words, his cut-off point, and his fluency from years
of writing. And he wrote. It is different from Kerouac's spontaneous
writing, in that Kerouac was recreating past experiences: the spontaneity of Kerouac's work was a way of recapturing the spontaneity
of the lived experiences. It was a spontaneity of expression. Lawrence
is like this in the long war-time flashback, 'The Nightmare'. But
Lawrence is also having to create fictional incidents, characters,
events. He is projecting himself and his ideas into a new environment
he does not know — an environment he discovers fictionally at the
same time — even before? — he discovers it in his afternoon walks
and his forays to the barber's shop at Thirroul.

In *Kangaroo*, then, Lawrence is drawing on the resources of dada
and surrealism, on the modernist commitments to spontaneity.
Naturally, the form of *Kangaroo* has found as few admirers as its
political meditation. Middleton Murry called it 'a chaotic book. It
has many passages of great descriptive beauty, but internally it is a
chaos' (238). Julian Moynahan said that 'from a formal point of
view the book is a heap of bits and fragments blown about on air
currents of emotion' (101). W.W. Robson assured us 'A judicious

admirer of Lawrence will not cite *Aaron's Rod* or *Kangaroo* as triumphs of originality of form. They are meandering, repetitious, padded-out' (268). Leavis remarked that the two novels,

> though very much open to criticism as novels and works of art, are yet most impressively the work of a novelist of genius; they are full of life and interest. Nevertheless, I put them apart from the works that show Lawrence's full creative power and on which his position as one of the greatest of all novelists is firmly based. (30)

In so far as *Kangaroo* is conceded as having power, it has been apart from, separate from, even despite, its form: a strange and unlikely concept. Yet no one stops to think, if the book conveys this power, maybe that is the result of the way it is written (what else?), maybe its form is indeed the appropriate form to convey that force.

Lawrence's formal innovations in his novels have long been recognized. His early letter to Edward Garnett is often cited for its statement of his theories of formal organization:

> Don't look for the development of the novel to follow the lines of certain characters: the characters fall into the form of some other rhythmic form, as when one draws a fiddle-bow across a fine tray delicately sanded, the sand takes lines unknown. (5 June 1914) (*The Collected Letters*, I:282)

Yet even those critics who are able to accept this formulation for the structure of the earlier novels, resist *Kangaroo*. Its rhythmic form is harder to detect. And Lawrence's letters mentioning *Kangaroo* imply that its formal qualities are different from his previous works. The gentler smoother regular rhythms of seed time and harvest are no longer the rhythms he is using. The modern world is more cut across, more disrupted.

'Heaven knows if anybody will like it,' he writes to his American publisher Thomas Seltzer; 'no love interest at all so far — don't intend any — no sex either' (9 June 1922) (*Letters to Seltzer*, 34-5). 'Funny sort of novel where nothing happens and such a lot of things *should* happen,' he writes to Catherine Carswell (22 June) (*The Collected Letters*, II:711). 'Even the *Ulysseans* will spit at it,' he writes to Koteliansky (9 July) (*The Collected Letters*, II:722). All the letters stress how the writing is 'going well'. Any peculiarities of form or disruption of form should not be put down to Lawrence's encountering difficulties, blocks or recalcitrant materials. The development and change in the nature of *Kangaroo* from his earlier work was conscious and deliberate. And the reference to the '*Ulysseans*' indicates his sense of the experimental nature of his new work; but it is an experimentalism 'even' they will spit at. It will not have the ordered, stylized, worked over, carefully woven structure of Joyce's novel. Its experimentalism will be in the line of the spontaneity of the dadaists, the surrealists and the beats. It is a tradition that will offend not only the Joycean avant-garde, but also the conservative realists; without action where there 'should' be action, without plot, love interest or sex, no wonder he wrote to Seltzer, 'I don't suppose you'll like it a bit' (18 July) (*Letters to Seltzer*, 40).

Lawrence comments within the novel on *Kangaroo*'s lack of action. It is an unusual intrusion for Lawrence, for any novelist at that time, when such nineteenth-century features were taboo for the 'modern'. But Lawrence has moved on beyond that conception of the modern — even if his critics haven't: Harry T. Moore complains that 'parts of the book repeat one of the faults of *Aaron's Rod* — the author's tendency to stop and chat colloquially with the reader' (218).

Lawrence first entered in chapter 14, 'Bits'. The novel's halting progress, leading towards events that never occur, came to an abrupt stop in chapter 12, 'The Nightmare', when the Australian political theme was suddenly dropped for the long account of the First World War years, the scarcely altered autobiography of Lawrence's experiences in Britain. The following chapter, 13, continued with this material, brooding on those experiences and relating their memory to the immediate Australian political context. With chapter 14 the reader expects the story to be picked up, expects to see what happens now that Somers has rejected the political appeals of both Struthers and Kangaroo. Instead, Lawrence offers 'Bits', a scrap book of cuttings from the Sydney weekly *The Bulletin* of unbelievable triviality, followed by Harriet's reactions to Australia. That Lawrence is not simply padding, as for instance William Tiverton asserts (64), marking time while he thinks how to develop his novel from its action's impasse, is suggested by the description of Harriet 'on the sofa, covered with an eiderdown, and reading a Nat Gould novel, to get the real tang of Australia' (14:306). Not many of Lawrence's readers would also be readers of Nat Gould, the popular novelist of the turf who lived for ten years in Australia, a non-literary figure definitely not for the *Ulysseans*. But the brief mention of him is one of the indications that Lawrence here is brooding on the problem of the appropriate form for his novel. When Harriet finishes the book she says, 'It's just like them — just like they *think* they are' (14:307). To capture Australia, is the Nat Gould type of novel, with its simple black and white structure of contrasts, and its strong story line, the appropriate form? A page later Lawrence announces, 'Now a novel is supposed to be a mere record of emotion-adventures, flounderings in feelings. We insist that a novel is, or should be, also a thought-adventure, if it is to be anything at all complete' (14:308). But thought-adventures produce a different sort of novel — Somers 'preached, and the record was taken down for this gramophone of a novel' (14:309). The tone shifts in these intrusions from the committed didactic to the defensively dissocia-tively ironic, ending up parodying and yet employing the Victorian novelist's 'dear reader' trope. 'I hope, dear reader, you like plenty of *conversation* in a novel: it makes it so much lighter and brisker' (14:311). The conversation is of Somers talking to himself.

These interjections are, as the chapter's title indicates, 'bits'. But the next chapter opens with two paragraphs of sustained comment on the novel's form.

Chapter follows chapter, and nothing doing. But a man is a thought-adventurer, and his falls into the Charybdis of ointment, and his shipwrecks on the rock of ages, and his kisses across chasms, and his silhouette on a minaret: surely these are as thrilling as most things.

To be brief, there was a Harriet, a Kangaroo, a Jack and a Jaz and a Vicky, let alone a number of mere Australians. But you know as well as I do that Harriet is quite happy rubbing her hair with hair-wash and brushing it over her forehead in the sun and looking at the threads of gold and gun-metal, and the few threads, alas, of silver and tin, with admiration. And Kangaroo has just got a very serious brief, with thousands and thousands of pounds at stake in it. Of course he is fully occupied keeping them at stake, till some of them wander into his pocket. And Jack and Vicky have gone down to her father's for the week-end, and he's out fishing, and has already landed a rock-cod, a leather-jacket, a large schnapper, a rainbow-fish, seven black-fish, and a cuttle-fish. So what's wrong with him? While she is trotting over on a pony to have a look at an old sweetheart who is much too young to be neglected. And Jaz is arguing with a man about the freight-rates. And all the scattered Australians are just having a bet on something or other. So what's wrong with Richard's climbing a mental minaret or two in the interim? Of course there isn't any interim. But you *know* that Harriet is brushing her hair in the

179

sun, and Kangaroo looking at huge sums of money on paper, and Jack fishing, and Vicky flirting and Jaz bargaining, so what more do you want to know? We can't be at a stretch of tension *all* the time, like the E string on a fiddle. If you don't like the novel, don't read it. If the pudding doesn't please you, leave it, leave it. *I* don't mind your saucy plate. I know too well that you can bring an ass to water, etc. (15:312-3)

And then he goes straight into Somers's thought-adventures again.

The tone is consciously unpretentious, even dismissive. The violin is called a fiddle — which could be contemptuous, or it could be the professional's term; the language of the craft, not of the alienated, mystified audience. The novel is compared to a pudding, which again could be contemptuous, like Henry James referring to the loose baggy monsters of Russian fiction, or it could be the realistic vision of someone who likes puddings.

The itemization of Jack's fishing catch makes its point about how boring and irrelevant it would be to fill the book with the trivial detail of bourgeois naturalism. Yet Lawrence at the same time uses those boring details in a dadaist way; he gives us an inexorable list of the fish. Suddenly it becomes amazingly interesting put in that absurd way. And Victoria going off to some old lover who is too young to be let languish? This is an item of that alternative fictional possibility to realism, romance. The earlier reference to Nat Gould and the novel of 'emotion-adventures' shows the other sort of novel Lawrence is avoiding, the romantic adventure with its strong 'plot'. But by putting plot suggestions in the dadaist anti-novel list, Lawrence gets the excitement of plot renewed again. So we have romantic possibilities and naturalistic details, both of them subsumed into being mere items of a dadaist list, the new fictional form that has superseded realism and romance.

This same categorization of the novel's two conventional extremes (naturalism and romantic adventure) and the same explicit intrusion into a novel to explain the avoidance of either of these courses we have noted in Meredith's *Beauchamp's Career*. An intrusion by the novelist was less disruptive to the novel's form in the 1870s than in the 1920s. But Meredith's comments were as disruptive, as revolutionary, as Lawrence's. Both of them are brooding over the problems of writing about politics in fiction; both of them are brooding over the nature of political action — is there any action that can be comprehended fictionally — is politics accessible to fictional analysis? Or does the fiction writer get fobbed off with or caught up with deliberate mystifications thrown out by the political people to obscure the nature of political power?

The aspect that is particularly remarkable is the avoidance by Meredith and Lawrence of external action. 'Chapter follows chapter, and nothing doing', Lawrence writes; and Meredith commented similarly, 'I am bound to forewarn readers of this history that there is no plot in it' (4:33). The essence of *Beauchamp's Career* is anti-climax, bathos; as it is of *Kangaroo*, a 'novel where nothing happens and such a lot of things *should* happen'. Politics 'should' be exciting and things 'should' happen in a political novel, conventionally. But for Meredith and Lawrence, this is not so. Indeed, Lawrence offers even less than Meredith: at least Nevil Beauchamp is shown trying to convert people to radicalism; whereas Somers's whole progress is away from conversion or commitment or action, an escape from the immediate political world. Somers finds no existing political position tenable. Political action, in the conventional political alignments, is futile, pointless, valueless. The external action in *Kangaroo* is non-existent, except where it is bathetic, because Lawrence is concerned to devalue the existing political possibilities. Somers arrives in Australia disenchanted with democracy – and his attitudes are paralleled in Lawrence's own letters from Australia. He wrote to Else Jaffe:

This is the most democratic place I have *ever* been in. And the more I see of democracy the more I dislike it. It just brings everything down to the mere vulgar level of wages and prices, electric light and water closets, and nothing else. You *never* knew anything so nothing, *nichts, nullus, niente*, as the life here. (13 June 1922) (*The Collected Letters*, II:707)

Once in Australia Somers is offered two alternatives to bourgeois democracy: Kangaroo's paramilitary Digger movement planning an armed take-over of Australia, and Struthers's socialism. Revolutionary politics represent the opposite of the slow process of speech-making, canvassing, persuasion that Meredith put as central to the political life.

But the issue of conversion, the theme of the individual's commitment, remains the basic action for the novel of politics. Somers is to be persuaded of the value of political activity (having in his rejection of democracy also rejected most of his concern with mankind), and the value of revolution. The novel's 'thought-adventure' is the attempted conversion, by others and by himself, of Somers to political involvement and, more specifically, to revolutionary politics.

Elections could be shown by the bourgeois realist, revolutions by

181

the romantic story writer; Meredith puts elections central to *Beauchamp's Career* to show how absurd and ridiculous they were; there were elections taking place in Australia at the time Lawrence was there, but they find no counterpart in the novel. Lawrence puts a revolutionary act at the climax of his novel; a bomb is thrown at a socialist meeting, fighting breaks out, people are killed, Kangaroo is fatally wounded; but it comes to nothing. There is neither a spontaneous revolutionary uprising nor are there repressive countermeasures. The political world remains unchanged. It all fizzles down, to use the reductive verb Lawrence used. For the bombs and revolutionary plans of existing political leaders are of no interest to Lawrence; they are as distant from true revolution as are the elections; and as irrelevant as the elections to true political power.

Kangaroo presents conventional political involvement and revolutionary political action as pointless, petty, incompetent, bathetic and banal. The true revolution has not yet arisen from the *zeitgeist*, the vertebral consciousness, the subconscious of society, the apocalyptic moment. The significant bomb, as Anais Nin points out (126-7), was Somers himself. Somers broods:

> I don't really like Kangaroo. The devil in me fairly hates him. Him and everybody. Well, all right then, if I *am* finally a sort of human bomb, black inside, and primed; I hope the hour and the place will come for my going off: for my exploding with the maximum amount of havoc. *Some* men have to be bombs, to explode and make breaches in the walls that shut life in. Blind, havoc-working bombs too. Then so be it. (8:184)

The inconsequent action, the lack of plot, has its meaning in the political scheme; conventional politics are inconsequent. We see Somers arrive in Australia, gradually come to know his neighbours, the Callcotts, become interested in Jack Callcott's schemes, and meet Kangaroo, leader of the Diggers. But instead of any further development at this point in the external narrative, there is stasis. Somers broods over Kangaroo's views, struggles with the conflicting demands of politics and marriage, meets Struthers, meets Kangaroo again. And again, instead of resolution or development, the narrative remains halted and we are given the lengthy chapter of flashback about the First World War. When we return to the present, it is to the perfunctory episode of the bomb outrage, to which Somers is merely an onlooker, which results in nothing, and after which Somers leaves the country. And in addition to this unresolved movement of the novel, this direction towards commitment and

action which is never resolved or fulfilled, there are red herrings like
the end of chapter 3. Somers, having set the rat traps, goes into the
garden for a last look at the moon. He hears a car arrive next door at
the Callcotts', a man 'giving a peculiar whistle' who 'went round to
the back door and knocked sharply, once, twice, in a peculiar way.
Then he whistled and knocked again' (3:58). It is Jaz conspiratori-
ally visiting Jack. Sinister, 'significant', this is an episode whose note
is dropped from the novel and the expectations of adventure and
mystery aroused here are never fulfilled. There is a similar bathetic
note over-all in the treatment of Jaz, William James Trewellah. We
are told in chapter 2 he married his brother's widow, and has a
Cornish mystery about him; in chapter 4 he visits Harriet to tell her
and Somers not to get involved with the Diggers; and he is shown in
an ambiguous relationship with both the Diggers and the socialists,
this presumably prompting Kangaroo to say of him that he is an
'instinctive traitor' (11:229). But nothing happens, he never does
anything, he never develops; but stands watching. As far as plot, as
far as external narrative is concerned, he is an excrescence. But for
the thought-drama he is necessary; he is one of the necessary components of the political novel: the potential traitor — or, the potential idealist spy. Exactly what he is is never clear, except that he is
mysterious and not to be trusted. But for the process of Somers's
arguments as to whether he should commit himself to political
involvement, then he is a necessary component of the traditional
revolutionary scene.

The novel's form repudiates available political action, presents it
as either bathetic or futile. But by undercutting the materials of
conventional narrative, it elevates the drama of the consciousness
above action, plot, conventional story. *Positively*, the form represents the movement of Somers's thought-adventure, his arguments,
the meditation on politics. Middleton Murry made this point,
though in a pejorative way: 'the internal chaos of *Kangaroo* is the
internal chaos of Richard Lovat Somers, who is Lawrence. It is
impossible that he should be a character any more. He is exploded
in fragments. Nothing in his being, at the end of the book, is more
important than anything else' (238). But that could be seen as a
great breakthrough, a demystification of false hierarchies of value.

The drama is the flux of Somers's views, his attraction to and
withdrawal from politics, his shifting between his reactions to the
demagogue-led bourgeois democracy of wartime Britain, to bourgeois democracy in general, to the idea of any political action, his
balancing the values of marriage and of social engagement. This is
why the most important chapter of the book — chapter 12, 'The

Nightmare' — is one unconnected with the 'story', unconnected with Australia and the direct political problem confronting Somers, but returning to his experience in wartime Britain.

In terms of a conventional structure for a novel, the nightmare chapter is an excrescence. It is, moreover, clumsily sewn into the book, as if Lawrence had insufficient faith in his thought-adventure formulation and wanted to integrate the chapter into the conventional narrative:

> Memory of all this came to him so violently now in the
> Australian night, that he trembled helplessly under the shock
> of it. He ought to have gone up to Jack's place for the night.
> But no, he could not speak to anybody. Of all the black
> throng in the dark Sydney streets, he was the most remote.
> He strayed round in a torture of fear, and then at last suddenly
> went to the Carlton Hotel, got a room, and went to bed, to be
> alone and think. (12:286)

After fifty pages on wartime England, this specifying of 'Australia', 'Sydney' and the 'Carlton Hotel' does not re-establish the Sydney setting; instead it draws attention to the contrivance of placing this nightmare into a particular time and place — trying to make the thought-drama part of a narrative drama.

Lawrence is simply perfunctory about it. He feels the need to make a narrative connection, but it is made as simply and quickly as possible. The need to make a narrative connection might possibly indicate a momentary, rare loss of faith in pure thought-adventure; but the perfunctoriness of the connection shows a happy use of his modernist aesthetic; if you need to do something, just do it. That is his basic procedure: that, and refusing the temptations of 'art' form. He refuses to structure Somers's thoughts into any neatness of predetermined pattern. Middleton Murry called Somers's mind a 'chaos', and certainly by avoiding the imposition of an arbitrary structure, Lawrence has laid himself open to this charge; he avoids patterning the changing attitudes of Somers to political life — of producing something like that figure eight pattern which Forster notes in *The Ambassadors*, or of following some mythic sequence. His comment that the *Ulysseans* will not like *Kangaroo* is relevant here. He is avoiding shaping his political material into anything approaching a recognized artistic form; he avoids fulfilling the formal expectations of the adventure romance or of the bourgeois realist novel; he avoids the symmetrical patterning of the thought-drama, or any mythic overlay.

What we notice about the novel's form are the continuous disruptions of whatever is momentarily achieved. Lawrence is suspicious of the values of 'art'. Caudwell has indicated something of the rationale behind this position:

It is inevitable that at this stage the conception of the artist as a pure 'artist' must cease to exist. For commercialized art has become intolerably base and negated itself. And equally art for art's sake (that is, the ignoring of the market and concentration on the perfect art work as a goal in itself) has negated itself, for the art form has ceased to exist, and what was art has become private phantasy. It is for this reason that since artists, such as Lawrence, Gide, Romain Rolland, Romains and so on, cannot be content with the beautiful art work, but seem to desert the practice of art for social theory and become novelists of ideas, literary prophets and propaganda novelists. They represent the efforts of bourgeois art, exploded into individualistic phantasy and commercialized muck, to become once more a social process and so be reborn. Whether such art is or can be great art is beside the point, since it is inevitably the pre-requisite for art becoming art again . . . . (48)

Instead of creating an autonomous work of art, Lawrence continually turns away from the aesthetically expected. The bathetic features of abandoned plot lines, the authorial intrusions, and the close relationship of Somers to Lawrence that allows Kangaroo to slip easily from fiction into autobiography, essay, harangue, and rave — all take *Kangaroo* away from the expected modes of fiction. Lawrence continually pegs the novel down to the everyday, the immediate unshaped experience of life. He incorporates an article on volcanoes from the Sydney *Daily Telegraph*, and snippets from *The Bulletin* to disrupt any tendency of the novel to achieve a neat and autonomous art shape. They disrupt the fictional form in order to relate the book directly to outward society. They are a response to the aesthetic of spontaneity, found objects, randomness as a mode of social perception, collage. They resist the hermetic tendency of the novel — whether a hermeticism of form (as in *Ulysses*) or of plot (as in Nat Gould), cutting off the novelist from social and political interests.

This novel is about politics, so this novel's form will not be hermetic and autonomous, but reaching into and absorbing the documentary. Critics have always praised the evocation of the Australian scenery, the bush especially, in *Kangaroo*. Richard

Aldington remarked that *'au fond, Kangaroo* is a travel book like *Sea and Sardinia'* (256). But the establishment of the bush should not be seen in isolation; it is only one aspect of the documentary; there is also the urban description of the Australian ugliness that, as Lawrence saw, becomes so expressive, transcends the concept of 'ugly'; and there is also the pasted-in journalism, catching certain of the quality of Australian life. Leavis remarked in *D.H. Lawrence: Novelist* that

> *Kangaroo* might be described as a day-dream in which he tests the idea of his becoming a leader in political action — might, if 'day-dream' didn't suggest an indulgence in irresponsible fantasy and an evasion of the conditions of real life. Actually, imagining, in this fiction, is rather an exposure of the idea to something like the full test of reality. (55-6)

Lawrence's day-dreaming is never without context. The fantasies are generated from found objects around.

The direct presentation of argument and information have generally been seen as the flat spots, the bad patches, the longueurs of *Kangaroo*. In chapter 5, 'Coo-ee', Jack describes the beliefs and organizations of the Digger clubs. The previous chapters have been leading up to this: Jaz's mysterious visit to Jack; the careful conversations glancing at politics. The build-up has been conventional and effective. Now Lawrence sets the simple conveying of information to Somers in a visual context, stressing beforehand the power of the sea:

> The sea's edge was smoking with the fume of the waves like a mist, and the high shore ahead, with the few painted red-roofed bungalows, was all dim, like a Japanese print. Tier after tier of white-frost foam piled breaking towards the shore, in a haste. The tide was nearly high. Somers could hardly see beyond over the white wall-tops of the breaking waves, only on the clear horizon, far away, a steamer like a small black scratch, and a fantastic thread of smoke. (5:37-8)

The sea blots out the shore almost totally, reduces a steamer to a scratch; when Jack starts to talk to Somers 'they had to shout at one another in unnaturally lifted voices, because of the huge noise of the sea' (5:100). The sea frames the political revelation, places it as trivial, transient, ephemeral in the movement of the cosmos. The setting itself is only sketched in; there is little more — but there are seven pages of Jack's explication, which are not made any more dramatic by such interjections as what, yes, heaven knows from Somers. There is no great emphasis on the setting here; it is evoked with minimal strokes; but it creates a critical perspective on the Digger fantasies. And the details of the fantasies are presented as directly as possible by Jack.

In the following chapter, 'Kangaroo', Jack takes Somers to meet Kangaroo and there is another long conversation piece — condemned by the critics. In one edition, James Gribble remarks that the 'long dialogues between Kangaroo and Somers [are] simply not assimilated into the novel' (383). He sees a disjunction, moreover, between Kangaroo at this first meeting, and the Kangaroo whom Somers visits to tell him he will not join his movement in chapter 11. 'In keeping with the first five chapters he is a colonial politician and in keeping with the following chapters he is a nightmare projection of Somers's mind. These two senses of Kangaroo don't coalesce, but conflict' (384). Keith Sagar has complained that 'Somers' quarrel with Kangaroo is not presented on the same level as his quarrels with Harriet or Jack, not convincingly enacted. His position has to be stated in the form of interpolated essays' (134). Lawrence the innovator is forgotten in these too-ready applications of the familiar critical tools. The complexity of irony, ambiguity, and the multi-lateral is the accepted literary complexity; it is a static model. Lawrence is aiming at a different and a freer complexity. He is not concerned with simultaneous multi-laterality: if it happens, good it happens; he doesn't *exclude* it, pare things away; but he does not seek it out. His mode is linear, his concern is the flux, the spontaneous rhythmic wave. Lawrence wants flux and change, not a stasis subsuming all possibilities. His is a dynamic aesthetic. He works from simple components, but to establish the flux and change he needs bulk to operate in. The flux of Somers's reactions, the complexity of his responses, emerges in the course of the long conversations. Jack, for instance, conveys simple information, linearly, one bit after another. Somers's emotional reactions to Jack are similarly linear, strung out in a process.

Somers was in a dilemma. Did he want to mix and make with this man? One part of him perhaps did. But not a very big part . . . . (6:119)

All his life he had cherished a beloved ideal of friendship — David and Jonathan. And now, when true and good friends offered, he found he simply could not commit himself, even to simple friendship. (6:119)

Yet he wanted *some* living fellowship with other men; as it was he was just isolated. (6:120)

He would never pledge himself to Jack, not to this venture in which Jack was concerned. (6:120)

There is the same flux of emotion in Somers's reaction to Kangaroo:

The luncheon passed frivolously. Somers was bored, but he had a shrewd suspicion that the other two men really enjoyed it. (6:122)

Kangaroo smiled slowly. And when he smiled like that, there came an exceedingly sweet charm into his face, for a moment his face was like a flower. Yet he was quite ugly. (6:123)

His face, with that odd look of a sheep or a kangaroo, took on an extraordinary beauty of its own, a glow as if it were suffused with light. (6:127)

This rather wicked idea came into Somers's mind: the lamb of God grown into a sheep. (6:127)

And yet even his body had become beautiful, to Somers — one might love it intensely, every one of its contours, its roundnesses and downward-drooping heaviness. (6:127)

The voice, slightly fat, very agreeable. Somers thrilled to it as he had never thrilled.
  'Why, the man is like a god, I love him', he said to his astonished self. (6:128)

The flux of attitudes, of withdrawls and commitments, occurs throughout the novel. Julian Moynahan complains of Somers that: 'from the beginning of his association with Kangaroo he lets the man think he may be able to commit himself eventually to the movement when he knows full well he will never commit himself' (106). But this is a misreading of the novel, and a misreading of Lawrence's method. Moynahan has taken one of the seemingly final statements in the novel out of its context of flux and possibility:

the statement that Somers 'would never pledge himself to Jack, nor to this venture'; but none of the statements in *Kangaroo* has finality, they are in continual flux. By not recognizing Lawrence's concern to present Somers's continually shifting attitudes, by not recognizing that statements of final intention are of final intention only at that particular moment of the novel and are likely to be changed later, *Kangaroo* has been much misrepresented.

The committedly linear flux of the novel creates problems for the reader approaching with other preconceptions. There are problems, especially for those who assume that the novelist must dramatize, or work through patterns of imagery. The conversations in *Kangaroo* tend to have no overriding image. Graham Hough sees it as a cause for failure in the novel

> that Lawrence has no adequate symbolism to hand, and in the atmosphere of rather easy-going everyday realism in which most of this book moves, it is practically impossible for him to devise one. Some of the conversations between Somers and Kangaroo are vaguely reminiscent of the Grand Inquisitor dialogue, which had always exercised a negative fascination on Lawrence, but the grotesque figure of Kangaroo himself is more like Chesterton's Man who was Thursday, to whom, I cannot help feeling, this part of Kangaroo owes something. The fact that Lawrence can fall back on these grotesque *espiègleries* shows that his imagination has not risen to the level of his task. (135)

Hough's objection is wrongheaded. Lawrence has come to suspect the single subsuming image, the coherent pattern of imagery, because these distort. Kangaroo shifts in appearance, aura, nature to Somers throughout the book, just as everything else shifts: Australia becomes ugly, repellent, attractive, beautiful. The image is generally too static a method of procedure. When it is used, it is used glancingly, evanescently — the sea framing the discussion between Jack and Somers in chapter 5. But in the Kangaroo episodes, Lawrence wants a direct (and shifting) confrontation: a direct exchange of opinions, of political attitudes. Critics brought up in the Jamesian dramatize or perish school have objected. Lawrence presents his discussions directly, in the way the newspaper cuttings are transcribed directly. Lawrence wants us to engage with the arguments, not to be diverted by the creation of neat fictions. There is almost no visual component in the Kangaroo discussions. There is some perfunctory description of Kangaroo's rooms, the 'handsome jarrah furniture, dark and suave, and some very beautiful rugs' (6:120), the study's 'big, deep leather chairs of a delicate brown colour' (6:123), but these create no strong visual impression. And when Somers visits Struthers in chapter 11, there is no description at all of the setting of their discussion.

Lawrence wants a direct exchange of opinion because he is writing a novel of political ideas; the ideas are a major component of the novel, not something to be hidden. *Kangaroo*, like Jack London's *The Iron Heel*, has been much misunderstood by critical commentators. The priority of political ideas, political discussion, has indeed upset the *Ulysseans*. Moreover, both London and Lawrence were concerned with *revolution*; how can a traditional and conventional novel form deal with what is new in politics? *Kangaroo* is dealing with the revolutionary — the abortive and false revolution which the Diggers offer, and the revolution in the individual consciousness which Somers is groping towards. So in so far as there was any nineteenth-century tradition of political fiction, Lawrence is rejecting its modes. In its progress *Kangaroo* has systematically disqualified itself as a political novel in conventional terms. The omission of the relationships between society and the political structures, the adoption of an alien as its central figure, the disregard of the actual pressures of citizenship and nationality, of economic factors and social classes — all these aspects put *Kangaroo* in a position of tension in relation to the traditional political novels. It is formally revolutionary. One of the limitations of *Felix Holt* for instance as a political novel is that, though subtitled 'the Radical', there is nothing radical about the form expressing the radicalism; it moves on the conventional apparatus of a love interest, of the will, of illegitimacy — the standard props of Victorian fiction; and not only are they traditional but they are unrelated to the political radicalism which is ostensibly the novel's theme.

In *Kangaroo* the flux, the change, the shifting ideas, the relativity of values that Somers struggles with, are represented in the novel's form. It is not a matter of the imitative fallacy; Lawrence is being exploratory, not merely imitative of Somers's thought processes. *Kangaroo* ends with a fugue, the recurrent Lawrentian flight, instead of participation. But the impulse to commitment, to political activity remains. On they sail. Despite the numerous potential disqualifications for *Kangaroo's* acceptance as a traditional political novel, it is properly to be read as a political novel because of its rejection of those conventional terms, and because of its one strong concern — the impulse towards political action. It is concerned with the basic issues of commitment and conversion. It attempts to relate the political to the domestic. And it does not offer a final statement. Its whole form of flux precludes its doing that. It is more a running commentary on the impulse to political commitment.

6

Darkness at Noon

A central feature of the political novel is the dialogue on politics. Gulliver talking with the King of Brobdingnag or with his houyhnhnm master, the narrator of *News from Nowhere* talking with Old Hammond, Richard Lovat Somers talking with Jack Callcott, Struthers and Kangaroo in *Kangaroo*: these discussions provide for the central political issues to be raised, considered, advocated and qualified. Amidst the dramatized action, the political issues are given explicit treatment.

This central dialogue depends on the assumption of an equality of position; not necessarily an intellectual or ethical or social equality — Gulliver's dialogues are designed to show discrepancies in just such areas — but an equality in free expression. The assumption is that each participant in the discussion has an equal right to his or her beliefs, and to the free expression of them.

But not all political situations are based on that assumption. How free are free societies? Jack London has Professor Cunningham's book suppressed in *The Iron Heel*: Ernest can give his political speech freely enough to the Philomaths — but soon he is in gaol. An interest in political novels of totalitarian societies develops as soon as doubts about the realities of the freedoms of free societies begin to develop. *The Iron Heel* and *Kangaroo* prepared the way for the acceptance of a novel like Arthur Koestler's *Darkness at Noon* (1940). The right could promote it as a shock revelation about what goes on under totalitarian socialism; others could wonder whether it was in fact *that* different from the politics of so called free societies. How many steps would it take?

The total situation of *Darkness at Noon* — not just the central episodes, but the totality — is an inquisition. The political issues arise from interrogation, not from free discussion. And this situational shift from free discussion to inquisition is soon taken up in the English political novel — notably in *Nineteen Eighty-four*. The shift at first sight marks a shift in political thinking, in political attitude. The political novel has moved from its preoccupation with the problems of bourgeois democracy, to exploring totalitarian societies. Yet it would be hard to assess whether over-all there was more totalitarianism in the twentieth century than in the nineteenth century. This preoccupation with totalitarian systems is predominantly the work of opponents of the Soviet Union. Whatever their original motives for such an opposition (whether a fear of socialism, or a belief that the revolution was betrayed) their hostility is directed primarily to post-revolutionary Russia. 'The central event of our century remains the Russian Revolution', Irving Howe writes (203): 'The contrast between early political hope and later disillusion becomes the major theme of the twentieth century political novel: Malraux, Silone, Koestler — all are obsessed by the failure, or betrayal, of the revolution' (205). John Strachey makes a similar point about the importance of Koestler's fiction in the literature of this century, though from a vastly different perspective; *Darkness at Noon* is 'the starting point of the literature of reaction', he wrote in *The Strangled Cry* (22).

The recurrent fictional analogy for the interrogation in the novels of this genre is one that suggests, however, not that the political world has entered a new phase, but that it is merely re-enacting history. There has been no change, merely cyclical repetition. The Spanish Inquisition serves as the standard analogy for the interrogations of the Stalin purges. In Zamyatin's *We* (1920), one of the earliest reactions to post-1917 society, a futuristic projection of tendencies already present, the comparison of the secret police to the Inquisition is presented as already a cliché: 'About five centuries ago, when the work of the Operations Department was only beginning, there were yet to be found some fools who compared our Operation Department with the ancient Inquisition' (15:77). And the analogy is implicitly present in the recurrent Christian metaphors and allusions throughout *Darkness at Noon*: 'No. 1's regime has besmirched the ideal of the Social State even as some medieval Popes had besmirched the ideal of a Christian Empire' (IV:2:205-6). Indeed the religious analogues are drawn from even earlier times.

'*Apage Satanas!*' repeated Ivanov and poured himself out another glass. 'In old days, temptation was of carnal nature. Now it takes the form of pure reason. The values change. I would like to write a Passion play in which God and the Devil dispute for the soul of Saint Rubashov. After a life of sin, he has turned to God —

to a God with the double chin of industrial liberalism and the
charity of the Salvation Army soups. Satan, on the contrary, is
thin, ascetic, and a fanatical devotee of logic. He reads
Machiavelli, Ignatius of Loyola, Marx, and Hegel; he is cold
and unmerciful to mankind, out of a kind of mathematical
mercifulness. (II:7:122)

The interrogation is seen now as a version of the temptation of the
Christian saints, that in its turn is a version of the original type,
Christ's temptation in the wilderness.

The Inquisition analogies are important to establish a touchstone
of cruelty — torture, burning at the stake. But it is important, too,
to establish a parallel of irrationality, and for this the images extend
beyond the implications of the Inquisition. Commitment to a
totalitarian system — and it is usually a marxist one — is by implication as absurd as commitment to a religious creed; it is a way of
opposing marxism's claims to be scientific, materialistic. It is a way
of presenting the totalitarian, marxist state as something irrational,
arbitrary, absurd; and as corrupt as medieval and renaissance religious
systems. And so the first leader after the revolution 'was revered as
God-the-Father, and No. 1 as the Son' (I:12:54), while we are told
of Rubashov: 'The Party's warm, breathing body appeared to him
to be covered with sores — festering sores, bleeding stigmata. When
and where in history had there ever been such defective saints?'
(I:12:52). The analogues are pervasive. Rubashov at the end of the
novel considers the current stage of political development in its
imperfections: 'Perhaps it was still only the second day of creation'
(IV:2:206). And in the future 'perhaps the members of the new
party will wear monks' cowls, and preach that only purity of means
can justify the ends' (IV:2:207). The way in which the religious
societies of the past have used lies for their ends is introduced as a
further analogy with totalitarian socialism. The epigraph to part II,
'The Second Hearing', is from Dietrich von Nieheim, Bishop of
Verden in 1411:

> *When the existence of the Church is threatened, she is released*
> *from the commandments of morality. With unity as the end,*
> *the use of every means is sanctified, even cunning, treachery,*
> *violence, simony, prison, death. For all order is for the sake of*
> *the community, and the individual must be sacrificed to the*
> *common good. (De schismate libri, III) (II:1:81)*

And Gletkin, Rubashov's second interrogator, defends the invention of 'saboteurs' to explain errors in industrial planning and production, by analogy with the practice of the church:

> Whether Jesus spoke the truth or not, when he asserted he was the son of God and of a virgin is of no interest to any sensible person. It is said to be symbolical, but the peasants take it literally. We have the same right to invent useful symbols which the peasants take literally. (III:4:182)

Both the church and the party have the same disregard of mere truth, something that is shocking to the ideology of liberal humanism, something utterly at odds with the official ethical theory of bourgeois democratic society.

The other analogy that recurs throughout *Darkness at Noon*, though somewhat less emphatically, is of the French Revolution and the Napoleonic era. Again the point is to emphasize the cruelty of a revolutionary regime, and the way in which the revolution is betrayed and moves into dictatorship. Robespierre, St Just, Danton, the Jacobins, Fouché, all are cited in Rubashov's discussions.

Though the totalitarian interrogation novel may purport to be responding to specifically twentieth-century realities, its structure of analogues provides the conservative message that totalitarian systems have always existed, that political progress is an illusion, that man is doomed to repeat history. The literary tactics introduced to shock the reader about contemporary totalitarian systems — or near future systems — contradictorily can be seen as conservatively reassuring: things are always the same. The French Revolution, the medieval church, even classical Rome (*Darkness at Noon* has its references to Nero and Sulla — II:7:125, 131) are types of this recurrent social model. The deduction the conservative writers and critics intend us to make from that, of course, is that we should not follow after the illusion of political systems that claim they will make life better. After every revolution in *Nostromo* things remains the same; maybe worse.

There is a central ambiguity here; the conservatives would argue for the unchangeability of human conditions, but to persuade us of the illusory nature of systems that offer improvement, they introduce a rhetoric that implies that change in fact means worse. There is no possibility of change; if you seek change, things get worse. But if things can change for the worse, then they can change for the better — the rhetoric of the conservatives ends up admitting that there can be change. Indeed, there must already have been change for the better from the benightedness of Roman tyranny, the Inquisition, the excesses of the French Revolution, if those periods are to be seen as a *threat* to what we have now.

The possibility of change is one of the issues that is central to the debate in *Darkness at Noon*. Rubashov, the fallen party official, speaks from disillusioned experience; his years in the centre of party activity give him the authority for his denunciation of the revolution:

> In order to defend the existence of the country, we have had to take exceptional measures and make transition-stage laws, which are in every point contrary to the aims of the Revolution. The people's standard of life is lower than it was before the Revolution; the labour conditions are harder, the discipline is more inhuman, the piece-work drudgery worse than in colonial countries with native coolies; we have lowered the age limit for capital punishment down to twelve years; our sexual laws are more narrow-minded than those of England, our leader-worship more Byzantine than that of the reactionary dictatorships. (II:7:129-30)

Ivanov argues in reply that though there is suffering, it is a suffering that is calculated for in the plan to improve the future; whereas under the old system there was random suffering that helped nothing.

> Every year several million people are killed quite pointlessly by epidemics and other natural catastrophes. And we should shrink from sacrificing a few hundred thousand for the most promising experiment in history?

> Yes, we liquidated the parasitic part of the peasantry and let it die of starvation. It was a surgical operation which had to be done once and for all; but in the good old days before the Revolution just as many died in any dry year — only senselessly and pointlessly. (II:7:131)

The discussion between Rubashov and his first interrogator, Ivanov, revolves round these issues of the possibility of change and lead on to the sensibilities of the bourgeois humanist conscience. 'Admit', Rubashov says, 'that humanism and politics, respect for the individual and social progress, are incompatible' (II:7:128). And Rubashov notes in his diary: *'we were the first to replace the nineteenth century's liberal ethics of "fair play" by the revolutionary ethics of the twentieth century. In that also we were right, a revolution conducted according to the rules of cricket is an absurdity'* (II:1:81). Those political novels about the tensions within bourgeois democracy, about the individual's adjusting or not adjusting to bourgeois democracy (*Felix Holt, Beauchamp's Career, The Rainbow*), were written for the bourgeois members of those societies. When the political novel shifted to dealing with totalitarianism the readership for whom it was written still remained the same. (Notice Koestler's references to English sexual morality and cricket for the English readership.) Both Koestler and Orwell are writing for the bourgeois democrat, warning him against 'false gods', pointing out how terrible it is 'over there' in totalitarian societies, building up the case that for all its weaknesses, bourgeois democracy is the best solution. Bourgeois democracy, hence, is still the theme of the totalitarian political novels. The debates are conducted with the same preoccupations; totalitarianism is introduced as a new term, but it is there not so much as a subject in its own right, as a way of underlining or illuminating the nature of bourgeois democratic society. It is another approach to the same themes with which George Eliot dealt.

Koestler handles it all very intelligently. He is a sophisticated enough writer to give his totalitarian devils (his imagery) a good tune. Ivanov says: 'History is *a priori* amoral; it has no conscience. To want to conduct history according to the maxims of the Sunday school means to leave everything as it is' (II:7:125). The debate is between the humanitarian morality, and the machine-like rigid rationality of the totalitarian society, a rationality undistracted by the irrelevancy of individual suffering when the 'common good' is the issue.

A series of sentimental vignettes serve to show the inhumane cruelties of the revolutionary regime; they provide the individualistic tear-jerking episodes underlining the broader themes of the betrayal of the revolution, the disregard for the individual, the cruelty of totalitarianism. It is in these that we see the individual human emotions. Whereas with Rubashov in the centre of the book's concerns, the emphasis is on the ideas, on the intellectual debate. This choice of emphasis enacts the emphases of Rubashov, Ivanov and Gletkin. They — accused and accusers — are central to the novel and their central concerns are intellectual, analytical, the abstraction of dialectic and of power. Human interest, individual feelings, are peripheral to their consciousnesses — and hence are made peripheral to the book's focus.

None the less the peripheral is still present — and is there to make important appeals to the bourgeois individualist reader.

Isolating various 'remarkable scenes' of the novel, Irving Howe picks one such incident:

> One remembers the terrible incident of the Communist who had been imprisoned in some wretched Balkan country and upon his release and arrival in Russia, imprisoned once more; he believes, with the literal sincerity of the damned, that he is not in Russia at all, he was put on the wrong train . . . . (228)

The point is succinctly, if melodramatically, made. Or there is the episode of the execution of Bogrov that follows immediately after the account of Rip van Winkle, to rub in the point. Bogrov, we are tellingly told, was a 'former sailor on the Battleship Potemkin' (II:6:114).

And there are the flashbacks of Rubashov's own past — his interrogation of Richard and expulsion of him from the party, his imposing the state's will on Little Loewy's party, resulting in Little Loewy's suicide after a lifetime of suffering for the party — and the suffering is presented in detail for us. These materials are all in vignettes, cameos, flashbacks. Structurally it is stressed that they are peripheral or secondary. The central concern of the novel is the central concern of Rubashov's consciousness — his intellectual commitment to the party, his logical debates with Ivanov and Gletkin.

The shift from free discussion to coercive interrogation as the centre of the political novel is dramatized within *Darkness at Noon* itself. The material of the novel is Rubashov's imprisonment and interrogation. But the interrogation itself is divided between Ivanov, the old revolutionary; and Gletkin, the new product of the revolution. Ivanov, an old comrade of Rubashov's, conducts his interrogation as a civilized discussion about the problem of ends justifying the means. Although imprisoned, Rubashov is treated by Ivanov as if he were participating in a free debate; Ivanov sets up the feeling — illusion as it is — that these two sons of wealthy landowners are having an intellectual argument late into the night — he offers Rubashov cigarettes at the first session, brings him brandy at the second.

But it is an illusion: the all-night-café dialogue is within the prison. The intellectual discussion is in fact a form of interrogation. And in so far as it approaches free, humane discussion, it results in Ivanov being relieved of the investigation, and shot. Once again, Koestler is having it both ways: it is not really a free discussion, it is held in prison. Yet those aspects that seem to be free result in

Ivanov's execution just to remind us that any moves towards freedom in this system are futile, will bring reprisals — even though we
have already got the message that such freedoms are impossible to
generate within this system. That is why Ivanov is a landowner's
son — he inherits pre-revolutionary ideas of bourgeois-liberal freedom: but they couldn't be produced from anyone born into this
revolutionary society.

The new investigator, Gletkin, has none of that aristocratic or
haut bourgeois elegant fascination with ideas for their own sake; he
is practical man, without speculative intelligence; his ideas are all
in the service of the specific aim of the party. 'Neanderthal' is
Rubashov's patrician word for him.

> 'Citizen Ivanov,' said Gletkin, 'belonged, as you do, to the old
> intelligentsia; by conversing with him, one could acquire some
> of that historical knowledge which one had missed through
> insufficient schooling. The difference is that I try to use that
> knowledge in the service of the Party; but Citizen Ivanov was
> a cynic.' (III:4:182)

And Rubashov reflects:

> One can deny one's childhood, but not erase it. Ivanov had
> trailed his past after him to the end; that was what gave
> everything he said that undertone of frivolous melancholy; that
> was why Gletkin had called him a cynic. The Gletkins had
> nothing to erase; they need not deny their past, because they
> had none. They were born without umbilical cord, without
> frivolity, without melancholy. (III:4:183)

Ivanov's civilized discussion is replaced by Gletkin's interrogations with the blazing light whose intensity can be increased or
reduced, glaring into Rubashov's eyes. Gletkin's techniques are
designed to achieve disorientation in the prisoner — waking up
Rubashov at any hour of the night for interrogation, returning him
to his cell, waking him after an hour for a further session. 'After
forty-eight hours, Rubashov had lost the sense of day and night.'
Gletkin is quite explicit about his methods. When his secretary
congratulates him on finally achieving the full confession from
Rubashov: 'Gletkin turned the lamp down to normal. "That," he
said with a glance at the lamp, "plus lack of sleep and physical
exhaustion. It is all a matter of constitution" ' (III:6:192). These
final words of 'The Third Hearing' section stress how Gletkin is

the complete materialist. His emphasis is on the mechanics, not on any individual prima donna interrogation act. The shift of interrogators represents, too, a class shift — intelligentsia 'acting on behalf of the people' now replaced by the people. Ivanov is superseded by Gletkin the peasant, Gletkin who 'was sixteen years old when I learnt that the hour was divided into minutes' (III:4:180), who 'read monotonously, without any intonation, in the colourless, barren voice of people who have learnt the alphabet late, when already grown-up' (III:3:151). The class war projected beyond the revolution: enough to frighten off any bourgeois liberal dabbling with marxism. It is a powerful trope; it is one of those themes of political art that reach back to quite primitive class terrors; it is the literary intellectual's fear of the mob, the people, that we find in Shakespeare, Milton, Dryden, Swift, Arnold and Orwell.

But the shift in interrogator also serves to add variety within the strict, classical unity of Koestler's novel. The shift dramatizes the class and style changes between the different interrogators; and those changes represent the changes that have occurred socially since the revolution. Koestler's formal techniques are economical, classical.

Indeed, he essentially observes the classical unities of time, place and action. The events are not restricted to twenty-four hours; but they do comprise basically a simple time-span — from Rubashov's arrest, to imprisonment, interrogations and execution. The place is the prison — with the brief prologue of the arrest in his apartment. The action is his interrogation: the arrest and execution are part of that process, the beginning and the inevitable end. Like a classical tragedy, the climactic action occurs in another place and is narrated at second hand, not portrayed: the public trial of Rubashov is presented to us only through the porter, Vasily, once a revolutionary soldier under Rubashov's command, being read an account of the trial by his daughter. The porter and his daughter form a chorus — a dual chorus of the two generations' different reactions — his old loyalty to the heroic, revolutionary officer, her new-style, party-oriented contempt for the traitor who has been tried and found guilty. Formally, Koestler's use of a classical model here makes some important political points. First of all, we might expect the execution of Rubashov to be the climax, not the trial. But in this non-individualistic society, the execution of an individual is unimportant; it is purely a mechanical detail — not a ceremonial as in Zamyatin's *We*, where executions are observed by the mass public with full ceremonials. The individual life is unimportant. 'The infinite was a politically suspect quantity, the "I" a suspect quality.

The Party did not recognize its existence. The definition of the individual was: a multitude of one million divided by one million' (IV:2: 204). The central event in this society is the public trial — that is the climax, that is the public, social occasion, with the reactions of the public present described in the newspaper report. 'The debate on the charge of the planned assassination of the leader of the Party had released storms of indignation among the audience; shouts of "Shoot the mad dogs!" were heard repeatedly' (IV:1: 197).

The logic of the society of *Darkness at Noon* requires that the climactic event is the public trial. The maximum political effect can be gained from this — explanations of errors in social planning can be ascribed to saboteurs, tighter security restrictions can be justified by the example of the Rubashovs and so on. But what happens to Rubashov afterwards is unimportant.

To the liberal bourgeois conscience, however, with its emphasis on the importance of the individual life, Rubashov's personal fate and experience is what is important. So Koestler gives us the execution directly — an epilogue to the strict, logical, cerebral classical drama. He writes a second climax directed to the readership of his book. There is hence a subtle and effective dual ending, an ambiguity of climax — to appeal to the two ideologies debated in the book, the two ideologies that Koestler has dramatized and presented for us. It is a skilful and pregnant manipulation of form — a powerful use and expansion of the basic classical model.

We have already briefly noted the other major formal component of the novel, the flashback. Rubashov's interrogation of Richard in the art gallery; his encounter with Little Loewy when he is sent to persuade the local party branch to lift the embargo on ships trading with the enemy. These are important episodes for filling out what we know of Rubashov — how in the past he was the interrogator and hatchet man, and now is the interrogated, waiting for his own dispatch. And they fill out what we know of the State, how the policies of No. 1 have overruled the beliefs and convictions of the individual party members and of parties in other countries, and have, in the eyes of many, betrayed the Revolution. The flashbacks provide a wider range of information, of event, of character than we would get if the novel were schematically restricted to the prison. But, it is important to stress, they remain limited to this illustrative aspect; they provide further evidence of the rigidity of party policy and they provide evidence of the sort of party apparatchik Rubashov was. And in Gletkin's interrogation further flashbacks are stimulated — Rubashov's encounter with Herr von Z., the diplomat from the reactionary state, who is alleged to have offered a deal to

Rubashov; and the encounter with Professor Kieffer and Hare-lip his son, in which Rubashov is alleged to have suggested the assassination of No. 1. These flashbacks that arise from the prodding of Gletkin's interrogation are analogous to the other flashbacks that arose spontaneously to Rubashov when he was first imprisoned.

The point to be stressed is that the flashbacks are clearly recollections from the past, and are subordinated to the dynamic of the present narrative of arrest-interrogation-execution. They are not there to create a structure like that of *Nostromo*, in which it becomes impossible to reconstruct a historical chronology of events and revolutions, in which the disrupted chronology serves to create the political message that nothing changes, nothing improves, one revolution is as bad as another. Koestler's Roman dictatorships-Inquisition-French Revolution group of analogies serve to create that message; his choice of a classical form indicates a conservatism; but his use of the form is dynamic. Rubashov has his dream of arrest and his past experiences of arrest, but these versions of reality are not there to intermingle with the present-time arrest to create a multilateral, multi-temporal confusion, shifting layers of versions of arrest like the shifting versions of reality in *Last Year at Marienbad*.

The dream and the history are dramatically proleptic of the present event of the novel — they predict the logical inevitability of Rubashov's fate. The form is dynamic, but the determinism has a negative, pessimistic conservatism that touches on Conrad's. The flashbacks are but steps in an inevitable progress to doom. Given his career as a party apparatchik, given his past experiences, inevitably he will be arrested; that is the logic of the society he is living in. And in case we do not accept the inevitability of this logic, Koestler provides a visual aid: the faces on the photograph of the delegates to the first congress of the party — of which only two or three remain alive, the rest of them all shot.

But the doom is a dynamic doom: that is the force of Koestler's novel. The dream and the memory are there to stress sequence, progression; they are not there to say that life in this society is a constant arrest, or that one arrest is indistinguishable from another. They predict and indicate what is going to happen. In this context it is important to notice the significance of Koestler's departure from strict classical unities; the totality of the action does not comprise only the prison experience. We see Rubashov before he is arrested, we see him after he is convicted. It would have been possible to have structured the whole novel within the prison — in which case the flashbacks would have had a somewhat different function. Horst Bienek's *The Cell* (1968), for instance, presents an experience of

202

imprisonment in which the prison life is the totality; we enter the novel at some indeterminate point in the character's sentence, and leave it at some indeterminate point; he might have been in gaol months, years; a past is created by his thoughts, but we have no touchstones outside of the prison to know whether it is a real, a fantasized, a paranoid, or an escapist set of experiences that float through his consciousness; Bienek's form stresses the timelessness, the non-dynamic nature of the experience.

By setting the action almost totally in prison, Koestler raises the image of, 'life in this society is imprisonment'. But that is the well-known rhetoric of political propaganda and it is presented by Koestler knowingly within that context: it is saying exaggeratedly though with some considerable justice that life here is like being in prison, as Hamlet says of Denmark.

But we know there are people unimprisoned — leading, maybe, limited lives, but none the less, unimprisoned. The prison isn't the *total* emblem for human existence, it doesn't totally contain human existence, as it does in Bienek's novel. It is a rhetorical warning — not an expression of human life *in toto*. Those individuals fighting the imprisonment — the officer in cell 402, or the barber — stress that there are other possibilities, there is still the will to resist, mankind isn't totally defeated: unlike the vision of Samuel Beckett, say, where the universe is pared down to utter limitation, alienation.

Koestler has structured his novel so that the dynamic is stressed; and with the dynamic stressed, the flashbacks become subordinate to the present time of the novel's action. It is not a reactionary obfuscation of the possibility of political change; it is not the alienated presentation of timelessness, meaninglessness — though it toys with that possibility. But for all that toying, it is none the less a form that through its dynamic stresses a belief in development, in the inevitable consequences of a course of action, in logical progression. It is still, that is, expressive of the possibilities of political action — in the way that, for instance, Conrad's work is not. For all his anti-Stalinism and more, Koestler retains a marxist understanding of dialectic, of dynamic; this is something that an English leftist like Orwell seems not to have acquired — certainly not acquired with any permanency, for it has slipped away by *Nineteen Eighty-four* when Orwell postulates a society in which no change is possible. It is the dynamic of this marxist dialectic that Koestler presents as leading Rubashov to his decision to confess.

Darkness at Noon tells a story, it has a direct, chronological narrative. Which is appropriate for the dynamic of a marxist politics. But it is also appropriate for the narrative of the individual fate of the bourgeois realist novel: for the universe in which one action leads to another, in which things are consequences of other things, in which (so it slides) bad actions lead to bad actions, an eye for an eye and a tooth for a tooth. In its basic form, therefore, *Darkness at Noon* is not alien to the form of a novel by George Eliot. A leads to B with the logical inevitability of an ethical system. If you do something, something else is bound to result. The rigidly logical, rational, materialistic world of No.1's regime is what Koestler is trying to capture — that is the system which his novel is demonstrating. And it is this logical inevitability of consequences that Koestler dramatizes in the novel to explain the confessions that were elicited in the purges.

> At their second or third meeting already, as it were, an unspoken agreement had come into existence between them: if Gletkin could prove that the root of charge was right — even when this root was only of a logical, abstract nature — he had a free hand to insert the missing details; 'to dot the i's', as Rubashov called it. Without becoming aware of it, they had got accustomed to these rules for their game, and neither of them distinguished any longer between actions which Rubashov had committed in fact and those which he merely should have committed as a consequence of his opinions. . . . (III:4: 178-9)

Rubashov ultimately signs his confession to having done things he had not done, because the logic of his beliefs, of his disagreements with No.1's policies, logically necessitated his doing such things, or analogous things. As he realizes earlier in Gletkin's interrogation:

> He who opposes a dictatorship must accept civil war as a means. He who recoils from civil war must give up opposition and accept the dictatorship.
>   These simple sentences, which he had written nearly a lifetime ago, in a polemic against the 'moderates,' contained his own condemnation. (III:3: 168)

Indeed, we come close to the proposition that Rubashov's real crime is his failure to act on his beliefs, to put his opposition to No. 1 into practice. Rather than act he prefers to leave the country and work for the state overseas — imposing its doctrines on parties in other countries, when he cannot bear to live in the state itself, cannot bear to encounter the consequences of its policies in practice. His secretary, Arlova, hence in this context becomes an indictment of Rubashov, for putting into practice the views she had known him to express constantly though never to act upon.

In one sense the party's disregard for 'actual' truth and replacement of it by what is symbolically true, or what might as well have been true, is a terrible affront to the assumptions of the liberal ethics of bourgeois democracy. Yet in another sense, there is a point of close contact. This world-picture of necessarily accepting the logical consequences of actions, of seeing the moral imperatives inevitably resulting from any particular position, is also the world-picture of the bourgeois individualist protestant ethic of George Eliot's fiction.

It is not, however, the world of Lawrence's political fiction; in *The Rainbow* Ursula is attempting to break out of inevitabilities, to find a spontaneous freedom: she rejects logical, social and ethical structures. It is not the world of *Kangaroo* either — where formally the novel shows a much more fragmented, tentative, movement; where formally we are given a field of possibilities, multi-directions, dead ends, incomplete movements. Lawrence is exploring a revolutionary individualism, an anti-bourgeois radical anarchism. All within a dynamic context: he still retains the realist linear narrative: but disrupts it, none the less.

But his disruptions are never in the direction of stasis; the disruptions are new starts, jerks forward, not imposed blocks. Koestler, though he resists stasis, is in tune with its appeals, he understands that language calling to him.

The formal conservatism of Koestler's fictional method is appropriate for bourgeois liberal readers as well as for 'official' marxist literary thinking at the time that it was written, and at the time of the society it portrays. It is a reduced canvas from the great spread of the nineteenth-century bourgeois realist novel, reduced and more strictly organized: it is a classical rewriting of realism.

The fact that it is a reduction is meaningful, of course — the argument is that No. 1 has reduced the quality of life from the richness of pre-revolutionary society — that life under the party is narrowed, limited; the library is purged of books, commodities are in short supply.

But the fact that the model is nineteenth-century realism, not modernism, is something totally in accord with official Socialist Realist theories on the novel, and on their promulgation in an academically conservative, elitist, traditionalist way by Georg Lukács. In utter contrast is the experimental modernism, the aesthetic progressivism, of Zamyatin's *We* — where the form of the novel is excitingly revolutionary, experimental, exploratory. But such experimentalism had been officially excluded as a possibility for communist writers by the 1932 proclamation on Socialist Realism.

And Koestler does not seem unhappy in his chosen form. He is not an experimentalist chafing at restrictions. There was no compulsion for him to use the form he does. His formal conservatism, rather, demonstrates his essential closeness to many of the party positions. Hence the unease someone like Irving Howe feels with *Darkness at Noon*.

The prefatory note to *Darkness at Noon* gives a strong pointer to how we are to read the book, directing us to see historical analogies with Stalin's purges.

> The characters in this book are fictitious. The historical circumstances which determined their actions are real. The life of the man N.S. Rubashov is a synthesis of the lives of a number of men who were victims of the so-called Moscow Trials. Several of them were personally known to the author. This book is dedicated to their memory. (6)

A number of commentators have read the book as a specifically historical account of the USSR. Kingsley Martin in his *New Statesman* review saw it as 'the thoughts of an Old Bolshevik, Rubashov, as he awaits death in a G.P.U. prison' (131). Irving Howe sees it in the same way:

> an account of the arrest of an Old Bolshevik, Rubashov, by the Stalin government and his gradual capitulation to its inquisitors; but it also carries a superimposed intellectual framework intended as an explanation of why the Old Bolsheviks confessed in the Moscow Trials of 1936-39. (227)

But to limit the novel to this reading alone, is to reduce it. Alan Swingewood offers an extreme case of such a limited reading. Aesthetic, structural, fictional issues never arise. The formal strategies of *Darkness at Noon* are ignored in favour of a crude reductionism of the fiction to an historical-political account of Koestler's career and the Stalin purges. Swingewood moves between the fictional Rubashov and the historical Bukharin too readily.

That sort of one-for-one substitutional approach strikes problems immediately; Jürgen Rühle, for instance, describes Rubashov as 'a Bolshevik revolutionary of the type of Bukharin or Radek' (436); Swingewood ignores Radek, ignores Koestler's claim of a fictional synthesis, ignores the possibility of fictional creation, and assumes Bukharin is Rubashov. Other interpretations of Bukharin, however, produce characters very different from Rubashov; Frank Hardy's

But the Dead Are Many (1975) draws on Bukharin too. There is a great deal of interest for the study of political fiction in looking at the novelist's fictional interpretations of historical characters: but the historical component is only a part of the fictional creation, and Koestler's and Hardy's fictional figures differ as much from each other as from their hypothetical original. Political meanings emerge in the choices taken in fictionalization: those fictional choices express the writer's politics. But Swingewood allows no autonomy to Koestler's fictional characters. He all too easily sees the novel as the transcription of a particular, somehow objective historical reality. In his final assessment documentary values are substituted for fictional ones: 'the strength of *Darkness at Noon* lies in Koestler's meticulous understanding of the bureaucratic *Stalinist* mind; its great weakness must ultimately rest with its selective and distorted historical grasp of Bolshevism and Stalinism' (189).

But *Darkness at Noon* is not limited to the USSR any more than *Heart of Darkness* is limited to the Belgian Congo. Both novels are carefully, pointedly set in unspecified places so that their political messages will not become reduced to historical specificities. In each case there is the intention of a widely applicable parable — though the parable does not in any way exclude the obvious specific applications. *Gulliver's Travels* had its specific political references but it survives because of the general transferability of its political and social understanding.

Koestler's careful unspecificness spreads through his fable and ends up demonstrating that disregard of the individual that characterizes his anonymous state. Most of the characters are given no names: they are either anonymous like the inhabitant of cell 402, given a pseudonym like Rip van Winkle, or a descriptive nickname like Hare-lip. The foreign diplomat who supposedly negotiated with Rubashov is merely Herr von Z. The leader of the anonymous State is simply No.1. This saves Koestler from inventing absurdly transparent nomenclature for the USSR and Stalin. But the device shows within the novel the disregard for the individual that characterizes the system: as if Koestler understands the system all too well, as if it has entered into the fabric of his novel in his all too ready disregard of individuals.

The disregard of the individual life is an important issue in explaining the trials and executions — how they can occur, how confessions can be elicited. The acceptance of the logical consequence of a belief, whether the consequence actually occurred or not, is one crucial habit of thought; and the consequent disregard of the mere individual. Ivanov expounds the principle to Rubashov:

Consider a moment what this humanitarian fog-philosophy would lead to, if we were to take it literally; if we were to stick to the precept that the individual is sacrosanct, and that we must not treat human lives according to the rules of arithmetic. That would mean that a battalion commander may not sacrifice a patrolling party to save the regiment. That we may not sacrifice fools like Bogrov, and must risk our coastal towns being shot to pieces in a couple of years. (II:7: 127)

The individual is held lesser than the mass, than the society. 'I' is subordinated to 'we' — hence the title of Zamyatin's novel that satirized the ideal of the soviet state: 'the things I think, or, to be more exact, the things *we* think. Yes, "we"; that is exactly what I mean, and *We*, therefore, shall be the title of my records' (1: 4). Zamyatin portrays a society in which 'we are a united, powerful organism of millions of cells' (24: 129). Hence the death of a few individuals means nothing:

A dozen Numbers represent scarcely one hundred millionth part of the United State. For practical consideration, that is but an infinitesimal of the third order. *Pity*, a result of mathematical ignorance, was known to the ancients; to us it seems absurd. (19: 102)

And so on the mass marches: 'we walked again — a million-headed body; and in each one of us resided that humble joyfulness with which in all probability molecules, atoms, and phagocytes live' (22: 121). It is quite a different vision from that one that Ursula has in *The Rainbow* when she looks at the cellular activity beneath her microscope, and sees the impulse to individual assertion in the single cell. Lawrence stresses the anarchic, assertive individualism. The theory behind the society of *Darkness at Noon* is the theory satirized by Zamyatin, the abandonment of individuality beneath the mass will. Even Rubashov's vision of the future is not one of anarchic individualism, but of a higher form of individual co-operation — higher, yet still a version of the subordination of the individual to the social totality — even if it is a subordination that allows for some expression of individuality; shared individuality.

Perhaps they will teach that the tenet is wrong which says that a man is the product of one million divided by one million, and will introduce a new kind of arithmetic based on multiplication: on the joining of a million individuals to form a new entity which,

no longer an amorphous mass, will develop a consciousness and
an individuality of its own, with an 'oceanic feeling' increased a
millionfold, in unlimited yet self-contained space. (IV:2: 207)

It is because of his acceptance of the interconnectedness of the individual with society, the mass of men, that Rubashov signs his confession. Individual wills are interconnected, if one can die for the benefit of those it is interconnected with, won't that be for the greatest
good? Rubashov agrees to the surrender of the individual will to the
party, for the good of the party.

Some were silenced by physical fear, like Hare-lip; some hoped to
save their heads; others at least to save their wives or sons from
the clutches of the Gletkins. The best of them kept silent in order
to do a last service to the Party, by letting themselves be sacrificed as scapegoats . . . They were too deeply entangled in their
own past, caught in the web they had spun themselves, according
to the laws of their own twisted ethics and twisted logic; they
were all guilty, although not of those deeds of which they
accused themselves. There was no way back for them. Their exit
from the stage happened strictly according to the rules of their
strange game. (IV:2: 201)

Rubashov outlines in his diary the choices open to someone who
opposes the dictatorship:

*In such situations the opposition has two alternatives: to seize the
power by a coup d'état, without being able to count on the
support of the masses; or in mute despair to throw themselves out
of the swing — 'to die in silence.'*
   *There is a third choice which is no less consistent, and which
in our country has been developed into a system: the denial and
suppression of one's own conviction when there is no prospect of
materializing it. As the only moral criterion which we recognize
is that of social utility, the public disavowal of one's conviction
in order to remain in the Party's ranks is obviously more honour-
able than the quixotism of carrying on a hopeless struggle.*
(III:1: 138)

This is the surrender Gletkin requires — and Gletkin makes explicit
the particular social utility that will arise from it for the party.

What we need is a complete, public confession of your criminal activities . . . The only way in which you can still serve the Party is as a warning example — by demonstrating to the masses, in your own person, the consequences to which opposition to the Party policy inevitably leads. (III:3: 156)

Still believing in the original ideals of the revolution, believing in the aim of a just society, believing in the ethic of surrendering the individual to the party, and of the irrelevance of specific truths to higher aims, Rubashov provides the confession. Tribulations over truth or the individual conscience are not an issue for the true revolutionary. As Ivanov spells out, 'sympathy, conscience, disgust, despair, repentance, and atonement are for us repellent debauchery' (II:7: 124-5).

The spare, classical rigour of the form is paralleled by the spare logical rigour of the arguments put up to, and by, Rubashov. But in opposition to that mode, Koestler employs various novelistic devices to suggest some tremors of individualist conscience in Rubashov. The gesture of the *Pietà*, runs throughout the novel, the image of religious compassion that has its specific point for Rubashov as a detail of the painting he was looking at while interrogating Richard and expelling him from the party. The other recurrent image, again of feminine love, is of the line of Arlova's breast — Arlova, secretary to him at the Aluminium Trust, whom he had made no effort to save when she was arrested on treason charges, whom he suspects was encouraged in her views by his sardonic comments. It is an image both sexual and maternal, Mary Magadalene and Mary mother of Christ,

> The outline of her large, well-shaped breast seemed as familiar against the darkness of the room as though she had always been there. Only the ear-rings now lay flat on the pillow. Her eyes had the same expression as ever, when she pronounced that sentence which could no more leave Rubashov's memory than the folded hands of the *Pietà*, and the smell of sea-weed in the harbour town:
> 'You will always be able to do what you like with me.' (II:3: 95)

The total surrender and trust: now a memory of betrayal, betrayal by Rubashov. It joins the *Pietà* and the smell of seaweed (evoking his part in the fate of Little Loewy) as images evoking remorse in Rubashov's memory. Writing for his liberal humanist readership, Koestler sketches in these somewhat schmalzy insignia of the torments of conscience. And they are not ineffective. But they are not, importantly, terms in the debates between Rubashov and Ivanov or Gletkin.

If Rubashov has pangs, they are the inevitable consequences of the revolutionary life. He is not like Richard Somers, toying with political commitment but preoccupied with keeping his hands clean, his conscience clear, refusing to make any compromises or commitments that might involve some overruling of the individual sensibility.

Though designed for a bourgeois democratic readership with liberal humanist ethics as an ideal, Koestler keeps the terms of the main debate of *Darkness at Noon* within the area of discourse of those revolutionaries who believe in the aim of creating a new society, who believe an ultimately just society justifies current cruelties, lies, slaughter. And the force of the novel lies in the way this attitude is unwaveringly, consistently, and sympathetically presented. It is assumed that for all the atrocities, the aim of No. 1 and the party is still to achieve this just society. Purges occur because of the centralized nature of the society, and the centralized nature of the society arises from the need to thrust a backward country rapidly into industrial efficiency.

> In all other countries, the peasants had one or two hundred years
> to develop the habit of industrial precision and of the handling of
> machines. Here they only had ten years. If we didn't sack them
> and shoot them for every trifle, the whole country would come
> to a standstill, and the peasants would lie down to sleep in the
> factory yards until grass grew out of the chimneys and everything
> became as it was before. (III:4: 181)

Error, imprecision, individual deviance and variation cannot be tolerated.

The interrogation, the logic of the purges and trials, is created with an inward understanding. The explanations are created from the logic of the system. Only once, early in the novel, does Rubashov consider the possibility of an individualistic explanation for what is happening: 'What went on in No. 1's brain? He pictured to himself a cross-section through that brain, painted neatly with grey water-colour on a sheet of paper stretched on a drawing-board with drawing-pins' (I:6: 19). And Rubashov day-dreams about a future time when materialist explanations can be given, with the teacher

> pointing with his ruler to a grey foggy landscape between the
> second and third lobe of No. 1's brain: 'Now here you see the
> subjective reflection of these factors. It was this which in the
> second quarter of the twentieth century led to the triumph of the

totalitarian principle in the East of Europe.' Until this stage was reached, politics would remain bloody dilettantism, mere superstition and black magic. . . . (I:6: 20)

But even this individualistic speculation remains couched in marxist language, in materialist terms. Explanations will be forthcoming.

None the less there is that implicit suggestion that everything can be explained by postulating that No. 1 is a mad dictator — the recurrent fantasy ogre of the bourgeois press and popular fiction. The novel never lurches right over into that world-picture; on the contrary Rubashov's worrying speculation is of No. 1's rationality. 'The horror which No. 1 emanated above all consisted in the possibility that he was in the right, and that all those whom he killed had to admit, even with the bullet in the back of their necks, that he conceivably might be in the right' (I:6: 18). But the mad dictator possibility is introduced none the less.

The strength of *Darkness at Noon* is in its systematic following through of a rigorous logic. The inquisition is like a true Inquisition, not our popular sense of the word as an investigation conducted by torture. It is like the Roman Catholic Inquisitions in that it not only investigates but persuades, gets the victim 'correct' again. The interrogation ends only when the interrogated accepts and believes the logic of the interrogation. *Nineteen Eighty-four* fails in this regard, although the theme is present: Winston Smith is defeated, broken at the end: nominally he loves Big Brother — but tonally Orwell presents him as crushed, fibreless, empty. We 'know' he is 'not the same man'. Whereas Rubashov accepts the logic of the Inquisition with his full intellectual faculties.

It is this quality that provokes the critical hostility of Orwell, Irving Howe and others. Sharing Koestler's hostility to socialist totalitarianism, having a cold war orientation in their anti-Sovietism, none the less Koestler's method deeply worries them. Orwell argues vigorously that Stalin's purges couldn't have operated as Koestler suggests they operated:

Naturally the whole book centres round one question: Why did Rubashov confess? He is not guilty — that is, not guilty of anything except the essential crime of disliking the Stalin régime. The concrete acts of treason in which he is supposed to have engaged are all imaginary. He has not even been tortured, or not very severely. He is worn down by solitude, toothache, lack of tobacco, bright lights glaring in his eyes, and continuous questioning, but these in themselves would not be enough to overcome a hardened

revolutionary. The Nazis have previously done worse to him without breaking his spirit. The confessions obtained in the Russian
state trials are capable of three explanations:
1. That the accused were guilty.
2. That they were tortured, and perhaps blackmailed by threats
to relatives and friends.
3. That they were actuated by despair, mental bankruptcy and
the habit of loyalty to the Party.

For Koestler's purpose in *Darkness at Noon* 1 is ruled out, and
though this is not the place to discuss the Russian purges, I must
add that what little verifiable evidence there is suggests that the
trials of the Bolsheviks were frame-ups. If one assumes that the
accused were not guilty — at any rate, not guilty of the particular
things they confessed to — then 2 is the common-sense explanation. Koestler, however, plumps for 3, which is also accepted by
the Trotskyist Boris Souvarine, in his pamphlet *Cauchemar en
U.R.S.S.* (CE, III:68: 275-6)

Orwell certainly uses the second explanation for the destruction of
Winston Smith in *Nineteen Eighty-four*. He cannot accept the
explanations Koestler offers, so postulates torture. A little later in
his essay on Koestler, he comes up with another possibility:

If one writes about the Moscow trials one must answer the
question, 'Why did the accused confess?' and which answer one
makes is a political decision. Koestler answers, in effect, 'Because
these people had been rotted by the Revolution which they
served', and in doing so he comes near to claiming that revolutions are of their nature bad. If one assumes that the accused in
the Moscow trials were made to confess by means of some kind
of terrorism, one is only saying that one particular set of revolutionary leaders has gone astray. Individuals, and not the situation,
are to blame. The implication of Koestler's book, however, is
that Rubashov in power would be no better than Gletkin: or
rather, only better in that his outlook is still partly pre-revolutionary. Revolution, Koestler seems to say, is a corrupting process. Really enter into the Revolution and you must end up as
either Rubashov or Gletkin. (CE, III:68: 277-8)

But this is not the tone of Koestler's explanation. 'Rotted' is
Orwell's metaphor for the very intellectual process Koestler is at
pains to describe. There is nothing to *rot*: the feel is of intransigent,
unchanging, adamantine logic — cold and steely, not something that

will rot or corrupt. Rubashov retains his intellectual integrity through till the end. He accepts the ideas of the party, retains his ideals, and is willing to take the risk that the society that will execute him still holds to those same ideals. In no sense can this conclusion make the case that revolution is a corrupting process, as Orwell claims. It concedes that things may go wrong, that the wrong policy may triumph: but it is the expression of a conflict of policies for the implementation of a social vision.

This resistance to Koestler's explanation of the abstract, intellectual, logical forces by which the confessions were reached is shared by Irving Howe. He complains that:

> It is precisely the apparent rigour of Rubashov's argument which renders Koestler's portrait of him suspect, for it assumes that Rubashov's gradual surrender to Stalinism is a dialectical process within his own thought, a valid deduction from the premises of his political career. But this is manifestly untrue to our sense of human behaviour, even the behaviour of Bolshevik politicians. Between the assumptions of theory and the conclusions of defeat there must lie a whole middle ground of Rubashov's experience, the gradual destruction of his will and integrity as he takes step after step toward acquiescing to the regime he knows to be vile. (229)

Howe talks of the logic of the confessions being 'manifestly untrue to our sense of human behaviour'. Yet having indicated (though not spelled out) his ideology of human behaviour in this comment, he then goes on to write of Koestler's expression of Rubashov's ideology as if 'ideology' was something Rubashov or Koestler had, like the flu, and Howe doesn't.

> A major part of his intention in writing *Darkness at Noon* must surely be to warn against the abstractions of ideology, those abstractions which, if allowed to spawn too freely, tend to dehumanize our lives — yet every line Koestler writes, and one doubts that he can avoid it, is suffused with ideology. He is like a stricken Midas yearning for the bread of life yet, with every touch, turning experience into the useless gold of ideology. (231)

In Orwell's and Howe's resistance to Koestler's analysis we see a major confrontation of ideologies. Koestler's difference from the tradition of English and American political fiction is dramatically indicated. For all his closeness to other aspects of the bourgeois

novel of politics, his absorption of a marxist dialectic strongly marks
out the difference in his consciousness from most English and
American political fictions. He has a self-consciousness about his
ideology that so much English political fiction lacks. Aware of the
ideological function of marxist thought within a centralized bureaucratic socialist society, he offers an explanation for those of other
ideologies of how seemingly inexplicable events occur, how they are
consistent with this 'foreign' ideology. This is his strength, his
ability to present a persuasive model of structures of thought or
behaviour. But to reject *Darkness at Noon* as simply 'ideology'
without recognizing that such a rejection comes from a competing
ideology, without using such a resistance to illuminate the ideological nature of the rejection, is to miss the point of his work.

7

Nineteen Eighty-four: rewriting the future

Of the many ironies of *Nineteen Eighty-four* (1949), one of the neatest is the way in which the novel's protagonist, Winston Smith, serves as a model of Orwell's own procedures in writing the novel. *The Times Literary Supplement* reported an exhibition of Orwell's papers at University College, London in which

> A notebook is open at a page giving a draft layout for *1984*,
> still called *The Last Man in Europe*. Is it merely coincidence that
> this thick quarto notebook of cream-laid paper, with the maroon
> binding just visible, is so like the notebook Winston Smith used
> for his diary? (7 March 1975, 250)

Winston used his diary for his secret thoughts. 'It was a peculiarly beautiful book. Its smooth creamy paper, a little yellowed by age, was of a kind that had not been manufactured for at least forty years past. He could guess, however, that the book was much older than that' (I:1: 8-9). But Winston's public life consists of rewriting news items to accord with changes in the society's political requirements. And that is the sort of thing Orwell is doing: Orwell's cream-laid paper notebook contains both the public and the private Winston. Orwell's procedure in *Nineteen Eighty-four* was a calculated, conscious rewriting of the political futures predicted in earlier utopian and anti-utopian fictions. Just as Winston rewrote past issues of *The Times* newspaper, so Orwell rewrote previous political fictions, adapting and transforming them to achieve a bleaker vision than anyone before had ever managed.

For some time he had been noting down ideas for his projected novel. He wrote in 1944 to Gleb Struve, thanking him for a copy of *Twenty Five Years of Soviet Russian Literature*, which had aroused his interest in Zamyatin's *We*: 'I am interested in that kind

of book, and even keep making notes for one myself that may get
written sooner or later' (CE, III:21: 118). Various commentators
have indicated 'sources' for *Nineteen Eighty-four*. But these are not
sources in the sense of material borrowed, rifled, plagiarized or
adapted. They are sources that are 'corrected'. Orwell is rewriting
utopian and anti-utopian fictions to accord with his vision of political possibilities. *Nineteen Eighty-four* is the product of a critical
intelligence that has ranged over previous political fiction and
commentary. Its incidents are not simple narrative, but to a large
extent the corrected versions of events and situations from previous
works. They are less invented fictions than documentary incorpora-
tions. And the documentation has been tampered with, it has been
'corrected'. It is this that contributes largely to the characteristic
tone of *Nineteen Eighty-four* — the bleak sense of closedness, the
dead end, the total negativity; the details of the society, the images,
the events of the narrative have no freedom for alternative development; the progressions are inexorable and remorseless. They have
been assembled and reduced from the creative possibilities of other
fictions; and shaped by an analytic intelligence so that their meanings and implications are totally controlled. Orwell's procedure is the
opposite of the creative artist whose fictions are created organically
and contain within them alternatives, contradictions, differing possibilities. The closed, static society which Orwell has presented is
achieved in large part by the willed, reductive rewriting of earlier
political fictions. The materials used are readily enough located from
Orwell's discussions of them in his four volumes of *Collected Essays,
Journalism and Letters*. Writing in 1946 on James Burnham's *The
Managerial Revolution* (itself an important non-fictional source for
Nineteen Eighty-four), he groups four of his major sources together:

Jack London, in *The Iron Heel* (1909), foretold some of the
essential features of Fascism, and such books as Wells' *The
Sleeper Awakes* (1900), Zamyatin's *We* (1923), and Aldous
Huxley's *Brave New World* (1930), all describe imaginary worlds
in which the special problems of capitalism had been solved without bringing liberty, equality or true happiness any nearer. More
recently, writers like Peter Drucker and F. A. Voigt have argued
that Fascism and Communism are substantially the same thing.
And indeed, it has always been obvious that a planned and
centralized society is liable to develop into an oligarchy or a
dictatorship (CE, V:46: 195)

The four novels he cites are all discussed in some detail in the course of his essays and reviews. And two further novels he wrote about also have an important role in the creation of the world of 1984, Swift's *Gulliver's Travels* (1726) and Koestler's *Darkness at Noon* (1940).

The super-city is a recurrent projection for both utopian and anti-utopian writing. Edward Bellamy's technological, automated society in *Looking Backward* (1887) and H. G. Wells's version in *A Modern Utopia* (1905) have super-urbanization as an ideal. But the negative implications of industrial urbanization have produced their alternative fictions. Zamyatin and Huxley both created anti-utopias from industrial urbanization − Zamyatin's in a totalitarian society, Huxley's in a projection of monopolistic capitalist society. In both *We* and *Brave New World* the mastery of technology has achieved commodity fulfilment, but the message is that man does not live by bread alone. The centralized control of the society offers satisfactions that cannot satisfy the individual, free, human spirit. Zamyatin's protagonist grows a soul and finds himself out of key with his society.

Orwell complained that Huxley's projection of 'the whole world . . . turned into a Riviera hotel' (CE, II:11: 46) lacked any persuasive rationale. The rationale which Huxley offers is a mixture of protected happiness and capitalist-industrialist consumerism. The controller, Mustapha Mond, runs a society based on mindless happiness, on the exclusion of the disturbing, on the satisfaction of satisfiable needs and the exclusion of the unsatisfiable needs. But the impulse is not, as Orwell's comments might seem to imply, mere benevolence. The basic economic rationale − the encouragement of consumerism − is stressed. The whole society is oriented to purchasing, throwing away and buying afresh. By conditioning and by mnemonic slogans, everyone is encouraged to spend, to consume.

Behind this capitalistic ethic, however, is the happy assumption that there will be sufficient wealth for everyone to be able to consume. Orwell's contention in *Nineteen Eighty-four* is that this will not be the case, and he inverts Huxley's society of mass-produced plenty into one of perpetual scarcity.

Though Orwell draws on and adapts features from both Zamyatin and Huxley, his major positive sources for the texture of the urban industrial world are H. G. Wells's *The Sleeper Awakes* and Jack London's *The Iron Heel*. In these two novels the super-cities are the product of oppression, of serf and slave labour, of subsistence and starvation economies for the proletariat. Orwell has looked at and rejected the prediction of commodity fulfilment in Zamyatin's and Huxley's anti-utopias; he responds to their accounts of the circumscription of the individual life, but for his own anti-utopia the circumscribed individual life is to be lived in physically and economically uncomfortable circumstances. He turns to Wells's and London's projections, in which the societies are run for the benefit of the power elite and the workers are kept in their place not by conditioning but by force, by physical and economic oppression. It is here that Orwell finds his model for the treatment of the proles. He makes one further cruel twist: in *The Sleeper Awakes* and *The Iron Heel*, the oppressors are the industrial capitalists; in *Nineteen Eighty-four* the oppressors are the party that operates in the name of state socialism, Ingsoc.

The societies of *We* and *Brave New World* are lacking in freedom and spirituality, but they offer physically comfortable conditions. In *The Sleeper Awakes* and *The Iron Heel* the comfort exists only for the capitalist elite. In *Nineteen Eighty-four* even the Inner Party do not live in great comfort, and the society shows none of the technological and architectural achievements of earlier predicitons. Jack London saw the super-city as the aim of both the socialist and the totalitarian capitalist societies. His socialists have a vision of a Bellamy-like future, while the oligarchy uses its captive proletariat to build a super-city that the proletariat will gain no benefit from. 'Ardis was completed in A.D. 1942, while Asgard was not completed until A.D. 1984. It was fifty-two years in the building, during which time a permanent army of half a million serfs was employed' (21: 913, n.3). The date of the completion of Asgard is significantly exploited in Orwell's title: another ironic rewriting. Asgard is the high technological and artistic architectural achievement of the brutal oligarchic society whose 'boot stamping on a human face' philosophy Orwell borrows, suitably adapted, for O'Brien. But whereas in *The Iron Heel* 1984 marks the year in which the oligarchy creates a monument to its efficiency by completing a second super-city, in Orwell's *Nineteen Eighty-four* the city is the old, unreconstructed city of the past, crumbling, collapsing, decaying. It has four modern buildings for the ministries of Truth, Peace, Love and Plenty, each 'an enormous pyramidal structure of glittering white concrete, soaring up, terrace after terrace, 300 metres into the air' (I:1: 7). But the rest of the city consists of 'vistas of rotting nineteenth-century houses, their sides shored up with baulks of timber, their windows patched with cardboard and their roofs with corrugated iron, their crazy garden walls sagging in all directions', together with bomb sites covered with weeds, or 'sordid colonies of wooden dwellings like chicken-houses' (I:1: 6-7).

His *Nineteen Eighty-four* cityscape is not so much like 1984

219

Asgard as like 1948 London — the year in which he wrote the novel, and the transposition of whose last two numerals it has often been claimed provided his title. But a pessimistic rewriting of the possibilities of 1948 only makes full ironic sense if the rewriting involves a further ironic reduction of the possibilities of a once projected 1984. *Nineteen Eighty-four's* 1984 is much worse than London's projected 1984 or than the contemporary 1948 Orwell wrote in.

The super-cities shown by Wells, Zamyatin and Huxley, and projected in concept by London, were all amazing glistening future visions, triumphs of technology. They are a pressing force in *Nineteen Eighty-four* — touchstones of what the future will not be like, touchstones of what Orwell saw as the naive optimism of earlier projections. But before considering why Orwell argues these visions will not come true, we need to look at Jack London's explanation for why he believed they would. As the plutocracy comes totally to control the society, the surplus from its capitalist industries will increase and increase. The plutocracy will not redistribute this surplus amongst the populace:

> When the oligarchs have completely mastered the people, they
> will have time to spare for other things. They will become wor-
> shippers of beauty. They will become art-lovers . . . wonder cities
> will arise that will make tawdry and cheap the cities of old time.
> And in these cities will the oligarchs dwell and worship beauty.
> Thus will the surplus be constantly expended while labour
> does the work. The building of these great works and cities will
> give a starvation ration to millions of common labourers, for
> the enormous bulk of the surplus will compel an equally enorm-
> ous expenditure, and the oligarchs will build for a thousand years
> — ay, for ten thousand years. They will build as the Egyptians
> and the Babylonians never dreamed of building; and when the
> oligarchs have passed away, their great roads and their wonder
> cities will remain for the brotherhood of labour to tread upon
> and dwell within. (14: 14-3)

All that Orwell borrows from the detail of this is the 1984 date and the Egyptian pyramidal shape and Babylonian terraces of the four Ministry buildings. But he also shares London's basic premise that the surplus has to be expended, that the oligarchy will never distri-bute wealth equally but will find ways to consume the surplus while preserving poverty. And the way in which Orwell suggests they will act is the complete opposite of London's way: the surplus will be expended not in building but in destroying, not by creating new cities but by continual war. The rocket bombs are incessant:

> There was a roar that seemed to make the pavement heave; a
> shower of light objects pattered on to his back. When he stood
> up he found that he was covered with fragments of glass from the
> nearest window.
>   He walked on. The bomb had demolished a group of houses
> 200 metres up the street. (I:8: 70-1)

This is Orwell's rewriting of Jack London's future. And just as London has Ernest Everhard spell out the rationale for the future expending of the surplus, so Orwell has his inversion of this projection spelled out in theoretical detail. The words are given not to a character but to Emmanuel Goldstein's book *The Theory and Practice of Oligarchical Collectivism*.

> The problem was how to keep the wheels of industry turning
> without increasing the real wealth of the world. Goods must be
> produced, but they must not be distributed. And in practice the
> only way of achieving this was by continuous warfare.
>   The essential act of war is destruction, not necessarily of
> human lives, but of the products of human labour. War is a way
> of shattering to pieces, or pouring into the stratosphere, or sink-
> ing in the depths of the sea, materials which might otherwise be
> used to make the masses too comfortable, and hence, in the long
> run, too intelligent. Even when weapons of war are not actually
> destroyed, their manufacture is still a convenient way of expend-
> ing labour power without producing anything that can be con-
> sumed. (II:9: 154-5)

'War is peace' indeed — peace meaning stability, stillness: war rages so that society will not change. Goldstein recalls how:

> In the early twentieth century, the vision of a future society
> unbelievably rich, leisured, orderly and efficient — a glittering
> antiseptic world of glass and steel and snow-white concrete — was
> part of the consciousness of nearly every literate person.
> (II:9: 153)

It is recurrent throughout *Nineteen Eighty-four* as a vision that has been eclipsed. But its aesthetic style is not derived from Jack London: he never describes his future cities. London provided the fictional projection of Marx's theory of the surplus which Orwell then

221

turned into an even bleaker, more negative, destructive vision. For the physical details of the city we need to go to Zamyatin, who probably borrowed details from Wells's 1899 vision of a glass-enclosed society with moving stairways, arching bridges and aerial transport; and both of them probably provided detail for Huxley. It is Zamyatin's portrayal of the shimmering colours, the abstract modernist poetry in the technological and architectural products of his future society, that lies behind *Nineteen Eighty-four*. The world of *We* was created satirically; the regimented, mathematical society is shown as oppressing the human spirit. The fantasies of mathematical designers are unsuitable for human use and life — but they are still appreciable as artistic abstractions.

> But the sky! The sky is blue. Its limpidness is not marred by a
> single cloud. (How primitive was the taste of the ancients, since
> their poets were always inspired by these senseless, formless,
> stupidly rushing accumulations of vapor!) I love, I am sure it
> will not be an error if I say *we* love, only such a sky — a sterile,
> faultless sky. On such days the whole universe seems to be
> moulded of the same eternal glass, like the Green Wall, and like
> all our buildings. On such days one sees their wonderful equa-
> tions, hitherto unknown. One sees these equations in everything,
> even in the most ordinary, everyday things. (2:5)

The satirical component is clear enough. But the aesthetic appeal of the ordered mathematical society is allowed and created; if it had no appeal, there would be nothing to satirize, after all; it would be self-evidently unappealing. And it seems that Orwell, too, recognized the appeal of this orderly futuristic world — that is the point of his denial of it in *Nineteen Eighty-four*. The rationale for the detail of the *Nineteen Eighty-four* world is the denial of whatever might seem appealing, the exclusion of any pleasant or attractive features.

At the same time, of course, Orwell exploits the negative associa-tions of this futuristic architecture to stress the totalitarian, brutal nature of the four modern government buildings that do exist in 1984. There is a similar doublethink ambivalence about his portrayal of the decaying city; its ramshackleness is a negative quality; its oldness is not a sign of tradition, of a valid past, but of decay and ruin. However, Orwell elsewhere does use old buildings to denote a good, liberal past now destroyed by totalitarianism. Like Huxley, Orwell sets his novel in London, and like Huxley he draws certain of his effects from the discrepancy between the London they knew and the London they projected. Orwell has Big Brother mounted on

Nelson's Column in Trafalgar Square, now renamed Victory Square. The renaming alludes satirically to the political renaming of Soviet cities — Petrograd becoming Leningrad, and so on. But both Huxley and Orwell draw on the cosy, trivial effects of seeing the permanent landmarks of the English bourgeoisie shockingly transformed. Orwell has the church at St Martin-in-the-Fields turned into a 'museum used for propaganda displays of various kinds — scale models of rocket bombs and Floating Fortresses, wax-work tableaux illustrating enemy atrocities, and the like' (I:8: 82-3). Huxley has his Westminster Abbey Cabaret with 'London's Finest Scent and Colour Organ. All the Latest Synthetic Music' (5:i: 67). Why any of this should be remarked upon by two such non-Church of England intellectuals is worth pondering: the effects are produced for some easy bourgeois-baiting, simple shocks for conformist and Christian readers — not out of any deep feeling. Huxley's name-games are, anyway, primarily facetious ('the Arch-Community-Songster of Canterbury') for all their easy satirical gestures. Orwell's use of the device is sardonic and bitter. And for his largest stroke in this area, Orwell adapted Wells rather than Huxley. In *The Sleeper Awakes* Wells looked forward to flying machines ten years before aircraft existed, and drew on contemporary theory that aircraft would need 'Flying Stages' for take off:

> The Flying Stages of London were collected together in an
> irregular crescent on the southern side of the river. They formed
> three groups of two each and retained the names of ancient
> suburban hills or villages. They were named in order, Roehamp-
> ton, Wimbledon Park, Streatham, Norwood, Blackheath, and
> Shooter's Hill. (356)

In this future totalitarian society with its centralized slave-based economy, London's suburbs have vanished and have become mere 'flying stages' for aircraft. In *Nineteen Eighty-four*, though the name of London survives, that of England is forgotten. Orwell's patriotism has been remarked on by a number of commentators; here it is the base from which a frisson of horror can be squeezed — how can Englishmen surrender the name of their land? 'This was London, chief city of Airstrip One, itself the third most populous of the provinces of Oceania' (I:1:6). Now the whole of England itself has become metaphorically a 'flying stage', an airstrip, for the world of perpetual war.

The drabness, decay and physical ugliness of the world of *Nineteen Eighty-four* has its further immediate sources in Orwell's projecting the perpetuation of conditions in England during and immediately after the Second World War — houses shored up after bomb damage, lifts that won't work, sinks that block — everyday breakdowns and commodity shortages and scarcity of maintenance workers are expanded into a total and seemingly irreparable condition. And he borrows too from accounts of conditions in the Soviet Union, drawing on Koestler's *Darkness at Noon* with Rubashov's bitter indictment of how conditions after the revolution are worse than before — an indictment lying behind Goldstein's account of the failure of the utopian vision and his comment that 'the world is more primitive to-day than it was fifty years ago' (II:9: 153). Rubashov declares: 'Acting consequentially in the interests of the coming generations, we have laid such terrible privations on the present one that its average length of life is shortened by a quarter' (II:7:129). Again, the source is not simply borrowed but critically reinterpreted and rewritten. No such consideration of future generations exists in *Nineteen Eighty-four*. The future generations will certainly not be more comfortably off, probably they will be worse off; the continual war is not to defend the existence of the country but to achieve and perpetuate privations, to absorb surplus production for ever. And to absorb it not by consumerism for any class, not by art, but by destruction. Jack London's materialist, economic projection has been transformed into a quasi-religious, metaphysical vision of perpetual destruction. It recalls the cosmic negativity of Milton's Satan: 'only in destroying I find ease' (*Paradise Lost*, IX: 129).

Orwell is more concerned with squeezing a further negative twist from anti-utopia than with exposing utopias in *Nineteen Eighty-four*. Utopias are inconceivable. Writing about Arthur Koestler he remarked:

> As an ultimate objective he believes in the Earthly Paradise, the Sun State which the gladiators set out to establish, and which has haunted the imagination of Socialists, Anarchists and religious heretics for hundreds of years. But his intelligence tells him that the Earthly Paradise is receding into the far distance and that what is actually ahead of us is bloodshed, tyranny and privation. . . . Since about 1930 the world has given no reason for optimism whatever. Nothing is in sight except a welter of lies, hatred, cruelty and ignorance. . . . (CE, III:68: 280-1)

The earthly paradise is present in *Nineteen Eighty-four* only as an absurdity. The visions of William Morris are cited only to be dismissed. Goldstein's book states:

> To return to the agricultural past, as some thinkers about the
> beginning of the twentieth century dreamed of doing, was not a
> practicable solution. It conflicted with the tendency towards
> mechanization which had become quasi-instinctive throughout
> almost the whole world, and moreover, any country which
> remained industrially backward was helpless in a military sense
> and was bound to be dominated, directly or indirectly, by its
> more advanced rivals. (II:9: 154)

With a world picture of basic military aggression, a shift to a non-
industrial society is for Orwell an impossibility. Urban industrial
society is terrible, but there can be no alternative since urban industrial society creates military strength. In *Brave New World* and *We*
the natural, rural, primitive life is presented as an alternative to the
organized urban industrial society. Huxley's Savage offers an individualistic critique, but can make no impact on the society. In *We*,
however, the rebels from behind the green wall infiltrate, find
increasing numbers of allies, and at the end of the novel are presenting a serious challenge to the stability of the urban society. Zamyatin presents an untamed jungle world, excluded from the ordered
society by a glass wall, 'the Green Wall', through which its seething
variety can be seen. He beautifully captures the magic of this natural
world through the stumbling traumatized perceptions of D-503.
(The three dots are in the original, this breaking off characteristic of
the stumbling expression of D-503 when he approaches the
unapproachable.)

> From beyond the Wall, from the infinite ocean of green, there
> arose toward me an immense wave of roots, branches, flowers,
> leaves. It rose higher and higher; it seemed as though it would
> splash over me and that from a man, from the finest and most
> precise mechanism which I am, I would be transformed into . . .
> But fortunately there was the Green Wall between me and that
> wild green sea. (17: 88-9)

Orwell borrows the structural opposition of urban society and
natural freedom, and reduces and anglicizes it. He had a strong
tradition in English fiction, anyway, of opposing the city of corruption to the life-enhancing countryside; and the countryside he presents is southern English woodland, not the vital protean primitivism
of Zamyatin. Yet without that primitive impulse, Orwell's country-

side is a very inert, Edwardian pastoral.

> Winston picked his way up the lane through dappled light and
> shade, stepping out into pools of gold wherever the boughs parted.
> Under the trees to the left of him the ground was misty with
> bluebells. The air seemed to kiss one's skin. It was the second of
> May. From somewhere deeper in the heart of the wood came the
> droning of ring-doves. (II:2:96)

For a moment Orwell leaves it undamaged. Soon, however, we find
that there may be concealed microphones and that the bluebells
have a 'faint sickly scent' (II:2:97); but it is one of the few areas of
the novel that is left comparatively unscathed by Orwell's obsessive
distastes. Julia and Winston only visit it this once, however. Other
times they make love in a deserted church tower which is 'hot and
stagnant, and smelt overpoweringly of pigeon-dung' (II:3: 106), or
in the seedy room above Mr Charrington's shop.

The countryside, Winston's recurrent dream of the 'Golden
Country', is a curiously fragile, undynamic image. It is a brief touchstone of nostalgia for a world of private relationships; but it has no
force in active opposition to the totalitarian regime.

In contrast, Zamyatin's nature was a much more forceful, disturbing, living presence, compelling D-503 to question his assumptions.

> The blunt snout of some unknown beast was to be seen dimly
> through the glass of the Wall; its yellow eyes kept repeating the
> same thought which remained incomprehensible to me. We
> looked into each other's eyes for a long while. Eyes are shafts
> which lead from the superficial world into a world which is
> beneath the surface. A thought awoke in me: 'What if that yellow-
> eyed one, sitting there on that absurd dirty heap of leaves, is
> happier than I, in his life which cannot be calculated in figures!'
> (17:89)

It is from beyond the Green Wall that the conspirators come. It is the
blowing up of the Green Wall that lets in the forces that may
undermine the society of *We*. Primitive nature bursts in, conditioned
restraints break down.

> The city seemed foreign, wild, filled with the ceaseless triumph-
> ant hubbub of the birds. It seemed like the end of the world,
> *Doomsday*.
> Through the glass of the walls in quite a few houses (this cut

into my mind), I saw male and female Numbers in shameless embraces — without curtains lowered, without pink checks, in the middle of the day! . . . (37:205)

But it is Orwell's case that the society of *Nineteen Eighty-four* is permanent, immovable. He sees nature from that traditional urban English standpoint — as a place for Sunday walks, not as a dynamic force. It is recreational parkland to catch a few fish in, not a repository of energy. The Party does not need to be shown to control or hold back nature in *Nineteen Eighty-four* — Orwell's own cultural conditioning has already discounted it.

So the magical challenging force of nature is rewritten from *We*. And there is another functional reason for the dismissal of nature as an alternative: Winston and Julia are the only two conspirators. In *We* there is an increasingly growing band of rebels who meet beyond the Green Wall. In *The Iron Heel* the romantic pastoral hiding place near Glen Ellen in Sonoma county is functional — the plutocracy is hunting down the socialists, who have to hide out. But with Orwell there is no primitive challenge from nature to encourage rebellion; and there are no rebels who need to seek out natural hiding places.

Orwell's 1946 *Tribune* review of *We* makes no mention of the glass wall, or of the vision of nature that Zamyatin presents. What was a major term in Zamyatin's vision was unimportant to Orwell. Orwell did, however, remark on another of the major terms, sexuality.

> At stated intervals they are allowed for one hour (known as 'the sex hour') to lower the curtains round their glass apartments. There is, of course, no marriage, though sex life does not appear to be completely promiscuous. For purposes of love-making everyone has a sort of ration book of pink tickets, and the partner with whom he spends one of his allotted sex hours signs the counterfoil. (CE, IV:17: 96)

As Orwell remarked, there are strong resemblances to *Brave New World*. Huxley takes the ration-book promiscuity further into a total freedom that becomes a total compulsion. 'Everybody belongs to everyone else'; 'Orgy-Porgy' becomes institutionalized. And in the earlier anti-utopia of Wells's, *The Sleeper Awakes*, there are explicit sex-shows on some quasi-movie apparatus, and 'Pleasure Cities' offering luxurious guilt-free sexuality to the upper classes.

Orwell offers a total, repressive opposite in his rewriting of these visions. In *Nineteen Eighty-four* promiscuity though not technically illegal is none the less punished by imprisonment: marriage is normative, though Party members have to have their proposed marriage vetted for approval or disapproval; and within marriage, sex is for breeding, not pleasure. If Orwell needed a source other than the expressed norms of English society, there was one in *Gulliver's Travels*. The houyhnhnms, Orwell wrote,

> practise strict birth control, each couple producing two offspring and thereafter abstaining from sexual intercourse. Their marriages are arranged for them by their elders, on eugenic principles, and their language contains no word for 'love', in the sexual sense. (CE IV:57: 2:5)

Orwell believed that Swift presented the houyhnhnms as an ideal, and it was an ideal that horrified him. They represented the frigid sexuality, the sexual repression, that was a part of English authoritarian systems. He projects what such houyhnhnm attitudes would be like in his account of the relationship of Winston and his wife, 'the frigid little ceremony that Katharine had forced him to go through on the same night every week. . . . "Our duty to the Party" ' (II:3:109). The aim of the party, O'Brien tells Winston, is to remove even the small amount of sexuality remaining.

> No one dares trust a wife or a child or a friend any longer. But in future there will be no wives and no friends. Children will be taken from their mothers at birth, as one takes eggs from a hen. The sex instinct will be eradicated. Procreation will be an annual formality like the renewal of a ration card. We shall abolish the orgasm. (III:3: 214-15)

In *We* the sex instinct is controlled; in *Nineteen Eighty-four* 'the Party was trying to kill the sex instinct, or, if it could not be killed, then to distort it and dirty it' (I:6: 56). Consequently in both *We* and *Nineteen Eighty-four* a fully sexual affair in which the partners are in love is in opposition to the norms of the societies. Zamyatin beautifully captures the love of D-503 for I-330; and the strength of the portrayal is in the dynamic quality of the love: D-503 initially resists, fearful of the illegality of his behaviour; in love he is consumed by terrible jealousies; and ultimately the jealousy is something he adapts to, accommodates and transcends. The protean, dynamic, developing quality of the love is in contrast to the static quality of official sexuality in the society of *We*.

Orwell predictably seizes on the negative features. He borrows the promiscuity motif; D-503 is tormented by jealousy and tormented by the absurdity of this throwback to old styles of feeling — but none the less through the jealousies the poignancy of ancient romantic love is re-established. Orwell, however, turns the motif into a sex-hate eroticism.

> Scores of times she had done it: he wished it had been hundreds
> — thousands. Anything that hinted at corruption always filled
> him with a wild hope. Who knew, perhaps the Party was rotten
> under the surface, its cult of strenuousness and self-denial simply
> a sham concealing iniquity. If he could have infected the whole
> lot of them with leprosy or syphilis, how gladly he would have
> done so! . . . "The more men you've had, the more I love you
> . . . I hate purity, I hate goodness! I don't want any virtue to exist
> anywhere. I want everyone to be corrupt to the bones.' (II:2:103)

Zamyatin and Huxley too are concerned with the irrational power of jealousy. But this does not involve their seeing sexual freedom as corrupt or diseased. That is Orwell's particular rewriting — though whether it is his conscious rewriting of utopian motifs or whether it is the product of his own personal obsessions is unclear. Certainly, it has its function in a rewriting the future context.

> In the old days, he thought, a man looked at a girl's body and saw
> that it was desirable, and that was the end of the story. But you
> could not have pure love or pure lust nowadays. No emotion was
> pure, because everything was mixed up with fear and hatred.
> Their embrace had been a battle, the climax a victory. It was a
> blow struck against the Party. It was a political act. (II:2:104)

In *We* the love of D-503 for I-330 threatens the state because it is something private between them. It further transpires that I-330 is part of the conspiracy, and D-503's confidence in the personal meaning of their love is shaken when the Well-doer suggests that she was merely using him since he was the Builder of the rocket ship. But D-503's own motives have been entirely romantic and sexual.

The pure love that D-503 feels is impossible in *Nineteen Eighty-four*. It is continually contaminated with negative feelings — like Winston's wish to crack Julia's skull with the glass paperweight. The highest expression of love Winston feels is immediately transformed into hatred (of purity), disease (thoughts of leprosy and syphilis), political instrumentalities (infecting party members). The politicization is central to Orwell's vision here. Though both Julia and Winston are hostile to the regime before their affair, they are not members of any 'conspiracy'. But immediately their affair has begun, they try to join the Brotherhood. Their affair inevitably leads to an attempt to join the conspiracy, because in the world of *Nineteen Eighty-four* love-making is immediately a political act, its emotion is immediately transformed. The state has permeated this last individual area. As in *We*, sexual activity that deviates from the social norms draws the lovers into political opposition. But by bitter irony, in *Nineteen Eighty-four* political opposition is the same as political conformity — firstly because the individual emotion is immediately sacrificed to the political; secondly, because the opposition, the 'Brotherhood' conspiracy, seems to be run by the state itself as a way to catch deviants. Big Brother's family and the Brotherhood are, as their names suggest, the same — whether or not Big Brother has any existence of his own. There is no way to escape the state.

The third term of the complex of opposition to the state in *We* is history. Orwell makes no mention of this in his review of *We*, but the role of history as a potential critique of the contemporary state is central to *Nineteen Eighty-four*. Part of the beauty of the love-making of D-503 and I-330 results from its setting in the Ancient House, the museum of the past ages;

> I turned around. She was dressed in a saffron-yellow dress of an ancient style. This was a thousand times worse than if she had not been dressed at all. Two sharp points glowing with rosiness through the thin tissue; two burning embers piercing through ashes; two tender, round knees . . . (10: 51-2)

There is a closely comparable scene in *Nineteen Eighty-four* when Winston turns round to Julia

> , and for a second almost failed to recognize her. What he had actually expected was to see her naked. But she was not naked. The transformation that had happened was much more surprising than that. She had painted her face.
>
> She must have slipped into some shop in the proletarian quarter and bought herself a complete set of make-up materials. Her lips were deeply reddened, her cheeks rouged, her nose powdered; there was even a touch of something under the eyes to make them brighter. It was not very skilfully done, but Winston's standards in such matters were not high. (II:4: 116)

Of course in Orwell's fiction it could not be very skilfully done; it had to be tawdry, and the scent Julia wears has to be the same scent that the fifty-year-old prostitute had used, another of Winston's traumatic memories. All the potentially high, erotic, magical moments in *Nineteen Eighty-four* are intruded upon by tawdriness, by the nausea of one sex fear or another, by corruption, decay, disease or debasement. And the setting for most of the love-making, the room above Mr Charrington's shop, is Orwell's ramshackle equivalent to Zamyatin's Ancient House. Even though the Ancient House is 'covered all around with a glass shell, otherwise it would undoubtedly have fallen to pieces long ago' (6:25) and even though it is described through the initially hostile perceptions of the mathematical, tabulating D-503, an extraordinarily powerful vision of historical beauty is created to set against the aesthetic of the future;

> She opened a heavy, squeaking, opaque door and we found ourselves in a somber disorderly space (they called it an 'apartment'). The same strange 'royal' musical instrument and a wild, unorganized, crazy loudness of colors and forms like their ancient music. A white plane above, dark blue walls, red, green, orange bindings of ancient books, yellow bronze candelabra, a statue of Buddha, furniture with lines distorted by epilepsy, impossible to reduce to any clear equation.
>   I could hardly bear that chaos. (6:26)

And though Mr Charrington's shop contains the relics of the past, embodies the missing history of the society of *Nineteen Eighty-four*, it is inevitably a reduced and tawdry history.

> In the fender was a battered tin oilstove, a saucepan, and two cups, provided by Mr Charrington. Winston lit the burner and set a pan of water to boil. He had brought an envelope full of Victory Coffee and some saccharine tablets. The clock's hands said seven-twenty: it was nineteen-twenty really. (II:4:112)

The past has been so obliterated in *Nineteen Eighty-four* that only these relics from the scrap-heap remain. They are the nearest Winston gets to recreating historical conditions; he tries to inquisition the old man in the pub but can recover nothing. Orwell has taken over Zamyatin's structure of oppositions in *We* and rewritten them to show how absurdly optimistic Zamyatin was. How could a future society let history remain even in a glass-enclosed museum? In *The Iron Heel* the socialist society of the twenty-sixth century that replaces the oligarchy has a National Library that preserves documents: Winston's job is to destroy documents and write new ones.

The location of nature, sex and history as the major forces opposed to the regimented state indicate *We* as a major source for *Nineteen Eighty-four*. Orwell takes over and 'corrects' the emphases, removes the dynamic significance from those three terms. But they are, of course, terms that exist elsewhere in political fiction. The romantic sexual bond between Ernest Everhard and Avis in *The Iron Heel* is one of the forces that keeps them strong in their rebellion against the state; it is the romantic archetype that Orwell reverses when he has Winston and Julia betray each other. And though the betrayal has its immediate source in *We*, Zamyatin was familiar with London's works, as he was with Wells's, so that D-503's betraying I-330 can be seen as a reversal of the strong romantic bonds of the rebels in *The Iron Heel* and *The Sleeper Awakes*. The state's hostility to history was something that Orwell found also in Huxley. The society of *Brave New World* dates from the year mass production of the Model T Ford began, A.F.1. And Our Ford's revered saying 'History is bunk' is the ethos of the society. The past has been systematically obliterated.

> Then came the famous British Museum Massacre. Two thousand culture fans gassed with dichlorethyl sulphide.

> Accompanied by a campaign against the Past; by the closing of museums, the blowing up of historical monuments (luckily most of them had already been destroyed during the Nine Years' war); by the suppression of all books published before A.F.150.
> (3: 50-1)

But there is also a less facetious, closer model in historical realities for the rewriting of the past — the rewriting of official histories and encyclopaedias in Stalinist Russia that Koestler refers to in *Darkness at Noon*. 'The official version of the events of the Revolution had gone through a peculiar change in these ten years, the parts played in it by the chief actors had to be rewritten, the scale of values reshuffled' (III:3:161). It was a topic that fascinated Orwell. He dealt with it in *Animal Farm*; and whatever his intentions, in effect it was just what Orwell was doing in his essays and in *Animal Farm* and *Nineteen Eighty-four* — writing a version of intellectual history that provided the ideology of the Congress for Cultural Freedom and the cold war. While some preferred to forget the left of the 1930s, others chose to re-write it, to present a counter image to the romantic attractiveness that it had presented. But so protective a system is doublethink, that though Orwell could see the doublethink in others, he was blocked from perceiving it in himself. His rewritings were the discoveries of truth; Winston Smith's rewritings were the creation of lies. But at a deeper level, a sardonic, tragic, painful level, the level at which he used his own notebook as the model for Winston's notebook, he must have sensed that his rewritings were just another version of Winston's rewritings, that in the end some big brother was going to get him, and he was going to love it.

A caste society is a common enough prediction for a future society. Orwell rejects Huxley's biologically controlled caste system; the possibility of non-sexual reproduction is raised by O'Brien — but in order to destroy sex, to remove family and personal attachments, not to breed uniform children. The horrors of *Nineteen Eighty-four* are horrors that could be applied immediately, not future horrors depending on as yet undeveloped scientific possibilities.

In *The Sleeper Awakes* and *The Iron Heel*, however, the segregating of the society into plutocracy and labour castes provides Orwell with his structure. In *The Iron Heel* the proletariat are abandoned to their own wretched life. 'Common school education, so far as they were concerned, had ceased. They lived like beasts in the great squalid labour-ghettos, festering in misery and degradation' (21:192). Orwell draws on London's people of the abyss, and derives, too, from the yahoos in *Gulliver's Travels*. The yahoos are called the 'houyhnhnms' cattle', and Orwell applies that metaphor to the proletariat. It is a metaphor that indicates how they are treated; they are not beasts, but they are treated by other people as beasts.

> Left to themselves, like cattle turned loose upon the plains of Argentina, they had reverted to a style of life that appeared to be natural to them, a sort of ancestral pattern. . . . Heavy physical work, the care of home and children, petty quarrels with neighbours, films, football, beer, and, above all, gambling, filled up the horizon of their minds. To keep them in control was not difficult. A few agents of the Thought Police moved always among them, spreading false rumours and marking down and eliminating the few individuals who were judged capable of becoming dangerous. (I:7: 60)

In *Gulliver's Travels* Gulliver is expelled by the houyhnhnms because they fear he will lead a rebellion of the yahoos. In *The Sleeper Awakes* the workers rebel. In *The Iron Heel*, though we see the defeat of the proletariat's rebellion in the Chicago Commune, their ultimate successful rebellion is predicted. 'In the end, who knows in what day, the common people will rise up out of the abyss'

(14: 143). But the idea of the proletariat rising is a hollow absurdity in *Nineteen Eighty-four*. Orwell's rewriting has removed that possibility totally from his future. '*If there is hope*, wrote Winston, *it lies in the proles*' (I:7:59). It is his desperate catch cry, and its repetition only confirms its hollowness. Goldstein's book asserts: 'From the proletarians nothing is to be feared':

> They could only become dangerous if the advance of industrial technique made it necessary to educate them more highly; but, since military and commercial rivalry are no longer important, the level of popular education is actually declining. (II:9: 168)

Orwell has accepted the prediction of a future caste society, and rewritten it as a totally undynamic structure, in which there is no possibility of change. He has projected the political defeat and economic demoralization of the English working class in the 1930s as a permanent future condition.

In the rebellions of the future, the fictional protagonists are usually involved in some sort of conspiracy against the state. But in Orwell's rewriting of this scenario, Winston and Julia join the 'Brotherhood' to conspire against the state — and fall directly into the hands of the Thought Police. During his interrogation afterwards, Winston asks O'Brien, 'Does the Brotherhood exist?' And O'Brien replies, 'That, Winston, you will never know. . . . As long as you live it will be an unsolved riddle in your mind' (III:2:209). This is one of the blackest of Orwell's rewritings; a totalitarian system so total that it even controls the only 'opposition' to it. Koestler postulates something approaching this horror in *Darkness at Noon* where the allegations of large scale conspiracies and organized saboteurs seem to have little objective basis; Gletkin indeed concedes that the society needs to create a myth of saboteurs to explain industrial errors and to motivate the workforce. But nothing in *Darkness at Noon* or *We* or *The Sleeper Awakes* or *The Iron Heel* is as final as *Nineteen Eighty-four* — a conspiracy created by the secret police as a way of forestalling any dissent, a deviant book critical of the regime actually written by the regime's inner party. The dynamic for any revolutionary change is totally blocked. The literary precedents for static totalitarian societies operate very differently from *Nineteen Eighty-four*. *Brave New World* has none of the brutal repressive apparatus in which Orwell delights. ' "In the end," said Mustapha Mond, "the Controllers realized that force was no good. The slower but infinitely surer methods of ectogenesis, neo-Pavlovian conditioning, and hypnopaedia . . ." ' (3:50). When Orwell sent Huxley a copy of *Nineteen Eighty-four*, Huxley wrote back a letter taking up some of the issues:

> whether in actual fact the policy of the boot-on-the-face can go on indefinitely seems doubtful. My own belief is that the ruling oligarchy will find less arduous and wasteful ways of governing and of satisfying its lust for power, and that these ways will resemble those which I described in *Brave New World*.
>
> Within the next generation I believe that the world's rulers will discover that infant conditioning and narcohypnosis are more efficient, as instruments of government, than clubs and prisons, and that the lust for power can be just as completely satisfied by suggesting people into loving their servitude as by flogging and kicking them into obedience. (604-5)

The society of *Brave New World* has a much more efficient and much less obtrusive apparatus of social order. Its effectiveness is demonstrated by the lack of any suggestion of rebellion. There is no need for surveillance. The rare dissidents are sent to remote island communities; the Savage's rebellion is purely private, internalized, and futile. But a society kept stable by genetic control and *soma*, was too benevolent for Orwell. He feeds his proletariat alcohol to keep them as unrevolutionary as the *soma*-zonked worker castes of *Brave New World*, but the stress is on the brutalization this causes, not any happy peace.

It was Orwell who pointed to the nature of 'the totalitarian society of the houyhnhnms, where there can be no freedom and no development' in *Gulliver's Travels* (IV:57:253) It is a totalitarianism that operates without any obvious brutalities. The language is limited, as in *Nineteen Eighty-four*, and this is one of their major instruments of control.

> They had apparently no word for 'opinion' in their language, and in their conversations there was no 'difference of sentiments'. They had reached, in fact, the highest stage of totalitarian organization, the stage when conformity has become so general that there is no need for a police force. (CE, IV:57:252)

But, except for the language limitation, this is not the form totalitarianism will take in Orwell's vision. It is too easy, too orderly. Perhaps he doubted the ability of the mandarins and rulers to be competent enough to run a *Brave New World* society — he didn't have Huxley's easy imperial, ruling class conviction that anything is possible, the servants will fix up the details. The world of *Nineteen Eighty-four* is one in which no one seems able to fix up anything; it is disorder, chaos — war, rocket bombs, crumbling buildings, arbitrary commodity shortages. The rationale of the party is not one of power demonstrated in efficiency. Efficiency would fail to consume the surplus generated by efficient industry; the surplus would have to be distributed amongst the people — as in *Brave New World*. O'Brien's stated aim is the exercise of power for its own sake; and the pleasure of seeing power demonstrated through the suffering it can create. Those highly organized static totalitarian systems that are shown to work efficiently, are rewritten for Orwell's future.

The futuristic architecture of *We* has its other, non-aesthetic function for a totalitarian society. 'We live beneath the eyes of everyone, always bathed in light. We have nothing to conceal from one another; besides, this mode of living makes the difficult and exalted task of the Guardians much easier' (4:19). So the Guardians watch through the glass walls of the buildings, peering through the observation tubes of their aircraft as they fly slowly past. Aerial surveillance is a motif in *The Sleeper Awakes*, too — aircraft with their occupants searching through field glasses for the escaped sleeper. So it is with a deliberate air of familiarity that at the opening of *Nineteen Eighty-four*

> a helicopter skimmed down between the roofs, hovered for an instant like a bluebottle, and darted away again with a curving flight. It was the police patrol, snooping into people's windows. The patrols did not matter, however. Only the Thought Police mattered. (I:1:6)

It is a deliberate allusion to Wells and Zamyatin; but an allusion that stresses that in this rewritten future, the most obtrusive surveillance Zamyatin or Wells could think of is now insignificant. Orwell borrows Zamyatin's 'street membranes' in his microphones concealed in bushes. But the telescreen has rendered obsolescent all earlier forms of future surveillance. With the telescreens, the Thought Police have a control undreamed of in the worst projections of earlier writers. And their name hints at a science-fiction fantasy of police who can read your innermost thoughts — telepathy, hypnosis, truth-drugs. 'Now psycho-analysis is being combined with hypnosis; and hypnosis has been made easy and indefinitely extensible through the use of barbiturates, which induce a hypnoid and suggestible state in even the most recalcitrant subjects' (604-5). Huxley's letter to

Orwell suggested this is how the society will be controlled, that was the method of his *Brave New World*. But Orwell borrows those possibilities only for his police — just to give them new, creepy powers. They operate in a brutal, repressive society — not in a society of zombie-like plenty. And they are everywhere: the Thought Police have become omnipresent.

The 'Guardians' are ubiquitious in *We*. But they do not set the total note of the society. Other components of the world are shown us. And the 'Guardians' are still called by their euphemistic name, they are 'protectors' rather than oppressors, your friendly neighbourhood cops. Orwell borrows the euphemistic nomenclature as a basic structure of Newspeak: Minipax or Ministry of Peace for the War Ministry, Ministry of Love for the Thought Police headquarters, joycamp for forced-labour camp. Zamyatin's dictator, variously translated as Benefactor or Well-doer, becomes Orwell's Big Brother.

But in the borrowing an ambiguity is introduced. Big Brother is watching you can mean the protective elder sibling looks on protectively, or the bullying bigger brother is looking for a chance to punch you. With the Thought Police, the adaptation is even greater and the ambiguity is removed. They are no longer labelled euphemistically. Unusual in the nomenclature of *Nineteen Eighty-four*, their identity is given explicitly, menacingly. In this future the forces of repression, interrogation and brutalization are explicit, open and dominant. They set the tone of the society — the diametric opposite of the covert, internalized conformity pressures in *Gulliver's Travels*. Writing of Koestler, Orwell remarked:

> England is lacking . . . in what one might call concentration-camp
> literature. The special world created by secret-police forces,
> censorship of opinion, torture, and frame-up trials is, of course,
> known about and to some extent disapproved of, but it has made
> very little emotional impact. One result of this is that there exists
> in England almost no literature of disillusionment about the
> Soviet Union. (CE, III:68:272)

Nineteen Eighty-four is Orwell's attempt to rectify this situation. *Darkness at Noon*, set almost totally in prison, provides a model for the imprisonment and interrogation of part III of *Nineteen Eighty-four*.

In discussing the Thought Police we have also to look at the rationale for the society of *Nineteen Eighty-four* — not the ideology of 'Ingsoc' but the rationale for the structure of power and control. For the Thought Police are not simply the means of maintaining a social end — they become pretty well the social end in themselves. Orwell complained of *Brave New World* that

> the hedonistic principle is pushed to its utmost, the whole world has turned into a Riviera hotel. But though *Brave New World* was a brilliant caricature of the present (the present of 1930), it probably casts no light on the future. No society of that kind would last more than a couple of generations, because a ruling class which thought principally in terms of a 'good time' would soon lose its vitality. (CE, II:11:46)

And he goes on to admire London's strategies in *The Iron Heel*. O'Brien tells Winston:

> Do you begin to see, then, what kind of world we are creating? It is the exact opposite of the stupid hedonistic Utopias that the old reformers imagined. A world of fear and treachery and torment, a world of trampling and being trampled upon, a world which will grow not less but *more* merciless as it refines itself. Progress in our world will be progress towards more pain. (III:3:214)

Writing of *We*, Orwell picked out the public executions as the

> intuitive grasp of the irrational side of totalitarianism — human sacrifice, cruelty as an end in itself, the worship of a Leader who is credited with divine attributes — that makes Zamyatin's book superior to Huxley's. (CE, IV:17:98)

It was something that strongly impressed him and he borrows public executions for *Nineteen Eighty-four*, rewriting them as even crueller. The 'guillotine' in *We* is a model of scientific execution — barbaric, but the barbarism of science.

> The prone body, covered with a light phosphorescent smoke; then, suddenly, under the eyes of all, it began to melt — to melt, to dissolve with terrible speed. And then nothing; just a pool of chemically pure water which only a moment ago had been so red and had pulsated in his heart. . . . (9:46)

Orwell regresses to eighteenth-century English style:

> 'It was a good hanging,' said Syme, reminiscently. 'I think it spoils it when they tie their feet together. I like to see them

kicking. And above all, at the end, the tongue sticking right out, and blue — a quite bright blue. That's the detail that appeals to me. (I:5:43)

He avidly draws on the available hints of brutality in his sources to elaborate them for the horror of *Nineteen Eighty-four*. The motif running through *Darkness at Noon* of being shot in the back of the head walking along a prison corridor recurs throughout *Nineteen Eighty-four*. But *Darkness at Noon* provides fewer physical horrors than *We*. Trials are public but executions are not. Orwell indeed complains of this lack of stress on physical horror in his comments on Rubashov's confession — 'He has not even been tortured, or not very severely': and he goes on to argue that 'the common sense explanation' for why people confessed to crimes in the Soviet purges is 'that they were tortured, and perhaps blackmailed by threats to relatives and friends' (III:68:276). He rejects the argument of Koestler's book, and for his own novel uses torture, cruelty, as the means by which the Party holds power in *Nineteen Eighty-four*. Further, he gives it as the motive for the Party's wanting power.

> 'You are ruling over us for our own good,' he said feebly. 'You believe that human beings are not fit to govern themselves, and therefore — —'
> He started and almost cried out. A pang of pain had shot through his body. O'Brien had pushed the lever of the dial up to thirty five.
> 'That was stupid, Winston, stupid!' he said. . . . 'Now I will tell you the answer to my question. It is this. The Party seeks power entirely for its own sake. We are not interested in the good of others; we are interested solely in power. . . . (III:3:211)
>
> How does one man assert his power over another? . . . By making him suffer. Obedience is not enough. Unless he is suffering, how can you be sure that he is obeying your will and not his own?' (III:3:214)

This becomes the extraordinary explanation for the society of *Nineteen Eighty-four*. This is the rewriting not only of the hedonistic utopias, but of the bleakest political novels like *Darkness at Noon*. In *We*, in *Darkness at Noon*, individuals suffer because the individual is dispensable for the greater good of the society. O'Brien expresses this same contempt for the individual: ' "Can you not understand, Winston, that the individual is only a cell? The weariness of the cell

239

is the vigour of the organism. Do you die when you cut your finger-nails?" ' (III:3:212). But in *Nineteen Eighty-four* the disregard of the individual is for the common ill. The sufferings of the individual are to increase the sufferings of the society.

Another borrowing from *Darkness at Noon* is the motif of confessing to crimes that were never committed.

> It was easier to confess everything and implicate everybody. Besides, in a sense it was all true. It was true that he had been the enemy of the Party, and in the eyes of the Party there was no distinction between the thought and the deed. (II:2:195)

But Rubashov also confesses because he believes in the revolutionary experiment, and believes that by surrendering to the party, he will avoid weakening the new society. He accepts the rationale of the society's repressions, as being necessary for an emergent society developing a new social structure and rapidly industrializing. Orwell found this explanation for the confessions unconvincing. He could not understand the force of ideas, the paranoid compulsion of systems. The confessions had to be induced by torture.

Ideas are without force for Orwell. Although O'Brien discusses things with Winston during the interrogation, there is none of the tension of debate that Koestler creates between Rubashov and his interrogators. All O'Brien ultimately does is tell Winston why ideas are unimportant, why physical torture, brutality, have become the total rationale of the party. Arguing against Koestler, Orwell wrote that if the confessions could be shown to be induced by brutality, this meant simply that 'one particular set of revolutionary leaders has gone astray' (CE, III:68:277). Yet the whole impulse of *Nineteen Eighty-four* is to argue that ideas can achieve nothing against organized brutality. Once power is achieved by those who have no other aim than to keep power by the most brutal, repressive means possible, mere ideas can never shake the society. Orwell here embodied the fullest expression of his hatred of intellectuals — the ultimate situation in which ideas stand for nothing against immutable physical violence. 'If you want a picture of the future, imagine a boot stamping on a human face — for ever' (III:3:215).

The image has a couple of sources. In *Gulliver's Travels* Gulliver envisions the houyhnhnms resisting an invading, colonizing army; 'Imagine twenty thousand of them . . . battering the Warriors' faces into Mummy, by terrible Yerks from their hinder Hoofs . . .' Orwell picks out the phrase in his essay on *Gulliver's Travels*, seeing it as a mark of Swift's 'secret wish to see the invincible armies of the Duke of Marlborough treated in a like manner' (CE, IV:57:244)

But a more specifically relevant source is *The Iron Heel*. The minor plutocrat Wickson, enraged by Everhard's predictions of the inevitable victory of the proletariat, expresses the plutocracy's intention to hold onto its power and privilege and resist change. 'We will grind you revolutionists down under our heel, and we shall walk upon your faces.' And he goes on to express the ethos of the image 'Not God, not Mammon, but Power' (5:63).

That the source of O'Brien's philosophy is so clearly to be found here would seem to contradict the contention that Orwell does not simply borrow materials but critically adapts them. However, Wickson's statement is not the full expression of the ideology of The Iron Heel plutocracy. As Orwell perceived,

> though he describes the caste of plutocrats who rule the world
> for seven [sic] centuries as inhuman monsters, he does not
> describe them as idlers or sensualists. They can only maintain
> their position while they honestly believe that civilization
> depends on themselves alone. (CE,II:11:46-7)

But when Orwell creates the ideology of his own power elite, he omits this 'ethical system' aspect. He removes the contradictions from his elite's ideology, reduces dialectic to a single static monolith: the 'boot stamping on a human face – for ever' – not claiming to preserve or better society, but just from the pleasure of power, brutally exercised.

And there is no reason why an ideology of power-with-brutality should be any more likely to survive than one of power-with-pleasures. The lack of 'a strict morality, a quasi-religious belief in itself, a mystique' (CE, II:11:46) applies no less readily to the ruling caste of *Nineteen Eighty-four* than to that of *Brave New World*. And what neither Huxley nor Orwell realize is that their systems are static, non-dynamic; whereas London thinks in dialectical, dynamic terms – there is the contradiction between the Iron Heel's ethos and its brutality, which generates tension; there is a conflict between The Iron Heel and the socialist underground; these are situations that allow for a dialectic, for a dynamic, for change. That is what distinguishes London's marxist vision from Huxley's and Orwell's bourgeois, static views. They have both postulated equivalent, parallel impossibilities. Orwell has projected a further negative twist on London's Iron Heel: O'Brien does not even claim to be doing it for anyone's good. But though this twist removes the last remaining positive aspect from the Iron Heel's ideology, it at the same time puts the *Nineteen Eighty-four* ideology into the same category which Orwell had previously attacked in *Brave New World*. He had reached the same place by a different process.

There is no doubt of the persuasive power of Orwell's vision of the future in *Nineteen Eighty-four*. Its images and phrases have entered into a wide and popular circulation — the telescreens, Big Brother is watching you, doublethink and such like. The novel encapsulated central aspects of a certain mood of its time; it found a ready acceptance in the cold war climate, and helped foster that very set of attitudes. It suited, too, the Tory propaganda against the English Labour party, and US policies of destabilizing post-war socialist governments. 'I am afraid some of the U.S. Republican papers have tried to use *1984* as propaganda against the Labour Party, but I have issued a sort of démenti which I hope will be printed', Orwell wrote to Vernon Richards (22 June 1949) (CE, IV:160:566). The 'sort of démenti' announced:

> My recent novel is NOT intended as an attack on Socialism or on the British Labour Party (of which I am a supporter) but as a show-up of the perversions to which a centralized economy is liable and which have already been partly realized in Communism and Fascism. (CE, IV:158:564)

But though Orwell claimed that English socialism was no part of his target, his naming of the official doctrine of the 1984 society as 'Ingsoc' directed readers to draw specific conclusions. *Nineteen Eighty-four* supported British and American right-wing propaganda that Stalinist totalitarianism was but the next step from the English Labour party.

Doublethink particularly captured qualities of intellectual leftists that Orwell hated: the capacity to believe two contradictory things simultaneously; the capacity to denounce fascist atrocities and fail to see anything disturbing in Stalin's purges. 'The sin of nearly all left-wingers from 1933 onward is that they have wanted to be anti-Fascist without being anti-totalitarian', he wrote in his essay on Koestler (CE, III:681:273). In isolating this habit of thought Orwell did something immensely valuable. But he extended his insights into less useful propagandist conclusions. It is one thing to attack the contradictions of those who denounce fascist atrocities yet ignore the Stalinist purges; but to go on to identify fascism with communism or state socialism is to draw a conclusion that obscures as much as it illuminates. It is a conclusion that is possible only if you totally reject the political beliefs or political ideologies; it is a position, indeed, that involves a rejection of the political. It recalls Swift's contempt for the confrontation of the Tramecksans and the Slamecksans, or Somers's refusal to choose between Kangaroo or Struthers, because they were both 'both right' and 'a choice of evils'.

Looking at Orwell's use of other political and utopian fiction, we notice the way in which he is consistently making two basic changes in them for *Nineteen Eighty-four*. Events, images, actions are drained of their political meaning, and they are made nastier, crueller. The emphasis is on the horror — at times reaching the grotesque as in the rat torture threatened to Winston. And yet the grotesque is the inevitable outcome of the *Nineteen Eighty-four* ethos — an ethos devoted to realizing its own power through the suffering it causes. Economic advantage, pleasure, ethics, religious zeal — none of these is allowed as an important factor in the politics of *Nineteen Eighty-four*. Just as Swift denied that any of these motivations was significant in any political position, and reduced all political action to absurdity, so Orwell denies them all and reduces all political action to the expression of cruelty. The ethical, benevolent approach of a Mustapha Mond, ensuring that people are happy; the ethical fanaticism of *Darkness at Noon*, tolerating suffering now for the ultimate achievement of the just society; the ideological deceptions of *The Iron Heel*, the plutocracy believing its role is to stave off anarchy, though in practical terms perpetuating its authority for economic privilege; the naked selfishness of a wealth and pleasure oriented caste as in *The Sleeper Awakes*: all these and every other example of political motivation are rejected, in favour of simple power.

Orwell's fictional absorption of James Burnham's thesis in *The Managerial Revolution* is important here: he postulates a power elite without hereditary privilege or wealth to preserve, without even a strongly economic or pleasure motivation, but concerned with the exercise of power. Orwell rejected the concept when he first reviewed the book in 1946 (CE, IV:46:192-215). By the time of writing *Nineteen Eighty-four* he had come to accept it as a possible future scenario. But as with his adaptation of the literary materials, he gave the thesis a further twist into horror. The rationale of the party in *Nineteen Eighty-four* is not simply the exercise and preservation of power; it is the exercise of cruelty by which it demonstrates to itself that it has power. That there are other ways of demonstrating power Orwell does not bother to consider. Power in *Nineteen Eighty-four* is simply the ideology for the practice of cruelty on a large scale.

The depoliticization of supposedly political motivations encourages a non-political explanation of Orwell's own motivations in writing the novel. The excess of horror, the reduction of all political motivations to the horrific have encouraged some commentators to explain the novel in terms of Orwell's own psychopathology. Indeed the novel might have been more persuasive had some psychopathological motivations for the cruelty imperative been offered within it – sexual explanations for fascist commitments are used in Sartre's story 'Childhood of a Leader' in *Intimacy* and in Moravia's *The Conformist*. But Orwell leaves the cruelty imperative totally unmotivated – as if the exercise of cruelty were in itself a basic drive.

The other major depoliticization at work in the novel is the removal of any dynamic from political and utopian themes. Orwell allows us no reason for challenging O'Brien's statement that this reign of terror will persist 'for ever'. There is no active conspiracy against it as far as we can see. The only individual rebellion of Winston and Julia is easily and totally crushed. Orwell has created a non-political political fantasy – a world in which stasis can be achieved, in which the last revolution has occurred. It is a belief derided in *We*. When D-503 voices the official belief that 'our revolution was the last one. No other revolutions may occur', I-330 asks him to 'name the last number'.

> 'But I-330, that's absurd! Since the last number of numbers is infinite, how can there be a last one?' 'And why then do you think there is a *last* revolution . . . their number is infinite. . . . The "last one" is a child's story. Children are afraid of the infinite, and it is necessary that children should not be frightened, so that they may sleep through the night.' (30:162)

Orwell's child's story was *designed* to frighten – to make his readers believe that certain social trends could result in a revolution that will be the last one, to warn against the digging in of the transitional stage. Writing in 1948 on the utopian vision of Oscar Wilde's *The Soul of Man Under Socialism* he commented:

> The trouble with transitional periods is that the harsh outlook which they generate tends to become permanent. To all appearances this is what has happened in Soviet Russia. A dictatorship supposedly established for a limited purpose has dug itself in, and Socialism comes to be thought of as meaning concentration camps and secret police forces. (CE, IV:118:484)

Orwell presents a transitional stage become permanent, from which

all hope is eliminated, from which all the dynamic that existed in
We, *The Iron Heel*, and *The Sleeper Awakes* has been removed. He
has created a future society in which political dynamic has been
stopped. Like Swift, Lawrence, and Conrad, he sees how the en-
trenchment of the political becomes corrupting, destructive, evil. His
final stance is an a-political anarchism, with strong reactionary
leanings: a writer as politically involved for as long as Orwell had
been could not but have known the use to which the reactionary
cold-war propagandists would put his novel. What Orwell wrote of
Swift applies closely to himself. He saw Swift as 'a Tory anarchist':
'Politically, Swift was one of those people who are driven into a sort
of perverse Toryism by the follies of the progressive party of the
moment' (CE, IV:57:243). The follies of English socialist intellectuals, their blindness to the realities of Stalinism, are in the forefront
of Orwell's consciousness in *Nineteen Eighty-four*. And the consequences for English socialism were, as Conor Cruise O'Brien has
pointed out, at the least ambiguous.

> The cant of the left, that cant which has so far proved indispen-
> sable to the victory of any mass movement, was almost destroyed
> by Orwell's attacks, which put out of action so much cant-produ-
> cing machinery in its factories: the minds of left-wing intellec-
> tuals. His effect on the English left might be compared to that of
> Voltaire on the French nobility; he weakened their belief in their
> own ideology, made them ashamed of their clichés, left them
> intellectually more scrupulous and more defenceless. (32-3)

Orwell did not stop at pointing out the follies; he was driven beyond
criticizing the progressive with which he had so long felt himself
allied, working from a position close to theirs; he moved into a
stance of virulent hostility towards the progressive. And the hostility
was all the more fierce because of Orwell's sense of his impotence.
Having been 'political' for so long, he could see no other world. He
could not simply reject the political world and offer rural anarcho-
communalism as in Morris's *News From Nowhere*, or domestic
privatism as George Eliot does for Felix Holt, or Christianity and the
hope of a better after-life like Swift, or the unorganized tribal primitive that Huxley considers in *Brave New World*, or simply sail away
to another country as Lawrence does in *Kangaroo*. Fiercely patri-
otic, Orwell allows himself no alternative to England; immersed in
the political he sees no other life but the political. He ends up with
a statement that is in part shared by so many of the English novelists
— politics are disgusting, degrading, destructive. But his vision is the

245

blacker because, unlike them, he is compelled to add the rider; yet everything is political.

Bibliography

Adams, Richard P., 'The Unity and Coherence of *Huckleberry Finn*', *Tulane Studies in English*, VI (1956), reprinted in Arnold Kettle, ed., *The Nineteenth Century Novel: Critical Essays and Documents*, London, Heinemann Educational, 1972.

Aldington, Richard, *Portrait of a Genius But . . .*, London, Heinemann, 1950.

Alexander, John C., 'D. H. Lawrence's *Kangaroo*: Fantasy, Fact or Fiction?', *Meanjin Quarterly*, XXIV (1965), pp. 179-97.

Atkins, John, *George Orwell* (1954), revised edition, London, Calder & Boyars, 1971.

Atkinson, Curtis, 'Was There Fact in D. H. Lawrence's *Kangaroo?*', *Meanjin Quarterly*, XXIV (1965), pp. 358-9.

Baldanza, Frank, 'The Structure of *Huckleberry Finn*', *American Literature*, XXVII (1955), reprinted in Arnold Kettle, ed., *The Nineteenth Century Novel: Critical Essays and Documents*, London, Heinemann Educational, 1972.

Barltrop, Robert, *Jack London, the Man, the Writer, the Rebel*, London, Pluto, 1976.

Bellamy, Edward, *Looking Backward 2000-1887* (1887), New York, Modern Library, 1951.

Berger, John, Blomberg, Sven, Fox, Chris, Dibb, Michael, and Hollis, Richard, *Ways of Seeing*, Harmondsworth, Penguin, 1972.

Bienek, Horst, *The Cell* (1968), London, Gollancz, 1974.

Borges, Jorge Luis, *Fictions* (1956), London, Calder, 1965.

Bottomore, T. B. and Rubel, Maximilien, eds, *Karl Marx: Selected Writings in Sociology and Social Philosophy* (1956), Harmondsworth, Penguin, 1963.

Bowden, Edwin T., *The Dungeon of the Heart*, New York, Macmillan, 1961.

Bibliography

Brantlinger, Patrick, 'News from Nowhere: Morris's Socialist Anti Novel', *Victorian Studies*, XIX (1975), pp. 35-49.

Burnham, James, *The Managerial Revolution* (1941), Westport Ct, Greenwood, 1972.

Caudwell, Christopher, *Studies in a Dying Culture* (1938, 1949), New York, Monthly Review Press, 1971.

Conrad, Joseph, *Heart of Darkness* (1902), ed. Robert Kimbrough, New York, Norton, 1971.

Conrad, Joseph, *Letters to William Blackwood and David S. Meldrum*, ed. William Blackburn, Duke University Press, 1958.

Cowley, Malcolm, *Exile's Return: a Literary Odyssey of the 1920s* (1934, revised 1951), New York, Viking, 1951.

Cox, James M., 'Remarks on the Sad Initiation of Huckleberry Finn', *Sewannee Review*, LXII (1954), reprinted in Charles Feidelson Jr, and Paul Brodtkorb Jr, eds, *Interpretations of American Literature*, New York, Oxford University Press, 1959, pp. 229-43.

Cox, James M., *Mark Twain: The Fate of Humor*, Princeton University Press, 1966.

Delavenay, Emile, *D. H. Lawrence and Edward Carpenter: A Study in Edwardian Transition*, London, Heinemann, 1971.

Deutscher, Isaac, *Heretics and Renegades*, London, Hamish Hamilton, 1955.

Dickens, Charles, *Our Mutual Friend* (1865), Harmondsworth, Penguin, 1971.

Eagleton, Terry, *Exiles and Emigrés: Studies in Modern Literature*, London, Chatto & Windus, 1970.

Eagleton, Terry, *Marxism and Literary Criticism*, London, Methuen, 1976.

Eagleton, Terry, *Criticism and Ideology: A Study in Marxist Literary Theory*, London, New Left Books, 1976.

Eliot, T. S., Introduction to Mark Twain, *Adventures of Huckleberry Finn*, London, Cresset, 1950.

Engels, Friedrich, *Socialism: Utopian and Scientific*, Peking, Foreign Languages Publishing House, 1975.

Fiderer, Gerald, 'Masochism as Literary Strategy: Orwell's Psychological Novels', *Literature and Psychology*, XX (1970).

Foner, Philip S., ed., *Jack London: American Rebel* (1947), New York, Citadel, 1964.

Foner, Philip S., *Mark Twain Social Critic* (1958), New York, International, 1972.

Forster, E. M., *Aspects of the Novel* (1927), Harmondsworth, Penguin, 1962.

Bibliography

Frye, Northrop, *Anatomy of Criticism*, Princeton University Press, 1957.

Geismar, Maxwell, *Rebels and Ancestors: The American Novel 1890-1915*, Boston, Houghton Mifflin, 1953.

Gerber, Richard, *Utopian Fantasy: A Study of English Utopian Fiction Since the End of the Nineteenth Century* (1955), New York, McGraw-Hill, 1973.

Goode, John, 'William Morris and the Dream of Revolution' in John Lucas, ed., *Literature and Politics in the Nineteenth Century*, London, Methuen, 1971.

Hardy, Frank, *But the Dead Are Many*, London, Bodley Head, 1975.

Hardy, Thomas, *Jude the Obscure* (1895), Introduction by Terry Eagleton, London, Macmillan, 1974.

Harrison, John R., *The Reactionaries. Yeats, Lewis, Pound, Eliot, Lawrence: A Study of the Anti-Democratic Intelligence*, London, Gollancz, 1969.

Henderson, Philip, *William Morris: His Life, Work and Friends* (1967), Harmondsworth, Penguin, 1973.

Hill, Christopher, 'The Norman Yoke' in *Puritanism and Revolution*, London, Secker & Warburg, 1958.

Hogan, Robert, 'The Amorous Whale: A Study in the Symbolism of D. H. Lawrence', *Modern Fiction Studies*, V (1959), pp. 39-46.

Hough, Graham, *The Dark Sun: A Study of D. H. Lawrence* (1956), Harmondsworth, Penguin, 1961.

Howe, Irving, *Politics and the Novel* (1957), London, Stevens, 1961.

Hulse, James W., *Revolutionists in London: A Study of Five Unorthodox Socialists*, Oxford, Clarendon Press, 1970.

Huxley, Aldous, *Brave New World* (1932), Harmondsworth, Penguin, 1972.

Huxley, Aldous, *Letters of Aldous Huxley*, ed. Grover Smith, London, Chatto & Windus, 1969.

Hynes, Samuel, ed., *Twentieth Century Interpretations of 1984*, Englewood Cliffs, Prentice-Hall, 1971.

Kaplan, Justin, *Mr Clemens and Mark Twain: A Biography*, London, Cape, 1967.

Kateb, George, 'The Road to 1984', *Political Science Quarterly*, 81 (1966), pp. 564-80.

Kateb, George, *Utopia and Its Enemies*, New York, Free Press, 1963.

Kermode, Frank, *Lawrence*, London, Fontana, 1973.

Kettle, Arnold, *An Introduction to the English Novel* (1951), 2 vols, London, Arrow, 1962.

Koestler, Arthur, *Darkness at Noon*, trans. Daphne Hardy (1940), Harmondsworth, Penguin, 1972.

Bibliography

Laurenson, Diana, and Swingewood, Alan, *The Sociology of Literature*, London, Paladin, 1972.

Lawrence, D. H., *The White Peacock*, London, Heinemann, 1911.

Lawrence, D. H., *Sons and Lovers* (1913), Harmondsworth, Penguin, 1969.

Lawrence, D. H., *The Rainbow* (1915), Harmondsworth, Penguin, 1961.

Lawrence, D. H., *Women in Love* (1921), Harmondsworth, Penguin, 1960.

Lawrence, D. H., *Kangaroo* (1923), Harmondsworth, Penguin, 1963 (quoted in text).

Lawrence, D. H., *Kangaroo*, ed. James Gribble, Melbourne, Heinemann Educational, 1963.

Lawrence, D. H., *Studies in Classic American Literature* (1924), London, Heinemann, 1964.

Lawrence, D. H., *Lady Chatterley's Lover* (1928), Harmondsworth, Penguin, 1960.

Lawrence, D. H., *Apocalypse* (1931), Harmondsworth, Penguin, 1974.

Lawrence, D. H., *Phoenix*, ed. Edward D. McDonald, London, Heinemann, 1936.

Lawrence, D. H., *The Collected Letters*, ed. Harry T. Moore, 2 vols, London, Heinemann, 1962.

Lawrence, D. H., *Letters to Thomas and Adele Seltzer*, ed. Gerald M. Lacy, Santa Barbara, Black Sparrow, 1976.

Leavis, F. R., *The Great Tradition* (1948), Harmondsworth, Penguin, 1962.

Leavis, F. R., *D. H. Lawrence: Novelist* (1955), Harmondsworth, Penguin, 1964.

Lee, Robert A., *Orwell's Fiction*, University of Notre Dame Press, 1969.

Lindsay, Jack, *William Morris: His Life and Work*, London, Constable, 1975.

Lindsay, Jack, 'D. H. Lawrence and *Women in Love*', in *Decay and Renewal: Critical Essays on Twentieth Century Writing*, Sydney, Wild & Woolley, London, Lawrence & Wishart, 1976.

London, Jack, *The Iron Heel* (1907), London, Journeyman Press, 1976.

London, Jack, *Letters from Jack London*, ed. King Hendricks and Irving Shepard, London, MacGibbon & Kee, 1966.

Jack London issue, *Modern Fiction Studies*, XXII, i, (1976).

London, Joan, *Jack London and His Times: an Unconventional Biography* (1939), Seattle, University of Washington Press, 1974.

Bibliography

Lukács, Georg, *The Historical Novel*, London, Merlin, 1962.

Lukács, Georg, *The Meaning of Contemporary Realism*, London, Merlin, 1963.

Lukács, Georg, *Writer and Critic*, London, Merlin, 1970.

Mackail, J. W., *The Life of William Morris* (1899), World's Classics, London, Oxford University Press, 1950.

Maddison, Michael, '*Nineteen Eighty-four*: A Burnhamite Fantasy', *Political Quarterly*, XXXIII (1961), pp. 71-9.

Mailer, Norman, *Miami and the Siege of Chicago*, New York, New American Library, 1968.

Mailer, Norman, *The Prisoner of Sex*, London, Sphere, 1972.

Mannheim, Karl, *Ideology and Utopia* (1963), London, Routledge & Kegan Paul, 1972.

Mao Tse-tung, *On Art and Literature*, Peking, Foreign Languages Press, 1960.

Martin, Kingsley, 'Bourgeois Ethics', *New Statesman*, 8 February 1941, pp. 130-2.

Marx, Karl, *Capital*, trans. Eden and Cedar Paul, Everyman, 2 vols, London, Dent, 1930.

Marx, Karl, *Grundrisse*, trans. Martin Nicolaus, Harmondsworth, Penguin, 1973.

Marx, Karl, *Selected Writings in Sociology and Social Philosophy* (1956), ed. T. B. Bottomore and Maximilien Rubel, Harmondsworth, Penguin, 1963.

Marx, Karl and Engels, Friedrich, *Manifesto of the Communist Party* (1888), trans. Samuel Moore, Moscow, Progress Publishers, 1973.

Marx, Leo, 'Mr Eliot, Mr Trilling and *Huckleberry Finn*', *American Scholar*, XXII (1953), reprinted in Charles Feidelson Jr and Paul Brodtkorb Jr, eds, *Interpretations of American Literature*, New York, Oxford University Press, 1959, pp. 212-28.

Maud, Ralph, 'The Politics in *Kangaroo*', *Southerly*, XVII (1956), pp. 67-71.

Meredith, George, *Beauchamp's Career* (1875), World's Classics, London, Oxford University Press, 1950.

Millett, Kate, *Sexual Politics* (1969), London, Sphere, 1972.

Moore, Harry T., *The Life and Works of D. H. Lawrence*, London, Allen & Unwin, 1951.

Morris, William, *News from Nowhere* (1890), in A. L. Morton, ed., *Three Works by William Morris*, Berlin, Seven Seas, 1968 (quoted in text).

Morris, William, *News from Nowhere or an epoch of rest, being some chapters from a utopian romance*, ed. James Redmond, London, Routledge & Kegan Paul, 1970.

Morris, William, *Political Writings*, ed. A. L. Morton, Berlin, Seven
    Seas, London, Lawrence & Wishart, New York, International,
    1973.

Morris, William, Review of Bellamy, *Looking Backward*, *The
    Commonweal*, 22 January 1889; excerpted in A. L. Morton, *The
    English Utopia* (1952), Berlin, Seven Seas, 1968.

Moynahan, Julian, *The Deed of Life: The Novels and Tales of D. H.
    Lawrence* (1963), Princeton University Press, 1966.

Murry, John Middleton, *Son of Woman*, London, Cape, 1931.

Nin, Anais, *D. H. Lawrence: An Unprofessional Study* (1932),
    London, Spearman, 1961.

O'Brien, Conor Cruise, *Writers and Politics*, New York, Vintage,
    1967.

O'Flinn, Paul, *Them and Us in Literature*, London, Pluto, 1975.

Orwell, George, *Nineteen Eighty-four* (1949), Harmondsworth,
    Penguin, 1961.

Orwell, George, *The Collected Essays, Journalism and Letters* (1968),
    ed. Sonia Orwell and Ian Angus, 4 vols, Harmondsworth, Penguin,
    1970.

Pinto, V. de Sola, 'D. H. Lawrence', in George A. Panichas, ed., *The
    Politics of Twentieth-Century Novelists*, New York, Hawthorn,
    1971.

Prichard, Katherine Susannah, 'Lawrence in Australia', *Meanjin
    Quarterly*, IX (1950), pp. 252-9.

Raskin, Jonah, *The Mythology of Imperialism*, New York, Random
    House, 1971.

Raskin, Jonah, *Underground: in Pursuit of B. Traven and Kenny
    Love*, Indianapolis, Bobbs-Merrill, 1978.

Rideout, Walter B., *The Radical Novel in the United States 1900-
    1954* (1956), New York, Hill & Wang, 1966.

Robbe-Grillet, Alain, *For a New Novel: Essays on Fiction*, New
    York, Grove Press, 1965.

Robson, W. W., *Critical Essays*, London, Routledge & Kegan Paul,
    1966.

Rühle, Jürgen, *Literature and Revolution: A Critical Study of the
    Writer and Communism in the Twentieth Century* (1960),
    London, Pall Mall, 1969.

Russell, Bertrand, *Portraits from Memory and other essays*, London,
    Allen & Unwin, 1965.

Sagar, Keith, *The Art of D. H. Lawrence*, London, Cambridge
    University Press, 1966.

Sanders, Ed, *Shards of God*, New York, Grove Press, 1970.

Sanders, Ed, *Investigative Poetry*, San Francisco, City Lights, 1976.

Sanders, Ed, *The Family* (1971), London, Panther, 1973.

Sinclair, Andrew, *Jack: a biography of Jack London*, London, Weidenfeld & Nicolson, 1977.

Smith, Henry Nash, *Mark Twain: the Development of a Writer*, Cambridge, Harvard University Press, 1962.

Smith, Henry Nash, ed., *Mark Twain: Twentieth Century Views*, Englewood Cliffs, Prentice-Hall, 1963.

Speare, Morris Edmund, *The Political Novel: its Development in England and in America*, New York, Oxford University Press, 1924.

Stansky, Peter and Abrahams, William, *The Unknown Orwell*, London, Constable, 1972.

Stone, Irving, *Jack London, Sailor on Horseback* (1938), New York, Signet, New American Library, 1969.

Strachey, John, *Literature and Dialectical Materialism*, New York, Covici Friede, 1934.

Strachey, John, *The Strangled Cry*, New York, William Sloane Associates, 1962.

Struve, Gleb, *Russian Literature under Lenin and Stalin 1917-1953*, London, Routledge & Kegan Paul, 1972.

Swift, Jonathan, *Gulliver's Travels* (1726), vol. IX, *The Prose Works of Jonathan Swift*, ed. Herbert Davis, Oxford, Blackwell, 1941.

Swingewood, Alan, *The Novel and Revolution*, London, Macmillan, 1975.

Thompson, E.P., *William Morris: Romantic to Revolutionary* (1955), London, Merlin, 1977, revised edition.

Thompson, Paul, *The Work of William Morris*, London, Heinemann, 1967.

Tiverton, William, *D. H. Lawrence and Human Existence*, London, Rockliff, 1951.

Trotsky, Leon, on Jack London, in Joan London, *Jack London* (1939), Seattle, University of Washington Press, 1974, pp. 313-15.

Twain, Mark, *The Adventures of Tom Sawyer* (1876), New York, Crowell-Collier, 1962.

Twain, Mark, *Life on the Mississippi* (1883), New York, Signet, New American Library, 1961.

Twain, Mark, *The Adventures of Huckleberry Finn* (1885), ed. Peter Coveney, Harmondsworth, Penguin, 1966.

Twain, Mark, *Mark Twain's Notebook*, ed. A. B. Paine, New York, Harper, 1935.

Wells, H. G., *The Sleeper Awakes* (1899), revised edition, The Atlantic Edition of H. G. Wells, vol. II, London, Fisher Unwin, 1924.

Bibliography

Wells, H. G., *A Modern Utopia* (1905), Lincoln, University of Nebraska Press, 1967.

Williams, Raymond, *Culture and Society 1780-1950* (1958), Harmondsworth, Penguin, 1961.

Williams, Raymond, *The Long Revolution*, London, Chatto & Windus, 1961.

Williams, Raymond, *The English Novel from Dickens to Lawrence* (1970), St Albans, Paladin, 1974.

Williams, Raymond, *Orwell*, London, Fontana, 1971.

Williams, Raymond, *The Country and the City* (1973), St Albans, Paladin, 1975.

Williams, Raymond, ed., *George Orwell: Twentieth Century Views*, Englewood Cliffs, Prentice-Hall, 1974.

Williams, Raymond, *Marxism and Literature*, Oxford University Press, 1977.

Winstanley, Gerrard, *The Law of Freedom and Other Writings*, ed. Christopher Hill, Harmondsworth, Penguin, 1973.

Woodcock, George, *The Crystal Spirit: A Study of George Orwell*, Boston, Little Brown, 1966.

Zamyatin, Eugene, *We* (1924), trans. Gregory Zilboorg, revised edition New York, Dutton, 1959.

Zwerdling, Alex, *Orwell and the Left*, New Haven, Yale University Press, 1974.

Index

action, 6-8, 35, 56, 116-18, 121, 123,
    150, 159, 177-8, 181-3, 190,
    192, 203
Adams, Richard P., 31, 247
adventure, 7-8, 18, 35, 37-41, 45,
    102-6, 115-16, 121-4, 177-81,
    183, 184; see also thought
    adventure
aesthetics, 5, 8, 9, 11, 34, 43-4,
    52-73, 89, 90, 101, 106-7, 120,
    124, 131, 147, 184-91, 206,
    221-2, 231, 236
Africa, 98
agents provocateurs, 111, 117, 159,
    165, 230, 233
aircraft, 104, 223, 236
Alcatraz, 105
Aldington, Richard, Portrait of a
    Genius But . . . , 186, 247
alienation, 15, 19, 21-2, 25, 31,
    47, 55, 58-67, 76, 84, 87, 88,
    96, 101, 131-3, 141, 143, 147,
    149, 160, 174-5, 180, 203
allusion, 60-1, 80, 193, 236
ambiguity, 9, 21, 24-6, 30, 33, 36,
    39, 41, 57, 61, 77, 100, 105,
    172, 174, 183, 187, 195, 201,
    222, 237, 245
America, see USA
anarchism, 85-6, 87, 97, 124, 136,
    141, 155, 164-5, 168, 205,
    208, 224, 243, 245
annotation, 9, 10, 93-9, 106, 110-11,
    120-5
anti-novel, 52-3, 180, 248
anti-utopia, 20, 94, 96, 119, 216-19,
    224

apocalypse, 16-17, 148-9, 170-1,
    174-5, 226-7, 250
aristocracy, 6, 8, 9, 34-5, 38, 42,
    85, 86, 114, 133, 138, 153,
    199, 245
Arnold, Matthew, 135, 200
art, 3, 9, 43, 50-75, 81, 83, 89, 90,
    107, 112, 118, 122, 124, 125,
    127, 140, 176, 177, 184-91,
    200-1, 217, 219, 220-2, 224;
    see also aesthetics; fiction; music;
    painting
Asia, 93
Asquith, 157
assassination, 121, 201-2
Austen, Jane, 2, 54; Emma, 149
Australasia, 93, 111
Australia, 9, 16, 151-60, 165, 171,
    178-9, 182, 184, 185-6, 189,
    252
authorial intrusion, 7, 178-81, 195
authoritarianism, 137, 138, 165,
    172, 228
authority, 18, 23, 154, 155, 158,
    174, 243
autobiography, 15, 178, 185
automatic writing, 176
avant-garde, 8, 73-6, 122, 178,
    184-5

Babylon, 220
Baldanza, Frank, 42-3, 247
Barltrop, Robert, Jack London,
    the Man, the Writer, the Rebel,
    114, 247
beats, 176, 178

255

beauty, 57, 61, 77, 81, 220, 222, 230-1
Beckett, Samuel, 19, 203
Bellamy, Edward, *Looking Backward: 2000-1887*, 51-2, 54, 65-6, 74, 82, 85, 86, 91, 92, 94, 96, 105, 218, 219, 247, 252
Berger, John *et al.*, *Ways of Seeing*, 55, 57, 247
Berkeley, 99, 101, 121, 123
betrayal, 3-4, 108, 183, 193-7, 201, 210, 229, 232, 238
Bible, the, 32, 36, 98, 170-1, 187
Bienek, Horst, *The Cell*, 202-3, 247
Blackwood, William, 14, 248
Bloody Sunday (13 November 1886), 78, 124
bolshevism, 155, 168, 174, 206-7, 213, 214; *see also* communism; marxism
Borges, Jorge Luis, *Fictions*, 122, 247
Bottomley, Horatio, 156, 158
Bottomore, T.B. and Rubel, M., *Karl Marx: Selected Writings in Sociology and Social Philosophy*, 135, 141, 247
bourgeoisie, 3, 4, 5, 7-8, 9, 15-18, 30, 45, 49, 52-7, 67, 70, 75, 90, 93, 100-1, 106, 110, 117, 125, 126, 127-49, 152, 157, 158, 164, 168, 169, 172, 173, 176, 180-5, 193-201, 204, 205, 211, 212, 214-15, 223, 241
Bowden, Edwin, *The Dungeon of the Heart*, 12, 247
Brantlinger, Patrick, 52-3, 248
Brecht, Bertolt, 6
Brett, George, P., 124
British Museum, 48, 232
brutality, *see* violence
Bukharin, 206-7
Bulletin, The, 178, 185
Bunyan, John, *Pilgrim's Progress*, 32-3
bureaucracy, 6, 9, 84, 156, 207, 215
Burnham, James, *The Managerial Revolution*, 217, 243, 248, 251
Butler, Samuel, *The Fair Haven*, 122

capitalism, 15, 17, 51-60, 63, 67-9, 75, 78, 81-4, 86, 91-126, 128, 130-45, 152, 158, 162, 172, 174-5, 217-20, 251
Carlyle, Thomas, *Sartor Resartus*, 122
Carswell, Catherine, 177
Casement, Roger, 14
cash relationships, 127, 144
caste, 75, 123, 233-4, 235, 243; *see also* class
Caudwell, Christopher, *Studies in a Dying Culture*, 127, 128, 141-2, 146, 152, 185, 248
censorship, 14, 71, 101, 144, 157, 158, 192, 205, 232, 237
centralization, 51, 82, 211, 215, 217, 218, 223, 242
Cervantes, *Don Quixote*, 35
change, 8, 49, 53-4, 61-2, 71, 73-8, 87, 94, 118, 119, 148-9, 155, 163, 166, 187-91, 193-6, 200, 203, 221, 234, 241
character, 1-2, 10, 22, 52, 73, 77, 87, 100-1, 106-8, 118-23, 125-6, 158-61, 177, 179-81, 183, 189, 197-202, 205-8
Chaucer, Geoffrey, 143
chauvinism, 105-6
Chesterton, G.K., *The Man who was Thursday*, 189
Chicago anarchists, 124
Chicago commune, *see* commune
child labour, 56, 98, 121
chivalry, 33, 35, 36
Christian socialism, 97, 107-8
Christianity, 12, 23-30, 32-5, 36-7, 39, 44-5; *see also* religion
chronology, 73-4, 200-4; *see also* cyclic repetition
CIA, 93, 242; *see also* Congress for Cultural Freedom
cities, 57, 59, 60, 75, 82, 84, 95-6, 104, 112, 115, 122, 129-30, 186, 218-25, 226, 254
civil war, 78, 118, 204; American Civil War, 13, 14, 31, 36; *see also* USA, South; English Revolution; French Revolution; revolution; USSR
civilization, 15, 21-4, 26, 28-34, 36-8, 42, 45-7, 51, 75, 112-15,

129-30, 137-9, 146, 148, 199,
241
Clarkson, Lawrence, 12
class, 5-6, 14-15, 18, 55, 57, 67-70,
74, 75, 99, 100, 108-18, 122,
123, 132, 135, 137, 138, 141,
147-8, 152, 155, 158, 161-2, 168,
190, 198-200, 224, 227, 236
class struggle, 11, 76, 108-18, 121,
168, 172-6, 198-200
classics, 9, 20, 71-2, 195, 202, 205,
210; classical unities, 200-1
Cockaigne, Land of, 103
colonialism, 1, 11-12, 15, 131,
136-9, 152, 196, 240; *see also*
imperialism
cold war, 212, 232, 242, 245
collage, 9-10, 20, 176, 185
commerce, commercialism, 30,
55-6, 58, 82, 84, 127, 129,
143-4, 162, 185, 234
commitment, 3, 4, 6, 9, 14, 32, 48-9,
54, 90, 94, 95, 99, 106, 115,
119, 136-7, 140, 149, 150-3,
159, 160-6, 171, 175, 181,
182-3, 188-91, 194, 198, 211
commodity production, 54-6, 58,
81-4, 144, 205, 218
commodity shortages, 224, 236
common good, 68, 81-2, 194, 197,
239-40
Commonwealth, The, 48, 51-2, 252
commune, 84; Chicago commune,
104-5, 117, 118, 122-3, 124,
233
communism, 8, 18, 49, 51-2, 54, 60,
62-9, 71-2, 78, 85, 87, 93, 117,
127, 155, 164, 165, 168, 193-4,
196-8, 205-6, 217, 242, 245, 251
conceptual fiction, 122
Concord, 14
conditioning, 26, 55, 226-7, 233-4
confession, 26, 204, 210, 212-13,
240
conformity, 36-7, 38, 40
Congo, 11-12, 14, 207
Congress for Cultural Freedom, 232
Conrad, Joseph, 9, 202, 203, 245;
Heart of Darkness, 11-12, 14,
131-2, 138, 207, 248; *Letters*, 14,
248; *Nostromo*, 9, 19, 43, 171,
175, 195, 202; *Under Western*

Eyes, 19
conscription, 156-8
conservatism, 9, 11, 12, 13, 17, 18,
19, 43, 125, 142, 173, 178,
195-6, 202, 205-6
conspicuous consumption, 68
conspiracy, 9, 163, 167, 183, 226,
227, 229-30, 233, 244
consumer goods, 54, 84, 218, 224
contradictions of capitalism, 36, 113
conversion, 106, 152-3, 160, 181,
190
co-operation, 62-6, 76, 152, 208-9
countryside, 57, 78, 80-1, 84,
128-30, 142, 145-6, 185-6,
225-6, 254
coups, 166, 169, 209
Cowley, Malcolm, *Exile's Return*,
176, 248
Cox, James M., 30, 248; *Mark Twain:
The Fate of Humor*, 12-13, 40,
248
cyclic repetition, 43, 193-6, 202-3

dada, 176, 178, 180
Danton, 195
Darwin, Charles, 52, 76, 98, 112
debate, 9, 48-9, 69, 74-7, 84-5,
87, 107-8, 179, 186-90, 192,
196, 198-9, 203, 210-11
decadence, 17, 70
decentralization, 84, 94
decorative art, 18, 63-4, 70
demagoguery, 156-7, 183
democracy, 14, 18, 48, 82, 86,
139-41, 146, 152, 153, 155-6,
158, 159, 162, 164, 168, 172,
181, 183, 193, 195, 197, 205,
211, 249
demystification, 8, 16, 75, 88, 161,
183
depoliticization, 12, 13, 16, 18,
243-5
destabilization, 93, 240
determinism, 202
dialectic, 9, 76-7, 85, 93-4, 118,
166, 175, 197, 214-15, 241,
253
Dickens, 1, 52, 80, 254; *Our Mutual
Friend*, 80, 248
dictatorship, 123, 153, 154, 174,
202, 204, 209, 212, 217, 244

Diderot, 5
Diggers: in English Revolution, 17,
66-7, 87, 254; in *Kangaroo*,
151, 153, 156, 159, 164-70,
181, 187, 190
diplomacy, 2, 201-2, 207
disappearance, 123-4
disinformation, 116
Disraeli, 5
documentary, 6, 8, 9-11, 106, 119,
120, 125, 178-80, 185-6, 207,
217
domestic, 150, 166-7, 171, 190, 245
Dostoevsky, 5, 19, 189
doublethink, 222, 232, 242
dream, 19-20, 40-1, 49, 51, 53, 55,
57, 73, 75, 78-80, 86, 89, 94,
123, 186, 202, 221, 225, 226,
249
Drucker, Peter, 217
drugs, 60-1, 235, 236
Dryden, John, 200
dynamic, 15, 43, 54, 62, 77, 78, 79,
94, 121, 187, 202, 203, 205,
226-7, 228, 232, 234, 241,
244-5

Eagleton, Terry, *Criticism and
Ideology*, 17-18, 248; *Exiles and
Emigrés*, 147, 248
economics, 2, 13, 14, 15, 16, 22,
24, 30, 36, 56, 68, 75, 84, 96,
100-2, 108-10, 113, 116, 132,
135, 137-9, 143, 152, 159,
160, 190, 218-19, 234, 243
education, 2, 6, 11, 15, 18, 19, 26,
55, 58, 66-7, 101, 111, 142-5,
147, 165, 174, 176, 199-200,
233-4, 241
egalitarianism, 52, 71, 86-7, 110,
126, 139, 140, 169, 173, 192,
217
elections, 92, 101, 102, 111, 181-2
Eliot, George, 5, 11, 19, 52, 100,
197, 204-5; *Felix Holt*, 5, 100,
175, 190, 197, 245; *Middlemarch*,
130, 149
Eliot, T.S., 11-12, 249, 251
elites, 1, 2, 6, 16, 59, 61, 67, 68,
74-5, 85, 87, 153, 172, 205,
219, 234-5, 241
emotion, 1-3, 26, 42, 49, 63, 153,

160, 166, 179, 180, 187-8, 230
endings, 39-46, 53-4, 105, 124,
148-9, 171, 190
ends and means, 194-8
Engels, Friedrich, 19, 117; *Socialism:
Utopian and Scientific*, 82,
84, 92, 108-9, 248; with Marx,
German Ideology, 141, *Holy
Family*, 135, *Manifesto of the
Communist Party*, 117, 251
England, 1, 4, 5, 6, 15, 16, 17, 18,
52, 66, 86, 87, 103, 104, 128,
137, 140, 155-8, 171, 172,
178, 183-4, 193, 196, 197,
214-15, 222-4, 228, 238-9, 242,
245
English Revolution, 12, 17, 67,
86-7, 103
epic, 9, 65, 71-2, 128
establishment, 6, 68, 103, 104, 158,
160, 164
ethics, 36, 113-15, 192, 195, 196-7,
204-5, 209, 210, 211, 218, 241,
243
Europe, 19, 92, 154, 159-60
evolution, social, 48, 98, 112, 173
execution, 29, 111, 121, 198-9,
200-2, 207, 214, 238-9
exile, 55, 160, 248
experimentalism, 18, 19, 20, 74-6,
118-19, 122, 125, 178-81, 205-6
exploitation, 31, 36, 67, 68, 75,
91-2, 98, 100-1, 131-3, 135,
137-9, 143

fable, 1, 4-6
factories, 50, 60, 82, 98, 143, 147,
153
fairy tale, 71
fantasy, 1, 5, 6, 7, 8, 11, 71, 73-4,
94, 103, 104-5, 108-9, 151, 172,
185, 186, 187, 203, 212, 236,
244, 249, 251
Farjeon, Eleanor, 161
fascism, 17-18, 92-3, 103, 114, 127,
139-40, 146-7, 151, 153, 154,
159-60, 165, 172, 213, 217, 243
feudalism, 6, 86
Fielding, Henry, *Tom Jones*, 9
folk tales, 65, 71-3
Foner, Philip, *Mark Twain Social
Critic*, 36, 248; *Jack London:*

American Rebel, 108, 248
force, 23, 24, 74, 82-3, 101, 105,
    120, 168-71, 219, 234-5
form, 6, 8, 18, 19-20, 53-4, 71-6,
    107, 118-26, 151, 173, 175-91,
    200-2, 205-6, 210
Fouché, 195
found manuscript, 20, 91-2, 95
found objects, 185-6
fragmentation, 17, 50-1, 57, 60, 62,
    91-5, 121-5, 152, 175, 178,
    183, 205
France, 5, 7, 18, 111, 143, 245;
    see also French Revolution
France, Anatole, 92
freedom, 2, 12-13, 22, 24-5, 27-32,
    36-7, 39, 40-7, 52, 60, 66, 73,
    80-1, 85, 87, 123, 129, 132,
    134, 140-1, 147, 151, 154,
    155, 158, 168, 175, 192-3, 198-9,
    205, 217, 218-19, 225, 229,
    235, 254
French Revolution, 34, 174, 195-6,
    202
Frye, Northop, *Anatomy of
    Criticism*, 53, 249
future, 8, 9-10, 16, 18, 48-9, 51,
    53-5, 57, 59, 60, 64, 66, 69-80,
    82-4, 86, 89, 90, 91-9, 104-5,
    108-13, 114, 122, 123, 148-9,
    193, 196, 216-24, 229, 233-4,
    236, 238, 243, 245

Garnett, Edward, 177
Gaskell, Mrs, *Mary Barton*, 54
Geismar, Maxwell, *Rebels and
    Ancestors*, 99, 120, 249
genetic control, 235
genocide, 117
Gerber, Richard, *Utopian Fantasy*,
    10-11, 249
Germany, 17, 18, 111, 160, 162
Gide, André, 185
Glen Ellen, 102-3
Goode, John, 80, 249
Gould, Nat, 178-9, 180, 185
government, 1, 34, 48, 74-5, 84,
    87, 105, 129-30, 137-40, 151,
    157, 206, 222, 235
gradualism, 96
Greece, 9
Greek art, 71-2

Gribble, James, 187, 250
Grimm, Jacob, 71

Hammersmith, 54, 57
Hampstead, 68
Hardy, Frank, 206-7, 249
Hardy, Thomas, 11, 138, 175;
    Jude the Obscure, 88, 249
Harrison, John, *The Reactionaries*,
    153, 249
Hegel, 194
Henderson, Philip, *William Morris:
    Life, Work and Friends*, 18, 249
hierarchy, 140, 153, 169, 183
high art, 59-65
high seriousness, 59
Hill, Christopher, *Puritanism and
    Revolution*, 86-7, 249; *Law of
    Freedom*, ed., 66-7, 254
historical inevitability, 91, 109, 112,
    116, 117
historical novel, 1, 45, 73, 76, 251
history, 1, 2, 4-6, 9, 11, 17, 36,
    48, 54, 66, 67, 71-3, 75-6, 88,
    91, 98-9, 108-9, 114, 118, 120,
    125-6, 130, 146, 173, 193-6,
    197, 199, 206-7, 230-2
Hitler, 154
Hoffman, Abby, 104
holiday, 62, 78
homosexuality, 167
Horrebow, Niels, *Natural History of
    Iceland*, 74
Hough, Graham, *The Dark Sun*,
    157, 189, 249
Howe, Irving, *Politics and the Novel*,
    2-5, 18, 193, 198, 206, 212,
    214-15, 249
Hulse, James, *Revolutionists in
    London*, 85, 249
Huxley, Aldous, 4, 5, 76; *Brave New
    World*, 5, 15, 74, 96, 105, 113,
    217-20, 222-3, 225, 227, 229,
    232-8, 241-2, 245, 249; *Letters*,
    235

ideas in fiction, 1-4, 8, 50-2, 106-7,
    190, 197, 240
ideology, 3-4, 8, 10, 11, 12-14,
    17, 22-6, 29-30, 33-6, 56, 67, 68,
    71, 75, 83, 93, 98, 101, 113-17,
    128, 138-9, 141, 144-5, 150,

152, 157, 167, 168, 195, 200,
214-15, 232, 237, 241-3, 245,
248, 251
Ignatius of Loyola, 194
image, 13, 24, 27, 32, 35, 189,
210, 217, 226, 242
imaginary book, 9-10, 20, 74, 122
imaginary worlds, 73, 99, 217
imitative fallacy, 190
imperialism, 12, 14, 15, 36, 54, 67,
84, 136-9, 141, 145, 147, 162,
171, 236, 252
imprisonment, 13, 24-5, 27-8, 30,
32, 33-4, 39-40, 42, 46, 101,
102, 111, 115, 154, 158, 192,
198-200, 202-3, 227, 235, 237,
239
India, 137-8
individual, 22, 26, 39, 42, 52, 82, 83,
85, 120, 131, 132, 133, 136-7,
139-41, 145, 147-8, 149, 152-4,
158, 168, 175, 181, 196-7, 203,
218-19, 230, 239-40
individualism, 6, 17-18, 52, 62-5,
85, 87, 119-20, 185, 200-1,
205, 207-12, 213, 225
industrialism, 15-16, 51, 53, 55,
57-9, 62, 69, 80-4, 85, 86, 100,
117, 128-49, 158, 162, 165,
173, 175, 194, 195, 211, 218,
220, 221, 225, 234, 240
intellect, intellectual, 6, 9, 16, 45,
49-50, 61, 63, 127, 133-5, 137,
140, 142-9, 164-6, 169, 192, 197,
198-9, 200, 212, 214, 223, 232,
242, 245
intellectual art, 63-6, 69, 70
interrogation, 9, 189, 192-6,
198-200, 201, 202, 210, 211,
212, 237, 240
irony, 21, 33, 37, 99, 107, 179, 187,
216, 219-20, 230
Italy, 16, 17, 18, 57, 73, 111, 151,
161, 186

Jacobins, 195
Jaffe, Elsa, 181
James, Henry, 1, 95, 180, 189;
The Ambassadors, 184; *The Turn
of the Screw*, 95
Japan, 56, 186
John Bull, 156

journey, 4, 22, 32, 41, 46, 54,
59-60, 80, 88, 90, 104
Joyce, James, 8; *Ulysses*, 177-8,
184, 185, 190

Kafka, Franz, 19
Keats, John, 61
Kelly's Army, 99
Kelmscott, 18, 54
Kermode, Frank, *Lawrence*, 17,
103, 249
Kerouac, Jack, 176
Kettle, Arnold, *Introduction to the
English Novel*, 128, 139, 144,
146, 249; *Nineteenth Century
Novel*, ed., 31, 42-3, 247
KGB, 104
Koestler, Arthur, *Darkness at Noon*,
9, 13, 19, 105, 106, 120,
192-215, 218, 224, 232, 234,
237, 239-40, 242, 243, 249
Koteliansky, S.S., 177
Kropotkin, 85-6

labour, 51, 56-60, 62, 66-7, 75, 80,
81-4, 96-8, 101-2, 103, 108-18,
119, 123, 137, 154, 174, 196,
218-19, 220, 221, 233, 237,
242
language, 21, 25-6, 40, 73, 115, 235;
see also vernacular
Laurenson, Diana and Swingewood,
Alan, *Sociology of Literature*,
128, 250
Lawrence, D.H., 13, 14-18, 19, 101,
103, 245, 247, 248, 249, 250,
251, 252, 254; *Aaron's Rod*, 154,
177, 178, 250; *Apocalypse*, 170-1,
250; *Collected Letters*, 146, 161,
177, 181, 250; *Democracy*, 140,
156, 250; *Kangaroo*, 2, 6-8,
9, 11, 17, 105, 106, 120, 125,
145, 146, 150-91, 192, 205, 243,
245, 250; *Lady Chatterley's
Lover*, 158, 250; *Letters to
Thomas and Adele Seltzer*, 151,
156, 177, 178, 250; *Phoenix*,
140, 250; 'The Prussian Officer',
162; *The Rainbow*, 11, 15-17,
101, 127-49, 158, 162, 174, 175,
197, 205, 250; *The Sisters*, 175;
Sons and Lovers, 15, 54, 128,

132, 133-4, 158, 250; *Studies in Classic American Literature*, 147, 250; 'The Thorn in the Flesh', 162; *The White Peacock*, 15; *Women in Love*, 11, 128, 133-4, 158, 167, 169, 175, 250
leadership, 2, 7, 8, 87, 150-4, 159, 172, 174, 182, 186, 244
Leavis, F.R., 5, 19; *D. H. Lawrence: Novelist*, 16, 128, 147, 148-9, 164, 171, 177, 186, 250; *The Great Tradition*, 5, 19, 20, 52, 250.
leisure, 58, 62, 67, 132, 221
leisure class, 68, 99, 116
Lenin, 19, 93, 253
Leningrad, 223
Lesage, 5
liberalism, 17, 75, 106-7, 155, 194, 195, 196-7, 199, 205, 210, 222
libertarianism, 169
Lindsay, Jack, v; *Decay and Renewal*, 128, 250; *William Morris: Life and Work*, 72-3, 124, 250
logic, 17, 161, 162, 166, 173, 194, 198, 201, 202-5, 207, 209-13
London, Jack, 4, 13, 18-19, 78, 248, 253; *The Iron Heel*, 5, 8-9, 10, 18-19, 36, 55, 56, 75, 76, 83, 91-126, 143, 190, 192, 217-21, 224, 227, 231-4, 238, 241, 243, 245, 250, 253; *Letters*, 124, 250
London, Joan, *Jack London and His Times*, 99, 118, 250, 253
love, 9, 53, 56, 127-8, 139, 163, 165-70, 177-8, 188, 210, 219, 226-32, 237
Lucas, John, ed., *Literature and Politics in the Nineteenth Century*, 80, 249
Luddites, 83
Lukacs, Georg, 6, 17, 19; *The Historical Novel*, 4-5, 251; *The Meaning of Contemporary Realism*, 160-1, 251; *Writer and Critic*, 17, 231
London, 54, 78, 80-1, 82, 124, 216, 220, 222-3, 249
lynching, 29

Machiavelli, 194

machinery, 51, 59, 81-4, 85, 86, 96, 103-4, 109-12, 130-5, 137, 139, 142-5, 148, 156, 158, 160, 175, 197, 200, 211, 225
Mackail, J.W., *Life of William Morris*, 18, 251
Mailer, Norman, *Miami and the Siege of Chicago*, 124, 251; *The Prisoner of Sex*, 154, 251
Malraux, André, 192
Mammon, 135, 241
managerial class, 16, 130-40, 248
Mannheim, Karl, *Ideology and Utopia*, 93, 251
Manson, Charles, 103
Mao Tse-Tung, *Talks at the Yenan Conference*, 168, 251
marriage, 54, 88, 106, 154, 167, 171, 182, 183, 227-8
Martin, Kingsley, 206, 251
Marx, Karl, 19, 76, 81, 93-4, 96, 102, 106, 109, 117, 163, 194, 221-2, 247, 251; *Capital*, 81, 102, 251; *Grundrisse*, 71-2, 251; with Engels, *The German Ideology*, 141, *The Holy Family*, 135, *Manifesto of the Communist Party*, 117, 251
Marx, Leo, 37, 39, 251
marxism, 5, 6, 9, 17, 18, 19-20, 45, 54, 71-3, 76, 93-4, 97,102, 108-18, 143, 144, 168, 174-5, 193-4, 200, 203, 205-6, 212, 215, 241, 247, 248, 251, 254; *see also* bolshevism; communism
masses, 2, 175, 208-10, 218, 221, 245
materialism, 17, 87, 103, 120, 144-5, 168, 194, 200, 204, 211-12, 224, 253
mateship, 167, 169
mathematics, 194, 208-9
medievalism, 33-5, 53, 54, 56, 65, 70, 71-3, 84, 86, 194-5
melodrama, 101, 198
Meredith, George, *Beauchamp's Career*, 5, 6-8, 76, 120, 149, 152, 160, 175, 180-2, 197, 251
military, 6, 16, 111, 120, 136-7, 151, 156-8, 162, 165-70, 172, 181, 200, 225, 234, 240-1
millenarianism, 103, 170-1

Miller, Henry, 161
Milton, John, 200; *Paradise Lost*, 224
mining, 128, 130-5, 158
Mississippi, 12, 30, 31, 32, 34-6, 38, 46
mixed mode, 6, 8-9, 11, 20
mob, 157, 174, 200
modernism, 10, 19, 125, 160-1, 176-81, 184, 205, 222
Moloch, 135
monopoly, 91, 109, 218
Moore, Harry T., *Life and Work of D. H. Lawrence*, 178, 251; *see also* Lawrence, *Collected Letters*, ed.
Moravia, Alberto, *The Conformist*, 244
More, Thomas, *Utopia*, 52
Morel, E.D., 14
Morris, William, ix, 4, 18, 93, 101, 131, 147, 224-5, 249, 250, 251, 253; 'The Aims of Art', 50; 'Art under Plutocracy', 58-9, 63, 67; *Dream of John Ball*, 50; 'A Factory as it Might Be', 50; 'How We Live and How We Might Live', 50, 81; *News from Nowhere*, 2, 5, 6, 8, 16, 18, 48-90, 91, 94, 95, 96, 110-11, 124, 144, 192, 245, 251; *Political Writings*, ix, 58-9, 63, 67, 68, 81; 'Useful Work versus Useless Toil', 50, 68
Morton, A.L., 68; *The English Utopia*, 51-2, 252; *see also* William Morris, *Political Writings*, ed.
Moscow trials, 206-7
Mosley, Oswald, 154
Mountsier, Robert, 156
Moynahan, Julian, *The Deed of Life*, 176, 188-9, 252
multilaterality, 187, 202
multinational corporations, 93, 111
murder, 89, 124, 169-71
Murry, John Middleton, *Son of Woman*, 176, 183, 184, 252
music, 8, 64-6, 96, 223, 231
Mussolini, 17
mystification, 12, 17, 46, 74, 138, 180

myth, 6-7, 12, 15, 54, 71-2, 77, 86, 129-30, 184, 234, 252

Napoleon, 2, 3, 195
narrative, 7, 8, 9, 10, 13, 36, 39, 54, 78, 89, 91, 92, 97, 99, 105, 106, 108, 120-6, 182, 184, 187-9, 202-6, 217
nationalization, 165
naturalism, 4, 158, 180; *see also* realism
nature, 15, 57, 61-2, 66, 76, 78-9, 80-1, 96, 102, 146, 224-7, 232; *see also* countryside; pastoral
negation, 46-7, 51, 55, 79, 86, 99
Nero, 195
New Statesman, 206, 251
newspapers, 9, 10-11, 100, 116, 153, 185, 189, 216, 231
newspeak, 9
Nietzsche, 76
Nin, Anais, *D. H. Lawrence: an Unprofessional Study*, 182, 252
nineteenth century novel, 1-2, 5, 6-8, 19, 26, 46, 51-5, 67-76, 89, 90, 95, 149, 175, 179-81, 190, 196-7, 205, 245, 247
noble savage, 15
Norman yoke, 86, 249

O'Brien, Conor Cruise, *Writers and Politics*, 245, 252
oligarchy, 76, 91-2, 95, 110-12, 114, 115, 123, 217, 219-20, 221, 231, 235; *see also* plutocracy
organic community, 128-30, 131
organic form, 175, 217
Orwell, George, 4, 92, 105, 106-7, 113-15, 116, 120, 125, 162, 197, 200, 247, 250, 251, 253, 254; *Animal Farm*, 5, 232; *Collected Essays, Journalism and Letters*, ix, 13-15, 96, 106, 110, 113, 114, 118-19, 123, 162, 212-15, 217, 224, 227, 228, 235, 237, 238, 240-1, 242, 243, 244, 245, 252; *The Last Man in Europe*, 216; *Nineteen Eighty-four*, 5, 9-11, 13, 19, 74, 75, 96-7, 105, 120, 203, 213, 216-46, 249, 252, 254
Oxford, 58

pacifism, 157

painting, 33, 55, 57, 59-60, 70, 73, 210

Panichas, George, ed., *The Politics of Twentieth Century Novelists*, 128, 252

paranoia, 203, 240

parliament, 1, 4, 6, 75, 84, 86-7, 92, 155, 156, 157, 159

parody, 42, 179

party, the, 11, 198, 199, 201, 206, 209, 213, 214, 219, 227-9, 236, 239-42, 243

party politics, 1, 2, 4, 6, 75, 92, 150, 152, 159, 162, 165, 196, 199, 242

pastiche, 69

pastoral, 16, 57, 59-61, 80, 102-4, 226-7

patriotism, 75, 156-7, 162, 233, 245

peace, 61, 77, 93, 96, 219, 221, 235, 237

Philby, Kim, 104

picaresque, 19, 73

Pieta, 210

Pinto, V. de Sola, 128, 252

poetry, 50, 59-61, 69, 70, 80, 143, 157, 222, 252

police, 15, 23, 124, 158, 164, 165, 193, 233-7

political novel, 1-11, 18, 19-20, 43, 45, 48, 52, 74-6, 87, 91, 106-7, 116-17, 125-6, 129-30, 149, 150, 166, 175, 180-7, 190, 192-3, 198, 205, 206, 207, 214-15, 217, 232, 239, 243, 245-6, 249, 253

popular fiction, 101-5, 212

power, 82-3, 96, 108-15, 159, 166, 180, 197, 235, 236, 239-42, 243; *see also* force: violence

Plekhanov, 19

plot, 7-8, 29, 46, 52-4, 55, 74-6, 88-9, 178-85

plutocracy, 36, 58, 63, 82, 101, 102, 104, 105, 110-15, 117, 118, 122, 123, 126, 220, 227, 233, 241, 243; *see also* oligarchy; capitalism

pollution, 80-2

positive hero, 106-7, 125-6

poverty, 30-1, 67, 69, 74-5, 101, 165, 220

pre-Raphaelites, 18, 81

primitivism, 15, 127, 146-7, 225-7, 245

profit motive; 30, 36, 57-8, 74-5, 82, 109-10, 131

profits, 109-10, 132; *see also* surplus

promiscuity, 88-9, 133, 169, 227-9

propaganda, 1, 10-11, 15, 52, 83, 92, 97-9, 108, 115, 150, 185, 203, 223, 242

property, 8, 13, 55, 56, 75, 85, 88, 97, 98, 111, 145, 165, 174

Proust, Marcel, 43

publishers, 14, 69, 101, 121, 151, 156, 157, 177, 178

purges, 204, 206-7, 211-15, 239-40, 242

racism, 29, 39-40, 155, 162-3

Radek, 206-7

radicalism, 6, 11, 13, 14, 16-20, 45-6, 54, 66, 86, 101, 103, 127-8, 152, 162, 172, 181, 190, 205, 252

Raskin, Jonah, *Underground*, 104, 252

rationality, 127, 134, 144-5, 166, 197, 204, 212; *see also* intellectual; logic; mathematics

reactionary, 16, 19, 34, 42, 69, 76, 91-3, 128, 148, 153, 193, 201, 203, 245

realism, 3-11, 15-16, 19, 52, 53, 55, 70-6, 79, 83, 88, 89, 90, 107, 119-21, 125, 133, 134, 173, 178-82, 184, 189, 204-6, 251; *see also* naturalism; nineteenth-century novel

rebellion, 8, 12-13, 36, 37, 40, 42, 105, 227, 232-4, 235, 244, 248, 249; *see also* revolution

reformism, 118, 149, 152

reification, 96

religion, 11-12, 17, 23-6, 28, 29-30, 32-4, 35, 36-7, 39, 44-5, 52, 54, 55, 67, 77, 84, 86, 88, 97, 98, 107-8, 113-15, 137, 143, 144, 146, 149, 160, 163, 170-1, 188, 193-5, 210, 223, 224, 238, 241, 243, 245

repetition, 42-5, 57, 177, 193

repression, 18, 76, 86, 91-3, 105,
110, 111, 113-15, 117, 123, 127,
156, 158, 175, 182, 227, 237, 240
Resnais, Alain, *Last Year at
Marienbad*, 202
revolution, 4, 9, 13, 14, 16-17,
18, 20, 34, 43, 50, 53, 76, 78,
81, 84, 86, 91, 94, 95, 103, 104,
105, 107, 108, 111, 113, 114,
115, 119, 120, 122, 125, 135,
141, 142, 143, 144, 148-9, 152,
159-67, 169, 170, 174, 175,
180-3, 190, 193, 195-202, 210,
211, 213-14, 232, 234, 241, 244,
249, 252, 253, 254
rhythm, 128, 177, 187
Rideout, Walter, *The Radical Novel
in the United States*, 105, 252
Robespierre, 195
Robson, W.W., *Critical Essays*, 176-7,
252
Rolland, Romain, 185
Romains, Jules, 185
romance, 1, 6-10, 12, 18, 48-55, 65,
71-6, 83, 99-107, 118-25, 173,
180
romantic, romanticism, 8, 12, 17,
33-9, 42, 44-6, 50, 59, 76, 86,
87, 99-107, 119-25, 133, 140,
141, 143, 149, 180-2, 227, 229,
232, 253
royalty, 2, 4, 8, 14, 28-9, 32, 38,
42, 71-3, 86, 87, 98
Rühle, Jurgen, *Literature and
Revolution*, 206-7, 252
rule, 37, 38, 40, 44-5, 55-6
ruling class, 12, 113, 236
Ruskin, John, 59
Russell, Bertrand, 153, 157, 252
Russia, *see* USSR

Sagar, Keith, *The Art of D.H.
Lawrence*, 164, 187, 252
St Just, 195
San Francisco, 102, 176
Sanders, Ed, *The Family*, 103, 253;
Investigative Poetry, 45-6, 252;
Shards of God, 124, 252
Sartre, Jean Paul, 'Boyhood of a
Leader', 244
Satan, 193-4, 224
science, 17, 48, 50, 75, 92, 96-7,
101, 103, 108-9, 117, 121,
134, 144-5, 146, 172, 194, 238,
249
science fiction, 103, 105, 236
Scotland, 33
Scott, Walter, 34-7, 41, 42, 44;
Ivanhoe, 35
sculpture, 59, 63-4
secret societies, 37, 103
Seltzer, Thomas, 151, 156, 177, 178,
250
sentimentality, 34-5, 174, 197, 210
serfs, 95-6, 112, 218-19
servants, 57, 81, 82, 84, 96, 97,
143, 172, 236
sex, 15, 87-90, 99-100, 104, 105-6,
127-8, 133, 150, 154, 160-1,
165-71, 177-8, 179, 210, 226-32,
233, 251
sexism, 57
Shakespeare, William, 104, 203
Shaw, George Bernard, 19
Shelley, Percy Bysshe, 61
Silone, Ignazio, 193
Sidney, Philip, *Arcadia*, 52
slavery, 2, 11-14, 22-6, 29, 30, 31,
36, 39-40, 42, 44, 45, 46, 57, 59,
68, 81, 82, 85, 95-6, 98, 111,
112, 116, 121, 218, 223
slums, 101-2, 153, 219
small press movement, 69
Smith, Henry Nash, *Mark Twain:
the Development of a Writer*, 41,
253
Social Democratic Foundation, 48
socialism, 8, 18, 48-52, 55-9, 66, 69,
70, 76, 83-5, 91-108, 110-14,
117, 119, 125-6, 141, 152,
153-4, 158-66, 174, 181-3,
192, 205-6, 215, 224, 227, 231,
241, 242, 244-5, 249
Socialist Labor Party, 108
Socialist League, 48, 49, 52, 53, 85
socialist realism, 125, 205-6
sociology of literature, 69-70, 251
song, 64-5
Sonoma, 102-3, 104
South America, 16
Souveraine, Boris, *Cauchemar en
URSS*, 213
Speare, Morris Edmund, *The Political
Novel*, 1-2, 3, 5, 18, 253

spies, 104, 111, 162, 183, 236
state socialism, 51, 76, 84, 94, 110, 174-5, 219, 242, 244
Stendhal, 5, 8
Sterne, Laurence, 74
Strachey, John, *Literature and Dialectical Materialism*, 17, 253; *The Strangled Cry*, 193, 253
strikes, 97
structure: of novel, 43-5, 80, 173, 175-7, 184, 198, 206, 233-4; of society, 12, 15, 48-9, 71, 84, 86, 119, 152, 158, 173, 175, 205, 225, 233-4
Struve, Gleb, *Twenty Five Years of Soviet Russian Literature*, 216
subconscious, 176, 182
Sulla, 195
surplus, 54, 75, 110, 112, 113, 122, 220-2, 224, 236
surplus value, 109-10, 116, 117
surrealism, 176, 178
spontaneity, 65, 73, 84, 136, 147, 175-6, 182, 185, 187, 202, 205
Stalin, 193, 203, 206-7, 214, 232, 242, 245, 253
state, 76-7, 94, 136-40, 174-5, 208, 232, 234
Swift, Jonathan, *Gulliver's Travels*, 4, 5, 10, 74, 87, 98-9, 105, 116, 192, 207, 218, 228, 233, 235, 240-1, 243, 245, 253
Swingewood, Alan, *The Novel and Revolution*, 119, 206-7, 253; with Diana Laurenson, *The Sociology of Literature*, 128, 250
Sydney, 154, 155, 171, 176, 184, 185
symbolism, 38, 54, 80, 195, 249

technology, 54, 83, 84, 86, 95-6, 105, 109, 132, 134, 144, 218-20, 222-3
telepathic communication, 2, 172, 208-9, 236
Tennyson, 60-1, 78, 79
Thackeray, William Makepeace, 1, 52, 68, 69; *Vanity Fair*, 68
Thames, 54, 59, 80-1
theatre, 34, 36, 38, 39, 43, 61-2, 69
Thirroul, 176
Thompson, E.P., *William Morris:*

Romantic to Revolutionary, 50, 253
thought adventure, 7-8, 179-84
Times, The, 10-11, 124, 216
Tiverton, William, *D. H. Lawrence and Human Existence*, 178, 253
torture, 199-200, 212-13, 237, 239-40, 243
Tory, 4, 242
totalitarianism, 18, 92-3, 95, 107, 124, 154, 158, 192-7, 212, 218-20, 222, 226, 234-5, 236, 238, 242; *see also* dictatorship
Trafalgar Square, 124, 223
tragedy, 9, 88, 125-6, 233
transition stage, 196, 244-5
trial, 27, 200-1, 206-7, 211, 212-15, 239
Tribune, 227
Trollope, Antony, 52
Trotsky, Leon, 9, 19, 92; *The Revolution Betrayed*, 9; on *The Iron Heel*, 118, 252
Trotskyites, 213
trusts, 92, 102, 109-12; *see also* plutocracy; oligarchy; multinational corporations
Twain, Mark, *Adventures of Huckleberry Finn*, 2, 8, 11-14, 21-46, 54, 98, 103, 149, 247, 248, 251; *Adventures of Tom Sawyer*, 11, 40, 253; *A Connecticut Yankee*, 31; *King Leopold's Soliloquy*, 14; *Life on the Mississippi*, 30-1, 34-6, 253; *Notebooks*, 31, 253; 'What is Man?', 14
tyranny, 83, 85, 224

underground, 104, 123, 241, 252
unions, 111-12, 117
University of Texas at Austin, 151
USA, 24, 30-1, 32-6, 45, 46, 55, 92, 93, 98, 99, 104, 105, 111, 120, 156, 214-15, 242, 250, 253; the South, 2, 8, 11-14, 22, 24, 27, 30-6, 40, 46; *see also* civil war
USSR, 104, 180, 193, 206-7, 208, 212-14, 216, 223, 232, 239, 244, 253; Russian Revolution (1905), 91, (1917), 16, 174, 193, 198
utilitarianism, 68, 131

utopia, 1, 4, 5, 6, 8, 11, 20, 48-57,
61, 63, 71-9, 82-6, 88, 90, 91-9,
103, 108-9, 116, 119, 217, 218,
221, 224-5, 229, 238, 239, 244,
249, 253

variety of life, 51-2, 59, 94
Veblen, Thorstein, *Theory of the
Leisure Class*, 99
vernacular, 11, 19, 21, 25-6
vertebral consciousness, 2, 172-4,
176, 182
violence, 12, 28, 29, 33-4, 35, 38, 39,
45, 76, 78, 80, 93, 97-8, 114,
118, 157-8, 164-71, 194, 195,
197, 222, 224, 235, 237, 238-42;
see also authority; force; military;
murder
Voigt, F.A., 217
Voltaire, 5, 245
von Nieheim, Dietrich, Bishop of
Verden, 194
vote, 84, 92

war, 55, 67, 75, 104-5, 108-11,
117-18, 120, 121-4, 154, 156-8,
220-5, 236, 237; First World
War, 151, 156, 166, 169, 170,
176, 178, 182, 183-4; Second
World War, 15, 224
Washington, 99, 101
wealth, 55, 56, 57, 74-5, 108, 109,
155, 218, 221, 243
weather underground, 105
Wells, H.G., 4, 19, 94, 95, 105;

The Island of Dr Moreau, 95;
A Modern Utopia, 94, 218,
253; *The Sleeper Awakes*, 118-19,
217-20, 222, 223, 227, 232-4,
236, 245, 253
Whig, 4
Whitman, Walt, 14, 167
Wilde, Oscar, *The Soul of Man Under
Socialism*, 244
Williams, Raymond, 54, 114, 254;
The Country and the City, 145-6,
254; *Culture and Society*, 50,
115, 254; *The English Novel*,
128, 254; *Marxism and Literature*, 54, 254
Winstanley, Gerrard, 17, 66-7, 87;
Law of Freedom in a Platform
66-7, 254
withering away of state, 76-7, 94
work, 56-60, 62, 63, 66-7, 77, 78,
80-4, 95-6, 101-2, 130-9, 196
working class, 2, 15, 16, 18, 56-60,
67, 68, 78, 81-4, 95-6, 97, 99,
101-2, 108-18, 130-7, 147-9,
152, 153-4, 158, 161-3,
218-19, 220-5, 230, 233, 234,
235, 241

Zamyatin, Eugene, *We*, 4, 5, 94,
105-6, 120, 125, 193, 200, 205,
208, 216-20, 222, 225-32, 234,
236-9, 244, 245, 254
Zola, Emile, *Germinal*, 132, 133
Zwerdling, Alex, *Orwell and the Left*,
10, 254